WITHDRAWN

THREE USES OF CHRISTIAN DISCOURSE IN JOHN HENRY NEWMAN:

AN EXAMPLE OF NONREDUCTIVE REFLECTION ON THE

CHRISTIAN FAITH

AMERICAN ACADEMY OF RELIGION

DISSERTATION SERIES

Edited by

H. Ganse Little, Jr.

Number 10

THREE USES OF CHRISTIAN DISCOURSE IN JOHN HENRY NEWMAN:

AN EXAMPLE OF NONREDUCTIVE REFLECTION ON THE

CHRISTIAN FAITH

by

Jouett Lynn Powell

SCHOLARS PRESS
Missoula, Montana

THREE USES OF CHRISTIAN DISCOURSE IN JOHN HENRY NEWMAN:
AN EXAMPLE OF NONREDUCTIVE REFLECTION ON THE
CHRISTIAN FAITH

by

Jouett Lynn Powell

Published by
SCHOLARS PRESS
for
The American Academy of Religion

Distributed by

SCHOLARS PRESS
University of Montana
Missoula, Montana 59801

THREE USES OF CHRISTIAN DISCOURSE IN JOHN HENRY NEWMAN:

AN EXAMPLE OF NONREDUCTIVE REFLECTION ON THE

CHRISTIAN FAITH

by

Jouett Lynn Powell
University of North Carolina at Chapel Hill
Chapel Hill, North Carolina 27514

Ph. D., 1972
Yale University

Adviser:
Hans W. Frei

Copyright © 1975

by

The American Academy of Religion

Library of Congress Cataloging in Publication Data

Powell, Jouett Lynn.
   Three uses of Christian discourse in John Henry Newman.

   (Dissertation series - American Academy of Religion ; no. 10)
   Originally presented as the author's thesis, Yale, 1972.
   Bibliography: p.
   1. Newman, John Henry, Cardinal, 1801-1890.
I. American Academy of Religion. II. Title.
III. Series: American Academy of Religion.
Dissertation series - American Academy of Religion ; no. 10.
BX4705.N5P65   1975   262'.135'0924 [B]   75-29423
ISBN 0-89130-042-2

Printed in the United States of America
1 2 3 4 5 6
Printing Department
University of Montana
Missoula, Montana 59801

TABLE OF CONTENTS

		PAGE
PREFACE		ix
CHAPTER I.	INTRODUCTION	1
CHAPTER II.	NEWMAN AND HIS CRITICS: A HISTORY OF REDUCTIVE ANALYSIS	11
CHAPTER III.	THREE USES OF CHRISTIAN DISCOURSE: A DESCRIPTIVE ANALYSIS	67
CHAPTER IV.	THREE USES OF CHRISTIAN DISCOURSE: AN INTERPRETATIVE ANALYSIS	121
CHAPTER V.	THE COMPLEX UNITY OF THE CHRISTIAN FAITH: NEWMAN'S METATHEOLOGICAL PRINCIPLES	185
BIBLIOGRAPHY		213

FOR MEB AND KRISTEN

PREFACE

This essay emphasizes basic distinctions which John Henry Newman drew between three separate uses of Christian discourse and between the separate contexts in which each use functions. These three contexts are those of coming to faith or religious inquiry, exercising faith or the religious life, and explicating the faith or revealed truth and theology. Distinguishing between these three contexts is especially crucial because Newman's critics have continually reduced one or two of the uses associated with these contexts to another use or have so concentrated on one or two of the uses as to render others seemingly unimportant.

The second chapter of my study offers a descriptive typology of various reductions of Newman's work. Chapters three and four present evidence which invalidates any such limited approach to Newman. Chapter three surveys Newman's literature in order to indicate that he did, in fact, repeatedly recognize distinctions between these three uses of Christian discourse. In addition, the third chapter seeks to clarify the nature of those distinctions. Chapter four continues that clarification by dealing with possible interpretative difficulties for my thesis regarding the nonreductive quality of Newman's reflections on the Christian faith. First, the testimony of conscience is shown not to be, characteristically, an argument for God's existence but a model for understanding religious inquiry. Second, the role of imagination in faith is shown to be a rich but limited one. This conclusion is counter to proposals that Newman was concerned with subjective appropriation of the faith to the exclusion of questions of truth. Third, questions of meaning and truth are shown to be capable of resolution, in Newman's view, not only for the individual believer but also for the church and her theologians.

The fifth chapter analyzes the evidence in Newman reflecting his understanding of the nonreductive relationships between uses of Christian discourse. Though the suggestions of basic principles guiding these relationships are not systematically developed, the contours of Newman's conclusions

can be sketched with some assurance of accuracy. The uses of
Christian discourse are related in a complex unity, that is,
in a unity not dependent upon a reduction of the uses to some
one description but upon a conjunction of diverse uses. The
resulting picture confirms Newman's nonreductive approach to
the analysis of Christian discourse.

I have always been impressed with the similarity of the
closing sentiments of a preface like this one. Such familiarity
can breed contempt and even the suspicion of insincerity.
Involvement in such a project is the only fully effective
antidote. Indeed there are many persons who make such a project
possible and one does owe them a word of thanks. Hans W. Frei
has done more than any one person to stimulate my thinking
about the themes pursued in this study. Paul Holmer originally
suggested that Newman would be an interesting figure to consider and, along with Professor Frei, introduced me to some of
the philosphical methods used in my interpretation. As he has
in relation to other matters before, my colleague John Schütz
offered encouragement and support in the preparation of this
manuscript for publication. The Institute for Research in
Social Science of the University of North Carolina at Chapel
Hill has been most helpful with a special word of gratitude
due to Pat Sanford for her editorial advice. In addition, I
cannot forget the typists and the Departmental Secretary who
were so understanding and diligent during the preparation of
the manuscript--Susan Eckert, Meb Powell and Maxine Underwood.
To each of these persons and others, I am grateful. I must
offer my special gratitude to my daughter Kristen for many
enjoyable afternoons together this summer while her mother was
busy typing.

J.L.P.

Chapel Hill, North Carolina
August 4, 1975

CHAPTER I

INTRODUCTION

John Henry Newman's understanding of the relation between faith and reason has long been a subject of controversy. To designate the problem as one of the relation between faith and reason is itself often to understand the issue in the wrong way and, consequently, to foster distortions of Newman's work. By so stating the problem, one suggests that a close study of Newman's writings will yield a "position" or unified description of the relation of faith and reason attributable to Newman. The temptation is to limit one's discussion of Newman's views on this matter to an analysis of the Grammar of Assent and the Oxford University Sermons, referring to the latter only secondarily and occasionally because of their comparatively immature and unrefined treatment of the same issues considered in the Grammar.

Exclusive concentration on the Grammar is understandable. The book does set forth the problem in a fairly traditional manner even if the structure of the book and the solution offered are not so typical. Newman was concerned to describe the factors relevant to one's being able to believe or to assent rationally in matters of faith. In addition, the Grammar does represent Newman's mature reflections on the subject and, thus, demands as well as allows individual treatment. For these reasons, a treatment of the Grammar within its limited purposes is a worthy enterprise; in interpreting the Grammar, one might well offer an analysis of the way in which one can come to faith in a rational manner. The assumption that such an analysis provides a proper representation and evaluation of Newman's understanding of all the issues involved in delineating the relationships between faith and reason is, however, an error.

The assumption rests on a failure to distinguish the various points of view which Newman took toward the relation of faith and reason--at one time looking at the relation from the point of view of the non-believer inquiring into the meaning and validity of faith; on another occasion reflecting on the relation within the life of faith; and in yet another context viewing the matter from the perspective of the Church and her creed. A failure to distinguish these various points of view can result in a significant confusion, and a failure to give each its due place can result in a truncation of Newman's work. The *Grammar* itself adumbrates these distinctions, but only a study of Newman's literature as a whole can give those distinctions sufficient content to be helpful.

That Newman made these kinds of distinctions explicit can provide the reader with the assurance that I am not imposing an artificial and perhaps misleading structure on Newman's thought. More often than not, however, I shall have to make the point of view explicit. Though Newman was sometimes pointedly specific about his intentions, he was more often simply operating within one of these points of view without announcing the fact to his reader. In short, at times Newman was describing certain general ways in which Christian discourse functions, while more often he was simply using Christian discourse in a certain way.

For example, Newman gave no extended treatment of the nature of rationality, yet he made certain remarks on the subject throughout his writings. That Newman's observations have a consistency even though they are not systematically treated can be seen in the kind of *ad hoc* distinctions which he made in the use of the word "reason." To map the general pattern which these distinctions assume is perhaps the best way to clarify the type of concern guiding my study, while at the same time providing the reader with some guidelines to aid his investigation of this essay.

In the course of a study of Newman's literature, one will note that the Cardinal distinguished between several ways in which reason is related to Christian faith. First, Newman often referred to "reason" pejoratively. In these cases he always had in mind the view that rational criteria are entirely formal in character and, consequently, transferable without alteration from one context and from one body of subject matter to another. His concern with this distortion was twofold: one, he was interested, for apologetic purposes, in opposing certain schema of rational criteria prominent in his own time which he considered potentially inimical to religious faith; two, he felt that certain schema would not allow a proper and full explication of the content of Christian faith, even if they were not specifically critical of faith.

In addition to his attack on certain understandings of rationality, Newman was also concerned to characterize the appropriate ways in which rational criteria operated in the life of faith and in reflection on the content of the Christian faith. His important distinction between implicit reason and explicit reason involved these two concerns. By an explication of "implicit reason," Newman sought to account for unanalyzed modes of personal reflection in the individual who is inquiring into the faith or living the life of faith. Such personal reflection is rational but not rational in the same way that "explicit" theological reflection is. Newman was concerned to emphasize the importance of personal factors such as one's life history and personal dispositions and the importance of the imagination in implicit reason. In this sense, he claimed that the "imagination" or what he called "real assent" in the Grammar is normally more like faith than is reason. By the use of the term "explicit reason," Newman designated, in contrast to reason pejoratively described, the proper exercise of reasoned faith in the life of the Church, in her creeds, and by her theologians. The roles of the imagination and of personal dispositions are not centrally important for explicit reason which is concerned directly with the nature, meaning and truth of revelation.

Newman's most common distinctions may have escaped many critics since they were so seldom made explicitly even though their operation is evident again and again. I propose to emphasize these distinctions while, at the same time, giving adequate attention to their actual use. A recent study of the Grammar by David Pailin illustrates the kind of analysis which my essay seeks to correct. Pailin seems to realize that Newman's purpose in the Grammar is a limited one, viz., to demonstrate the nature of certainty possible to faith understood as an act of an individual's mind.[1] Yet, in the course of his book, Pailin tends to identify this limited purpose as the definitive expression of Newman's view of the relation of faith and reason. For example, in discussing Newman's understanding of the relationship of theology and religion, Pailin asserts that, for Newman, ". . . we start with our religious experience and derive our theology from it. . . ."[2] What Pailin should have recognized is that this kind of priority makes no sense as an indication of Newman's position but only as true for certain contexts within Newman's writings. This kind of distortion rests on Pailin's opposition of real assent and religion, on the one hand, and notional assent and theology, on the other hand, as if that opposition were simple and complete in all contexts and for all purposes.[3] For Newman, the relationships between them were much more complex than that. In order to understand that complexity, one must first understand the diversity of contexts and uses of language in Newman's work.

The attempt to describe and account for the complexity in Newman's use of Christian discourse is important for at least two reasons. First, since many of Newman's interpreters have sought to describe the nature of Newman's reflections on the Christian faith in terms of what proves to be only one aspect of his thought, a recognition of the complex unity of his reflections is necessary for overcoming certain false analyses fostered by these critics and for giving an adequate picture of Newman's work. I propose to take seriously the different contexts in which Christian discourse functions for Newman and the different rules governing the linguistic uses in those contexts. My conclusion is that the unity of Newman's thought is not identifiable with any one of these points of view or functions--what Newman sometimes called "aspects." Rather the unity of his reflections is the complex union of these aspects or functions. Edwin Burgum describes the kind of complex unity which I find in Newman's literature:

> The truth was complicated as only the wise man knew. It lay not in any one generalization, not even in the whole body of them, but in the whole body of relationships among them. No single generalization was true for any particular case, but only a particular combination of them.[4]

An understanding of this complex unity is useful, in the second place, because it has potential value as a methodological clue for contemporary analysts of Christian discourse whether philosophers or theologians. In this essay, however, I do not plan to explore how that value might be appropriated; I only intend to clarify what Newman himself was doing.

In order to reveal Newman's complex reflections, certain common misunderstandings of his work must first be eliminated.

Though they have had other effects, some helpful and some adverse, on Newman scholarship, these analyses have in common a distortion or oversimplification of the nature of the unity which characterizes Newman's reflections on the Christian faith. I shall consider these oversimplifications in the second chapter of this study. In instance after instance, Newman's critics--both friendly and unfriendly--have attempted to find some one factor that explains his work. Sometimes that factor was thought to be enunciated in Newman's writings and sometimes it was taken to be external to his writings altogether. In both cases, the result was a reduction of what I have called a "complex unity" to a simple or systematic unity. A "simple unity" is one in which the concepts of a given realm of discourse are taken to have a constancy of relationship and meaning no matter the context in which they function. For some, Newman's understanding of Christianity is always to be interpreted as a product of his personality and of his life history. In that sense, the concepts of Christian discourse always have their relationships and meanings determined by psychological and biographical matters. That same sort of simple unity is found by others in a philosophical persuasion or in a theological principle. In every case, however, these attempts have lost the richness of Newman's thought for the sake of simplicity and false unity.

The most persuasive form of these attempts to describe a simple unity consists in an analysis of Newman's understanding of the reality of conscience and of the role of moral dispositions as the clue to the nature of faith. I shall give studies of this kind the separate attention which they deserve. Even in the case of these important studies, however, I shall point to the danger of what Newman called the "fallacy of the leading idea."[5] This fallacy consists in seizing upon one idea to the exclusion of others so that material which suggests another point of view is either ruled out or explained in terms of that leading idea.[6]

After having described common reductive tendencies in interpretative works on Newman, I shall investigate Newman's corpus in order to establish that he did in fact make the kind of distinctions which I have indicated that he did. I am concerned to describe the consistency of Newman's understanding of the different uses of Christian discourse and the relationships between them. Newman reflected on the nature of faith and on the manner in which the language of faith operates in different contexts though, less directly, on the way in which these different uses and contexts are related to one another. In this sense, in addition to claiming that Newman himself had "metatheological" concerns, I am seeking to explicate those concerns more fully than Newman himself did.

In order to clarify what I mean by "metatheology," it is perhaps most helpful to indicate what certain writers have meant by "metaethics." William K. Frankena understands metaethics to consist of four areas of inquiry: one, the meaning of concepts, the nature of rules, and the propositions in which these function; two, the meaning of moral discourse as opposed to other strata of discourse; three, the analysis of concepts related to moral discourse; and, four, the possibility or nature of justifying moral judgments.[7] Paul Edwards, in more summary fashion, defines a "metaethic" as ". . . any theory which attempts to define or else to describe the way or ways in which moral judgments are <u>actually</u> used by human beings."[8] Provisionally, one may understand meta-theology to be a theory based on an analysis of Christian discourse that seeks to account for the ways in which its concepts function, mean, and are justified. The third chapter of this study traces the development of metatheological distinctions in Newman's literature.[9]

The purpose of this survey of Newman's literature is twofold: first, to establish what I have claimed, namely, that Newman did make explicit metatheological distinctions himself; second, to develop means for a more effective interpretation of Newman's mature reflections on the issues involved. We shall find that Newman isolated three contexts in which Christian discourse functions—the contexts of coming to faith, of exercising faith, and of asserting and explicating the faith. We shall also find that the diverse senses of "reason" and the various relationships between faith and reason which I have already introduced play important roles in distinguishing these contexts. With these distinctions in mind, I shall turn, in the fourth and fifth chapters, to a more detailed analysis of how these distinctions account for the complex unity of Newman's thought.

The distinction between these three contexts is not
unlike the kind of distinction one is apt to make between contexts of "knowing" and contexts of "imagining."[10] One realizes
that there are important differences between separate cases of
imagining and between separate cases of knowing, but one also
sees that there are just as clearly important, identifiable
differences between any case of knowing and any case of imagining. Though each broad context gathers up an infinite number
of possible speech acts significantly different from one
another, the more general designation is not without purpose.
Just as it can be helpful to distinguish between the variety of
uses of discourse in disciplines such as history, philosophy,
and theology, it can also be helpful to distinguish between general categories of uses within each discipline.

By making these kinds of distinctions, I simply mean to
indicate a description of the way in which language operates
in given contexts of use and, consequently, to reveal the rules
which govern those uses. Newman's definition of "grammar" represents what I have in mind; for Newman, grammar is ". . . the
scientific analysis of language, and to be conversant with it,
as regards a particular language, is to be able to understand
the meaning and force of that language thrown into sentences
and paragraphs."[11] As in other elementary studies, said Newman, the discipline of grammar calls for "accuracy of mind."[12]
Thus, by analyzing the uses of Christian discourse in Newman,
I am investigating Newman's writings so as to be accurate about
the kinds of distinctions which he took to exist between different uses of Christian discourse. That accuracy demands a
description of the "meaning and force" of the various uses.
Therefore, to describe Newman's metatheological observations is
to clarify his descriptions of the various uses of Christian
discourse and the diverse contexts in which it functions.

The three contexts which I have isolated reveal particular rules and concepts unique to each individual context as
well as concepts which operate with different meanings and in
different relationships to one another in different contexts.
Since some rules and some concepts function in one context in a
way in which they do not operate in another, their particular
function in any one context may not be informative in any way
for their function and meaning in another context. This lack

of transferal of function and meaning can be a source of misunderstanding for the unwary.[13] Not a few significant errors have been made by those who have sought to cross contextual boundaries in an illegitimate way. Just as confusion may exist about the way in which two particular disciplines relate or differ in their uses of a given concept, so confusion often abounds concerning the use of particular concepts and pieces of discourse within a given sphere of human activity and reflection. Newman understood the possibility of this kind of error and gave diligent, if not systematic, attention to avoiding it.

As an examination of these important distinctions in Newman's work, the study begins by isolating and describing overly simple analyses of Newman's use of Christian discourse. The central portion of the study affords analysis of the development of the complex unity of Newman's thought--an analysis that corrects the reductive interpretations of Newman. The essay concludes with a consideration of the metatheological framework which, though not elaborately explored by Newman, seems to inform his reflections on the Christian faith.

NOTES TO CHAPTER I

[1] Cf. David A. Pailin, *The Way to Faith, An Examination of Newman's Grammar of Assent as a Response to the Search for Certainty in Faith* (London: Epworth Press, 1969).

[2] *Ibid.*, p. 115.

[3] Pailin, *ibid.*, p. 122, summarizes what he considers to be Newman's view: "When we grant theological assent we are merely recognizing the truth of certain ideas. Our religious faith, in contrast, is a commitment to something we recognize to be real and actual."

[4] Edwin Berry Burgum, "Cardinal Newman and the Complexity of Truth," *Sewanee Review*, XXXVIII (July, 1930), 323.

[5] John Henry Newman, "The Development of Religious Error," *The Contemporary Review*, XLVIII (October, 1885), 466-469.

[6] To say this is not to claim that Charles Stephen Dessain is reductionist when he claims that Newman's literary efforts can be understood as permeated throughout by a dedication to revealed religion. Cf. Dessain's article "Newman's First Conversion," *Studies: An Irish Quarterly Review*, XLVI (Spring, 1957), 51. Though the dedication is a constant one, it is not always exercised in the same way or for the same purpose. Newman's dedication to revealed religion was not so much a "leading idea" as it was the circumscription of the province within which his reflections, in all their complexity, lie.

[7] William K. Frankena, *Ethics* (Foundations of Philosophy Series, Elizabeth and Monroe Beardsley, editors; Englewood Cliffs, New Jersey: Prentice-Hall, Inc., 1963), pp. 4-5, 78-79.

[8] Paul Edwards, *The Logic of Moral Discourse* (New York: The Free Press, 1955), p. 45.

[9] The use of the term "metatheology" can be very misleading in that it may suggest the very same kind of systematically reductive enterprise which this essay opposes. Therefore, it is important to note that the term is not intended to imply that some foundational structure or analysis is necessary in order to hold these diverse uses coherently and meaningfully together. Rather, the term indicates that this study is essentially descriptive and second-order in its explication of the variability in Newman's modes of theological activity; it is not an analysis of specific doctrinal opinions which Newman held. In no sense, moreover, is this analysis to be taken as a necessary logical or psychological prerequisite to the correct use of Christian discourse. To use Newman's terms, the explication of the distinctions is an exercise of "explicit" reflection, an exercise distinct from and unnecessary to "implicit" use.

[10] This kind of distinction is made by Gilbert Ryle in *The Concept of Mind* (New York: Barnes and Noble, 1961).

[11] John Henry Newman, "Elementary Studies," *The Idea of a University* (Garden City, New York: Doubleday and Company, Inc., Image Books, 1959), p. 314.

[12] *Ibid.*, p. 313.

[13] Of course the literature which informs this warning is extensive, but I am especially indebted to the following: J. L. Austin, "A Plea for Excuses," *Philosophical Papers*, J. O. Urmson and G. J. Warnock, editors (Oxford: The Clarendon Press, 1961), pp. 123-152; Austin, "Performative Utterances," *Philosophical Papers, op. cit.*, pp. 220-239; Gilbert Ryle, "Ordinary Language," *The Philosophical Review*, LXII (April, 1953), 167-186; Ryle, "Philosophical Arguments," *Logical Positivism*, A. J. Ayer, editor (New York: The Free Press, 1966), pp. 327-344; Friedrich Waismann, "Language Strata," *Logic and Language*, Antony Flew, editor (second series; Garden City, New York: Doubleday and Company, Inc., 1965), pp. 226-247; Ludwig Wittgenstein, *Philosophical Investigations*, trans. G. E. M. Anscombe (second edition; New York: The Macmillan Company, 1958), p. 33^e.

CHAPTER II

NEWMAN AND HIS CRITICS:
A HISTORY OF REDUCTIVE ANALYSIS

Samuel Parkes Cadman has correctly observed that:

> Newman was an exemplification of his own contention that the same object may be viewed by various observers under such different aspects as to make their accounts of it more or less contradictory.[1]

The history of critical studies of Newman reflects a series of figures each of which has been considered to be the "true" Newman.[2] Of particular interest for this study are the implications of the history of this reflection for a description of the unity of Newman's thought. I shall deal, therefore, with those studies that have consciously sought to describe that unity as well as those that have done so even if that was not their avowed purpose. We shall find that these discussions of unity show a tendency to isolate an aspect of Newman's thought as the determinative factor in understanding Newman's work as a whole. These efforts to find a simple unity in Newman actually constitute reductions of the complex unity of his thought-- that is the thesis guiding the investigations within this chapter.

In describing several types of reductive criticisms, this chapter clarifies the nature of an attempt to describe a simple unity and the errors to which it leads in the interpretation of Newman's work. Chapters three, four and five of this study present Newman's own testimony regarding the nature of complex unity and the metatheological distinctions which that kind of unity involved for him. Lack of regard for that testimony has issued in four separate and inadequate attempts to account for Newman's understanding of the nature of Christian faith. Each of these attempts fails to account adequately for the complex unity of Newman's reflections. These analyses disregard metatheological distinctions between different contexts in which Christian discourse is used either by purposeful coalescing of diverse contexts or by lack of attention to one context of use as the result of a misleading concentration on another.

Three of these attempts are of some long standing, dating in each case from Newman's own lifetime, while the fourth, though also having some place in the nineteenth century discussion, has largely been a recent development. The earliest and most characteristic attempts related Newman's work to his personality and life history or to philosophical and theological subjectivism. A more generally sympathetic group of interpreters emphasized Newman's apologetic interests. And, in recent years, critics have tended to concentrate on Newman's understanding of religious inquiry. I shall relate some of the history of each of these types of interpretation in turn, noting some of their obvious errors and later attempts to correct them.

I. BIOGRAPHICAL AND PSYCHOLOGICAL REDUCTIONS

In 1906, Ernest Baudin called for the separation of treatments of Newman's thought from studies of his life since, he claimed, no objective evaluation was otherwise possible.[3] His reasons for making this suggestion are apparent when one considers the early history of Newman research. That history is replete with evaluations characterized, on the one hand, by personal antagonism and vindictiveness and, on the other hand, by personal attachment and devotion. These critiques sought to explain Newman's beliefs by reference to certain personality traits and/or by reference to certain events in his life. In short, these kinds of evaluations attempted to unify Newman's thought by reference to his life alone. They did not take Newman's theological views seriously in and for themselves. To that extent, they are psychological and biographical reductions.

The attitudes of Newman's brother, Francis W. Newman, may be taken as characteristic of this form of reductive interpretation.[4] Francis' acerbic attack on the Cardinal read into the events of Newman's life a precocious ability to deceive, a love of authority, and a disdain for others. He pictured his brother as credulous, sly, and fanatical. He intimated that Newman was secretly a Papist before 1845 and issued this warning:

> Scholars . . . may read with profit my brother's
> works . . . . But parents who would be sorely grieved
> by their children becoming converts to Romanism will
> not be wise in exposing the young and inexperienced to
> the speciousness of his pleading.[5]

John, said Francis, could reason (after all, he is deceptive with words too); John could reason like any other wily priest seeking unwary prospects for conversion.

The most important and influential figure in fostering this view of Newman was Edwin A. Abbott. Abbott pictured Newman as a lonely, egotistical man who lived in a dream world and who, as he despised himself, despised mankind in general. Abbott considered that it was Newman's fear and self-doubt that led him to join the Roman church. In summary, said Abbott, he was a "born dogmatist."[6] For this critic, the understanding of faith found in Newman's later works is a grand deceptive scheme, actually serving as a mask for an impetuous decision and a credulous spirit, though meant to make the act of faith seem reasonable. This distorted notion of faith, asserted Abbott, renders the imagination predominant over reason and facts.[7] In this way, Abbott explained the burden of Newman's intellectual endeavors in terms of his personal fears and irrational behavior. Abbott compared Newman to Hamlet as ". . . not a deceiver of others except so far as he is a pre-eminent deceiver of himself."[8] For Abbott, Newman's credulity, his intense need to believe, was based in fear and his intellectual efforts were rationalizations of an essentially irrational act.

Abbott's views were attacked as early as 1892 by Walter K. Firminger, but the view which Abbott promoted persisted.[9] A legend arose which influenced Newman research in many ways. For some, Abbott's view was authoritative.[10] The most tortuous attempt to make this judgment respectably fair to Newman was that of Alfred Fawkes who claimed: "Never consciously insincere, Newman constantly gave the impression of insincerity."[11] A second and more influential group refined their analysis while maintaining an essentially psychological interpretation of Newman. Francis Newman and Abbott had suggested that Newman was both a sinister figure and a hopelessly confused thinker. Their one-sided, sometimes vitriolic, interpretation sought to make the most damaging case possible against Newman. On the one hand, they claimed that Newman

was blind to his rationalizations of his fears. On the other
hand, they claimed that he willfully sought to deceive others.
While that paradoxical state of mind may be a psychological
possibility, what seemed more plausible to most critics was
that Newman was either self-deceived or conscious of fulfilled
personal need and, thus, honest in his appeals to others; or
conscious of his own base motives and correspondingly cunning
in his appeals to others. In most cases, the latter interpretation like the analysis by Abbott has given way to the
former interpretation. Many have argued that Newman's personal
act of faith as well as his written understanding of faith
rested on personal need rather than on sound argument without
attributing to him a host of negative traits.[12] The conclusion
of these interpreters is:

> Newman was a convert because Catholicism was adapted to
> his temperament, because there was a pre-established
> harmony between his character and the Catholic system,
> because his soul was naturaliter catholica. In one
> word, the conversion of Newman is a psychological much
> more than a theological problem.[13]

The judgment that Newman interpretation involves psychological more than theological problems, whether the focus be
on his conversion or more general than that, continued to be
prominent among interpreters of Newman even though those interpreters have differed in many other respects. In 1931, G.G.
Atkins described Newman and his work as being guided by personal
need rather than argument.[14] And, in 1943, G.O. Griffith pictured Newman as reacting in great fear and disillusionment to
the revolutionary hopes of the day and, consequently, becoming
intolerant and absolutist.[15]

While Atkins and Griffith were negative in their judgment
of Newman on the basis of their psychological interpretations,
other critics have made more positive conclusions from a psychological point of view. These interpreters have fostered
what Francis Reade has aptly called the "sentimental myth."[16]
This myth pictures Newman as a sweet, though hesitant and perplexed, individual who made a kind of romantic submission to
Rome. The primary sources for this interpretation, says Reade,
are the poem and hymn "Lead, Kindly Light" and the Apologia
pro vita sua. Newman is described as gentle, tender, and full
of pathos, while other aspects of his personality pale in their
significance. Associated with the priority of these emotions

and personal traits, there is an evaluation of Newman's understanding of faith that suggests his subordination of reason to sentiment and feeling. Edwin B. Burgum offers the best summary of this sentimental portrait of Newman by indicating how Miss Emmeline Deane's actual painting of Cardinal Newman[17] illustrates that view of Newman.

> It presents him as a good weak man who needs the aid of authority, but is so perplexed by tepid feminine sensations, so lost in a maze of ideas, as scarcely to recognize his dependence. He sits protected, almost sustained, by the rich full folds of his priestly dress, of which only one thin aristocratic hand upon his knee is conscious. His trifling weight is thrown forward upon a slender black gold-headed cane, that the other aged hand clutches as though it were a crozier in disguise, withdrawn from its public and symbolic use for personal support, but retaining under the tact of its secular form the assurance of authority. His attention, meanwhile, is elsewhere. With his fine white hair in casual neglect and his tremulous mouth held firm by the discipline of habitual gentility, he looks forward with hesitant grandmotherly affection into a world of which he had a grandmotherly experience.[18]

Blatant errors concerning Newman's biography and personality as well as overly sentimental or romanticized views of his life have met with sterner opposition since the Second World War. Earlier reports and interpretations of Newman which challenge the negative psychological reduction and the "sentimental myth" have been revivified.[19] New biographical studies based on these materials and others have appeared.[20] Processes to establish the candidacy of Newman for canonization--with all the resulting research into and discussion of his life--have been inaugurated.[21] What is significant in these developments, for this study, has been the gradual separation of these issues from interpretations of his thought. Nevertheless, psychological and biographical reductionism is always a possibility in dealing with a controversial figure like Newman--a possibility to be avoided.[22]

II. SUBJECTIVISTIC REDUCTIONS

Biographical and psychological reductions have not been nearly so numerous in the history of critical reflection on Newman as has been a group of separate types of criticism that share in common the judgment that Newman was a subjectivist in his view of faith. That is to say, these critics understood

Newman to have depreciated the role of reason and to have lost the objective content of belief. Two major groups of critics fall under this designation. First, there were those critics who charged Newman with a subjectivism rooted in an intellectual scepticism. These critics are largely identifiable with intellectual traditions in nineteenth century England. Second, there were those critics whose work was generated by the modernist movement. The twofold effect of the modernist movement was an attempt to identify Newman with modernism and a resulting contrary attempt to show his essential harmony with the scholastic tradition. After having considered these two groups of critics, I shall turn to consider an individual critic, Ernest Baudin, who made a more persuasive case for Newman's subjectivism than most.

English Critics

An early reviewer of the Grammar of Assent described that book as espousing subjectivism or the view that truth is ". . . little more than that which each man troweth."[23] It was advocates of a view of intellectual rigor first set forth by John Locke who found this charge to be the most damaging criticism which they could level against Newman. In An Essay Concerning Human Understanding, Locke formulated the principal tenet of this view as

> . . . the not entertaining any proposition with greater assurance than the proofs it is built upon will warrant. Whoever goes beyond this measure of assent, it is plain, receives not truth in the love of it; loves not truth for truth's sake, but for some other by-end.[24]

In this sense, Newman was, according to these critics, a sceptic; he did not subscribe to the appropriate set of epistemological criteria.

The charge of scepticism was given its original vitality by Fitzjames Stephen and his younger brother Sir Leslie Stephen. In a review of the Apologia, the elder Stephen claimed that Newman, while no liar as Charles Kingsley had incautiously charged, was a superstitious man guided by sophistry. Stephen's criticisms went beyond these personal criticisms to more formally philosophical considerations. Stephen prized "reason" and felt that Newman depreciated its role in gaining truth. According to Stephen, Newman failed to distinguish religious need of dogma from the necessity of the existence of true

dogmas, accepting arguments and evidence more for the sake of
peace of mind than for their truth.[25] According to Stephen,
Newman accepted an ultima ratio by which he chose those probabilities that suited his whim and that served his fears and
fancies more than his reason. Stephen's final judgment was
that ". . . if Dr. Newman was thoroughly honest he would be
an atheist."[26] Presumably Stephen felt that the probabilities
were not favorable to theism and that personal need provided
no further justification for faith. In that case, atheism must
have seemed, to him, the only "rational alternative."

The philosophical issues were more completely separated
from personal innuendo by Leslie Stephen. For the younger
Stephen, scepticism was an attitude of mind which declares
truth to be unattainable.[27] He accused Newman of sanctioning
a dangerous mode of apology which destroys the validity of the
reasoning process itself in order to evade reasonable conclusions.[28] Since Newman found the world to be devoid of evidence
for God's existence and since he found no other tests of its
truth, argued Stephen, the Cardinal appealed to the history of
what he considered to be the demonstrable unity, efficacy, and
persistence of the Church.[29]

In short, concluded Stephen, Newman was able to escape
complete scepticism only by accepting an authority that is outside the sphere of justification and whose presumptive existence depends on the sceptical assumption that the preservation
of truth demands a continuing miracle.[30] For the younger Stephen, Newman illustrated the principle that the real sceptic is
the man who declines logical tests, who has lost confidence in
reason. This form of scepticism, said Stephen,

> . . . orders us to believe because, if we don't believe,
> we shall doubt. That is virtually to admit that doubt
> is the legitimate and normal result of reasoning, which
> is, I take it, the essential characteristic of scepticism.[31]

Newman implied, according to Stephen, not just that men do
sometimes believe on insufficient evidence but that they ought
to do so. The only conclusion from Newman's position was,
therefore, that rational agreement is impossible.

Newman's thought represented, for Stephen and other
advocates of these rational criteria, a complete rejection of
rational criteria by means of an individualistic and solipsistic faith and a submission to authority.[32] Newman's

scepticism led him, in their view, to exalt subjective, personal need over more strictly rational criteria. Submission to an untested authority was possible only on the basis of this subjectivism. The exploration of the various uses of the word "reason" in Newman will reveal in what sense he can be said to have rejected reason as a guide. On the other hand, such an examination will also reveal the highly positive evaluation which Newman made of the rational enterprise. The kinds of criticisms which the Stephens made of Newman will not stand up against the results of such an analysis. While they were certainly right that Newman did not accept the rational criteria which they espoused, they failed to see that this fact did not constitute sufficient reason for understanding him to be a sceptic or a subjectivist.

Modernist Reductions and Thomist Responses

The modernist movement of the early twentieth century and Pius X's condemnation of the movement in his encyclical Pascendi dominici gregis fostered another set of evaluations to the effect that Newman showed subjectivist tendencies. Modernists sought to make Newman their progenitor, even if some admitted that the Cardinal was unconscious that modernism was the logical result of his theological principles. Those who sought to defend Newman against this association did so at that time by attempting to show his essential harmony with scholastic theology, increasingly identifiable by then with Thomist philosophy and theology. The particular issue on which the discussion centered was the relation of man's knowledge of God's revelation to his general experience. Those who found elements of the modernist position in Newman claimed that Newman held that religious beliefs are to be accounted for in terms of experience rather than in relation to acts of revelation.[33] Newman's defenders responded by detailed analyses showing points of agreement between Newman and Thomas on the matter of the relation of faith and human experience.

Modernism was no monolithic movement nor were modernists even in essential agreement regarding their methods of interpretation and procedure.[34] B.D. Dupuy suggests that three separate forms of modernism can be identified.[35] First, there were those modernists who emphasized the symbolism of Christian revelation in such a way as to suggest that one's personal faith was the constant and the content of one's faith the variable element. Modernists like George Tyrell and Alfred Loisy might be included in this group. A second group assimilated Newman to a type of French philosophy now commonly called the "philosophy of action." This school of thinkers emphasized the activity of the whole self in the attainment of truth. In addition, however, they maintained that the approach to the supernatural is through the natural--that one's thinking, willing, and feeling, closely scrutinized, demand an object beyond the natural order.[36] Perhaps the most prominent members of this group were Leon Olle-Laprune and Maurice Blondel. This group was less interested in direct analysis of Newman's position than in developing certain elements in Newman which they felt to be in agreement with their position. A third group emphasized the psychological, historical, and moral elements of Christianity dealt with by Newman as an antidote to scholastic thought. Henri Bremond was the prominent figure in this group. I shall consider only the first and third groups since the second group did not concern itself directly with Newman.

<u>Symbolism and fideism.</u> George Tyrell argued that Newman was the unwitting father of the modernist movement. Tyrell wrote:
> The solidarity of Newman with Modernism cannot be denied. Newman might have shuddered at his progeny, it is none the less his.[37]

Tyrell claimed that it is the liberals and the modernists--just those for whom Newman would have felt the greatest antipathy--that found in Newman's understanding of religious belief hope for communicating with the modern world.[38]

Tyrell bemoaned, however, what he felt to be the opposition between Newman's historical method and his scholasticism. In Newman's sermon of 1843 on "The Theory of Developments in Religious Doctrine," claimed Tyrell, the Cardinal showed essential agreement with liberal theology's contention that the formulation of the object revealed is not the subject matter of revelation but the object itself ever present to human experience.[39] In <u>The Essay on the Development of Christian Doctrine</u>, on the other hand, the development theory, as Tyrell understood it, was made subservient to the notion of a <u>depositum fidei</u> as a record of bygone supernatural experience.[40] Obviously Tyrell was more attracted to the former notion than to the latter; he also believed that Newman would have been more consistent with the larger body of his work if he had not held to the latter idea.

It is fairly apparent that Tyrell had Newman's understanding of faith and its relation to the matter of probabilities in mind when he mentioned the "larger body of his work." Certainly Tyrell felt that Newman's position on these questions aligned with the modernists and clearly made him subject to the condemnations of <u>Lamentabili sane exitu</u> and of <u>Pascendi dominici gregis</u>.[41] Tyrell was claiming that Newman's view of faith would mesh comfortably with a view of doctrine less defined and less concerned with questions of authority. Dupuy suggests that the notion of a symbolism of experience was often joined to a kind of fideism by this group of modernists. Tyrell sought to make that same connection in Newman. He was honest enough to note that at least one element of Newman's position did not align itself comfortably with this thesis. Tyrell regretted the loss of a unified view that might have been Newman's if he had simply not been concerned to find some <u>depositum fidei</u>.

Two other French critics shared Tyrell's interpretation of the two foci in Newman's thought that were essentially in harmony with modernism. Ernest Dimnet argued that dogma was relative and symbolic for Newman and that the conscience was an organ of intuition by which one perceived the divine.[42] It was another Frenchman, Alfred Loisy, however, whose similar claims were even more influential.[43]

<u>Psychology and personal experience.</u> The third form of modernism which I isolated above emphasized the psychological, historical, and moral elements of Newman's thought as opposed to the strictly theological elements. An English Roman Catholic Bishop, J.C. Hedley, presented an early development of this view:

> I have never been able to accept Newman's main thesis in the <u>Grammar of Assent</u>. This I take to be, that the real reasoning process by which men arrive at all their important convictions is not purely intellectual, but made up of imagination, association, probability, memory,

> instinct, feeling, popular persuasion and every kind of
> impression that the complexity of man's being is susceptible
> of. Doubtless, many minds do depend for their conviction
> on very mixed motives. But I should have thought it evident
> that no really intelligent mind would ever allow the
> validity of a conviction until it had reviewed, by the
> great controlling faculty of reason, the multitudinous
> impressions with which it had to deal. The only power
> by which the mind can really 'infer,' is the purely intel-
> lectual faculty. Feeling, associations, and personal
> character may incline a man to an inference; but until the
> intellectual faculty has reviewed, summed up and pronounced,
> there can surely be no inference. To say that there is
> an 'illative' sense, other than the intellect proper, is
> only to say that truth is subjective--which is intolerable.[44]

This criticism was taken as a positive recommendation of Newman's position by Henri Bremond. In his study, <u>Newman</u>: <u>Essai de Biographie Psychologique</u>, he pictured Newman as advocating the dominance of the imagination and the intuition over reason.[45] For Newman, said Bremond, that is most true which will produce virtuous acts.[46] For Bremond, Newman's defense of religion was always an unfolding of his personal experience; conscience is the ultimate sanction of religion.

Bremond's fellow Frenchman, Leonce de Grandmaison, who did not share Bremond's enthusiasm for these views, did agree with Bremond that Newman held them. His final warning was that Newman, though brilliantly suggestive as a psychologist, was not to be trusted as a theologian or as a philosopher.[47] He described Newman alternately as an anti-intellectualist, a conceptualist, a relativist, and an agnostic. While his list of accusations were not uncommon among Newman's critics, it was the judgment that Newman's genius was specifically psychological that came to characterize criticisms of Newman even more generally.[48]

The course of the controversy concerning Newman's modernist tendencies or his lack of them did lead Bremond and Dimnet to soften their claims, but they did not essentially change them.[49] Because of the modernist claims of association with Newman and because of papal warnings and condemnations, the controversy lingered and a pale of doubt lay over Newman's work.[50] Tyrell's judgment seemed sound to many both within and without the Roman Church:

> If the authors of the Encyclical had not Newman in mind,
> it must be concluded that, in total ignorance of his work,
> they did not recognize his theories, ideas, opinions,
> and his very words in the writings of his 'Modernist'
> followers. At all events, in the expert judgment . . .

of all who have studied Newman, not merely as literature but as philosophy and theology, his condemnation is written all over the face of the Encyclical.[51]

Even a letter of Pius X to the bishop of Limerick, Edward Thomas O'Dwyer, in which he expressly denied Newman's being condemned by the encyclical, did not quiet the controversy.[52]

<u>Thomist interpretations of Newman.</u> One form which the controversy assumed from the outset consisted in comparisons of Newman's views with the official philosophical and theological positions of the Roman Church. Not surprisingly, as one comes to expect in relation to Newman, the judgments differed on this question. Frederick Denison Maurice believed that Newman's was essentially a scholastic, propositional theology and that Newman did not distinguish between belief in a person and assent to a statement.[53] On the other hand, Father Thomas Harper, a leading scholastic scholar of the day, made elaborate criticisms of what he considered to be Newman's failures to understand and to appropriate a proper understanding of logic, conceptuality, and metaphysics. In each case, Harper's criteria were Thomist.[54] Other critics were not so wholesale in their rejection of Newman's work, believing some parts to be genuinely scholastic. In an early piece of criticism appearing in Germany in 1895, A. Bellesheim claimed that Newman's philosophy is essentially Thomist but that it is not free from the influence of Whately's nominalism and Reid's "common sense" theory.[55] Still other critics found Newman to be fully scholastic in his ideas, with the proviso on the part of some that his emphasis was subjective while that of Thomas was objective.[56]

Modern criticism that has assumed a scholastic point of view has shown similar schools of opinion. Martin Cyril D'Arcy subscribes to the view that Newman's errors, though never so general as Harper supposed, do stem from a defective theory of universals, in his case nominalist, which separates inference from assent and proof from certitude too sharply, introducing the illative sense only to make up for having deprived thought of some of its legitimate functions.[57] Erich Przywara sees Newman in total agreement with scholastic thought, only emphasizing subjective rather than objective categories. Przywara's cry is: "Not Thomas <u>or</u> Newman, but in faithfulness to Catholic polarity [a conjunction of objective and subjective emphases]

Thomas and Newman."[58]

The most damaging results of this kind of Thomist analysis are the tangles into which critics get themselves by fitting Newman too closely to a scholastic pattern. Let us examine two examples of these tangles. Thomas J. Gerrard argued that, though Newman seemed to exclude a middle term from informal reasoning, he actually used an implicit middle term and, thus, subscribed to Aristotelian rules of thought. Gerrard also concluded that, though Newman held that not all implicit reasoning is in fact capable of being made explicit, such explicitness is always theoretically possible.[59] In a second case, George P. Klubertanz argued that Thomas anticipated all of Newman's basic ideas and, therefore, that those ideas are sound. Klubertanz admitted that it is difficult to find an equivalent in Thomas to Newman's distinction between formal and informal inference. The best that Klubertanz could do was to argue from silence: Thomas does not per se exclude informal inference.[60] Such efforts make more understandable, if not entirely fair, Henri Bremond's retort to Father John J. Toohey: ". . . to transform Newman into a scholastic, is possible only for one who knows nothing about Newman or nothing about scholasticism."[61]

Bremond's argumentum ad hominem is, however, hardly appropriate in relation to Franz Michel Willam, a scholar whose work reveals his knowledge both of scholasticism and of Newman.[62] Adrian J. Boekraad has made the most direct and telling criticism of Willam's work and, coincidentally, of much of this kind of scholastic criticism. Boekraad praises Willam for his erudition but finds him so fascinated by the attempt to find the influence of Aristotle on Newman that he can find no other influence of importance.[63] As a consequence, Willam tends to use any piece of argument to make his case. He employs isolated passages in which Newman praised Aristotle but neglects those in which he lauded Plato, Butler, and others. Especially significant is that Willam does not give anywhere near the importance due to Newman's independent way of thinking. That Newman was influenced in his Dublin lectures by Aristotle is certain, but that he adhered to Aristotle in other matters, as in his epistemology, does not necessarily follow.[64] In his major study Aristotelische Erkenntnislehre bei Whately und Newman, Willam confesses that his translations of Newman are not literal but designed to bring out Newman's "true meaning." Since Willam places such great value on the use of the same term by Aristotle and Newman, such a manner of translation makes many of his arguments from the text without any value. Boekraad's summation of the difficulty of Willam's view indicates that his work is reductive at times: "We must not allow the interest in one question to obscure our view of the whole."[65]

Johannes Artz has also made pertinent observations regarding the limitations of any comparison between Aristotle or Thomas and Newman. He notes that Newman's conception of logic has nothing to do with Aristotelian formal logic, since Newman constantly lessened the role of verbal reasoning and failed to view an argument as incomplete even if it was not a perfect syllogism. For Aristotle, on the other hand, the only true induction was a complete induction expressible in a syllogism, and the only kind of probability proof was an abbreviated chain of reasoning that is rhetorically advantageous but imperfect. Aristotle did not pay attention to the matter of assent and made no use of the notion of _phronesis_, as Newman did, in relation to knowledge claims. Newman went far beyond Aristotle both by virtue of various influences on his thought and by virtue of his own originality.[66]

Perhaps a letter from Newman to Father Whitty, from the Birmingham Oratory on December 20, 1878, best indicates some of his own thoughts on the matter. The letter was written on the occasion of Leo XIII's exaltation of Thomism to a position as the official philosophy of the Roman Church. This decree had fostered speculation regarding the status of Newman's views of the nature of religious belief. Newman wrote to Whitty:

> Thank you for what you say about the _Grammar_ of _Assent_. If any one is obliged to say 'I speak under correction' it is I--for I am no theologian and am too old, and ever have been, to become one. All I can say is that I have no suspicions, and do not anticipate, that I shall be found in substance to disagree with St. Thomas. What is it exactly that the Pope has done?[67]

This humorous passage contains the words of a man unconcerned to be in essential agreement or disagreement with Thomas; his concerns were directed elsewhere. In response to the Jesuit Father Harper's criticisms, Newman wrote to a friend: ". . . I think I see that the main argument of my book does not fall within the philosophical and theological traditions of the society."[68] And, in another letter to the same friend on the same subject, Newman wrote:

> I began to read Fr. Harper's papers, but they were (to my ignorance of theology and philosophy) so obscure, and (to my knowledge of my real meaning) so hopelessly misrepresentations of the book, that I soon gave it over.[69]

Despite these "misrepresentations," Thomist critics have rendered an important service to the study of Newman. They have shown that he had real concern for the question of the content of the faith and for its reality as an objective revelation. Tyrell typifies the modernist reluctance to give those interests their full importance in Newman. Nevertheless, to study and to interpret Newman's work from any one philosophical position as some Thomists and others have, has limited value at best and becomes the occasion for the distortion of reductionism at worst.

<u>Ernest Baudin</u>. Although much superficial and misleading analysis has been done under the banner of exposing Newman's supposed subjectivism, some of the studies do raise significant questions for the interpretation of Newman's work. By far the most capable critic who charged Newman with subjectivism was Ernest Baudin, who published a series of papers on "La Philosophie de la Foi chez Newman" in 1906.[70] Baudin was free of the English tradition of personal accusation in the criticism of Newman. In fact, as I noted, he called for the separation of critical studies of Newman's thought from biographical studies.

In his own way Baudin repeated the common criticism that Newman developed a philosophical account that has no real value in comparison with his psychological observations. He went further to charge that Newman developed his philosophical account under the guise of a psychological description. The philosophical account, however, was not derived from facts of experience, depending instead on doctrines held prior to the facts. The belief in these doctrines itself rested on a need and a desire to believe; Baudin charged that Newman was, in this sense, a fideist. Baudin summarized: "Fideism, according to Newman, is first a need and an attitude, then a doctrine, then a psychology."[71] In fact, urged Baudin, Newman universalized a personal case, exalting his own passional self in such a way as to establish an affective dogmatism. According to Baudin, this dogmatism served Newman as a method of proselytizing and as a defense against the attacks of reason. A faith devoid of rational argument is not subject to rational rebuff; what is required for understanding it and appropriating it is a contagion of delicate sensibility.[72] The ultimate foundation of this affective dogmatism is an intuitionism, a mystical communion of the soul and God. The result of holding this position, claimed Baudin, is to limit one's audience to fideists. Such a defiant irrationalism allows no satisfactory criteria of justification, presupposing a rapport between beliefs and the meeting of religious needs which does no justice to the diversity of beliefs which might satisfy those needs.[73] The success of Newman's argument was based on his presupposing a Christian conscience rather than a conscience unaware of Christian ideas; the ideas which Newman took to be innate are endemic to a Christian culture only.[74] Baudin's final judgment was, therefore, that Newman's position was basically fideism that is culturally dependent.

The important questions which Baudin raised must be treated later, as many of them impinge on the question of the unity of Newman's thought which is our central concern in this study. Though I shall not always refer to Baudin directly, I shall attempt to answer the following questions which he raised. Did Newman confuse a particular life history with the only appropriate path to faith? Did he make faith subjective and solipsistic? Was faith finally an irrational act for Newman? Some of these questions were raised by others before Baudin, but they had never been asked with such care and with such power. I shall consider them below, however, to show that I do not think that even Baudin can make a case for Newman being a subjectivist. To attempt to do so is, by necessity, to overlook much that is in Newman, that is, to be reductive in one's analysis.

III. APOLOGETIC REDUCTIONS

Another interpretative clue has drawn considerable attention from critics of Newman. These interpreters, usually citing Newman's *Biglietto* speech, conclude that the unity of Newman's literature is his apologetic efforts in an age characterized by religious liberalism and by open hostility to religious matters.[75] Lawrence F. Barmann's judgment perhaps summarizes this interpretation best:

> This notion of the Christian combat [against the world] and the weapons for attaining the victory is the framework within which studies so diverse as the *Grammar of Assent* and the *Idea of a University* must ultimately be considered . . . . Newman's life and works, then, have a single motive--the triumph of Truth, Christ the Logos of God, in his battle against Satan for the minds and hearts of individuals and, ultimately, for the world as a whole.[76]

R.W. Church, Newman's close friend, made a similar judgment: "The leading subject of his modern thought is the contest with liberal unbelief . . . ."[77] The unity found in Newman's work by these critics is what Philip Hughes has called Newman's prophetic opposition to religious liberalism.[78]

A leading contemporary student of Newman, H. Francis Davis, is an advocate of this apologetic thesis. Davis views Newman's mission as one to the secularized world in which scientific theology is only a collection of notions. Newman asserted that religious truth cannot be approached scientifically since religion is a relation between two persons, the human and the divine, through a third person, the teacher or prophet, with whom one must be in contact if he is to realize the meaning of the religion. According to Davis, Newman understood that scientific language is incapable of bringing about such personal contact; only the language of literature is conscious of the individuals addressed.[79] The language of literature expresses reality as understood, valued, and loved or hated by a person.[80] It is in this way that Davis believes that Newman argued for the viability of religious discourse by first showing the incompleteness of scientific discourse for certain realms of experience.[81]

According to Davis, religious language is expressive of the reality of God and lives as a mystery in the Word of God ". . . below all the multiplicity and complexity of human expression as a deep inner unity."[82] Davis, in a cryptic passage, writes of this inner and saving word which makes Christianity what it is as having existence ". . . underneath and before all of the expressions which Christians have invented to expound it."[83] Davis understands Newman's notion of the development of doctrine to imply a kind of blossoming of this inner word in a man's mind, not an addition to knowledge but a deeper penetration and understanding.[84] Throughout his analysis Davis emphasizes what he finds to be Newman's anticipation of modern psychology and its understanding of the unconscious.[85] In the final analysis, Davis understands Newman to have made evaluative judgments of levels of discourse on the basis of a certain theory of language and ultimately on a certain view of the way in which the mind works. I would argue that neither aspect of the interpretation does justice to Newman's views. The interpretation devalues the role of dogma and tends to make appropriation of Christianity the central model for the description of its content.

A less recent, but more helpful and persuasive, form of this kind of analysis is found in Newman's able biographer Wilfrid Ward.[86] Ward argued that the variety of Newman's work was actually a function of his unity of purpose, which was his concentration on preserving religion against the tide of rationalism and infidelity.[87] "He did not touch history or theology for their own sake, but solely as bearing on his great aim. And he did not care to pursue them into regions which had no connection therewith."[88] That Newman's writings seldom directly deal with religious unbelief is a fact that Ward explained as a function of Newman's reluctance to disturb the habitual religious associations of the minds of believers by argument on the fundamental questions raised by modern unbelief. He preferred to strengthen the rational and spiritual supports of belief actually present in society and in individuals and its supports in their affections and in their imaginations.[89] Newman saw arguments as medicinal, as cures for diseased minds, which could, however, suggest difficulties for one who habitually practiced his faith and thus weaken his faith.[90] In Ward's view, Newman's writings were meant to strengthen the Church and the faithful. They were designed to prevent, not to discuss infidelity. Newman believed that such strengthening was best kindled, said Ward, by appeals to the whole man--his conscience, affections, and imagination--rather than by argument alone. Ward's conclusion was that Newman used his literary powers to make the story of Christianity and the power of its ideal live in the imagination and to form in his hearers and readers the Christian mind and the Christian character.[91]

The suggestiveness of Ward's analysis should not be

overlooked. He pointed to significant apologetic and pastoral concerns that were certainly important for Newman. He also illumined the place of literary efforts and the role of the imagination for the Cardinal. It is in giving this emphasis, however, that he suggested a negative verdict on the place of argument in Newman. I shall argue that Newman did not limit the role of argument to a "medicinal" effect and that his dedication to the Christian story was not only apologetic and pastoral.

IV. MORAL DISPOSITIONS AND THE ARGUMENT FROM CONSCIENCE: THE CONCENTRATION OF RECENT CRITICISM ON NEWMAN'S VIEW OF THE NATURE OF RELIGIOUS INQUIRY

In this section, I shall consider various, more recent works that interpret Newman's understanding of the nature of Christian faith. These works scrupulously avoid psychological and autobiographical reductionism. They refuse to attribute "subjectivism" to Newman. Their central purpose is to show how Newman understood the process of coming to believe. In some ways, they maintain elements of the apologetic thesis, but they are not interested in concentrating on the nature of religious liberalism. Their principal concern is to understand how Newman views religious inquiry rather than to describe what views he opposed.

Because of their freedom from the other types of reductionism which I have discussed and because of their importance in the contemporary discussion of Newman, the critiques which I take up in this section are highly significant for understanding the nature of the thesis which I have set forth regarding the complex unity of Newman's reflections on Christian faith. A consideration of these writers can provide a way in which to introduce the distinctive thesis which I seek to propose. As in the case of Ward's analysis, criticisms of these works should not, in every case, be taken to suggest a fundamental error in the interpretation of Newman within that study, but in every case, to imply that there is an incompleteness of analysis that is misleading.

<u>Maurice Nédoncelle.</u> Maurice Nédoncelle's book, <u>La</u>

Philosophie Religeuse de John Henry Newman, is one of the ablest
attempts to give an organic shape to Newman's scattered reflections on the nature of Christian faith. In any attempt to give
those reflections such treatment lies much wisdom and some danger. If one can gain an awareness of Newman's unity without
reducing his insights to an artificial structure, he has accom-
plished a great deal. Nédoncelle seeks this kind of balanced
view. He typifies Newman as a "philosopher of mystery" or a
philosopher who stood in wonder before all things, who began
with an initial problem rather than with evidence, and who,
though he posited an original clarity about matters of importance, soon perceived that clarity to be inadequate.[92] Newman,
says Nédoncelle, understood this lack of clarity to be the
result of a discontinuity, of a fall in man's existence which
is exhibited in his alienation from others and from the world.[93]

Yet, amidst the misery of man, there stands a primitive
"moral grandeur" or intuition of his spiritual being that is
inaccessible to discursive reason. This intuition is of the
moral law, according to Newman, and not of God. But the sense
of duty implies an object of authority, a being exterior and
superior to man. Thus, claims Nédoncelle, the intentionality
of conscience is religious and, even more, theistic, for Newman.[94] But Newman did not, says Nédoncelle, hold that such
intentionality reveals the Christian God. Newman held to an
anti-intuitionism and anti-mysticism in this respect--an initial
light is so seriously affected by sin that it is in constant
need of external assistance.[95] Although Newman emphasized
man's moral vocation, he did not describe man in terms of his
will alone; the ideas to which one commits himself impose conditions of their own upon him.[96] This second element, remarks
Nédoncelle, is also necessary for understanding Newman; the
economy of providence constitutes the ideas or symbolic percep-
tions of the real given to man by God and preserved by Him
from decline and error.[97]

Nédoncelle also helpfully points out that Newman's
understanding of the nature of assent and of the moral element
in knowing must be seen as a reaction to rationalistic and
evidential apologetics if one is not to jump to the conclusion
that they are sceptical or subjectivistic.[98] Newman's attack
was not on the intellect as such but on the aristocracy of the

intellect which leads to the view that the majority of men are involved in incurable irrationalism and prejudice.[99] I shall return to this point in chapters three and four as I unfold how Newman distinguished between several senses of the word "reason." Nédoncelle is careful to note that Newman's understanding of the promptings of the conscience and of the desire for revelation are not to be understood as meaning the opposition of reason and intuition but as a way in which to enlarge the province and nature of the intelligence and of logic.[100] According to Nédoncelle, Newman found no contradiction between nature and grace, only a disproportion. The expectations aroused by natural religion provide sufficient reasons for believing in the revelation once it comes.[101]

    The wisdom of Nédoncelle's attempt to understand Newman is that he makes clear the distinctions between the negative and positive aspects of Newman's judgment of reason, between reasons for believing and what one believes.[102] He even notes correctly, it seems to me, that one cannot understand the full implications of Newman's views on the basis of the <u>Grammar</u> alone.[103] The danger with which Nédoncelle flirts is the tendency to concentrate on Newman's distinctions in such a way that insufficient notice is given to his understanding of the content of faith. Newman had as many interesting things to say about the question of revelation as he does about the human appropriation of faith. And, even if Nédoncelle's book is designed to deal with Newman's philosophical insights, surely his view of how these distinct matters relate is of philosophical interest. Yet Nédoncelle does not give attention to this interesting metatheological question. It is one thing to concentrate on Newman's understanding of the role of dogma in relation to the inadequacy of man's understanding in natural religion. It is another thing to concentrate on how that revealed truth shapes his vision and action. And it is still another to consider that revelation in and of itself apart from the question of its appropriation and use. Newman had observations regarding each matter. Not only that, he had important observations regarding the relationships between these various functions of Christian discourse. Nédoncelle's analysis proves especially inadequate on this level.

Adrian J. Boekraad. At the outset of his study of Newman, The Personal Conquest of Truth, Adrian J. Boekraad writes that:
> Of all the problems that surround, and are involved in, the consideration of the human soul, one of the most baffling and yet most important, is the fact that truth and its acceptance is dependent on, and relative to, the individual mind.[104]

How that relativity is related to the universality and objectivity of truth is, for Boekraad, the issue for understanding Newman. Boekraad makes two important points: one, that Newman distinguished between "universal truth" and the "personal characteristics in the method of acquiring and possessing it;" two, that it would be a regrettable error to confine Newman's importance within the limit of his treatment of the question of personal appropriation.[105]

Boekraad evidences, therefore, a clear desire to avoid a reduction of Newman's work or life.[106] For example, he argues against the attempt to describe Newman's conversion in terms of one element of what was a complex "multiplicity of data." Boekraad himself finds the unity of all the elements in Newman's thought in his personal Platonism, i.e., in his view that ". . . a soul lives only to use all its forces for the most glorious task that man can undertake, that of conquering and possessing truth in love."[107] Such a conquest consists in the realization of an invisible world behind but impressing itself upon the visible world. In this way, notes Boekraad, Newman understood knowledge to be the result of a personal effort of thinking.[108] This personal conquest of truth which is the subject of the Grammar is capable of being analyzed, a process necessary in fact if errors are to be avoided.[109] The result of Boekraad's interpretation of that analysis seems, however, less than satisfactory if one wants to avoid a misleading one-sidedness in understanding Newman.

Boekraad accounts for the universality of the Gospel on the basis of the nature of man. He argues that Newman understood the origin of all assents to be ultimately based in experience.[110] The root of that experience he takes to be universal elements in the nature of man. The most important of these elements for Newman, says Boekraad, was the conscience.[111] In this way, knowledge of one's nature leads to knowledge of God. In short, Boekraad maintains that, for Newman, truth is to be found by means of a reflexive act of concentration on one's own being. The question of God's existence becomes inseparable from the question of man's nature. The goal of this identification, says Boekraad, was to make atheism self-contradictory. One could not deny God without also denying his own nature, specifically the testimony of his conscience.[112]

Several questions can be raised about this interpretation of Newman. First, Boekraad's analysis does not give sufficient attention to the negative judgments which Newman made regarding the conscience. Second, that interpretation, while acknowledging the presence of other factors in Newman's analysis of faith, seems to concentrate in an exaggerated fashion on the matter of personal appropriation. In another study of Newman, largely from Boekraad's hand, Boekraad describes the matter of implicit or personal thinking as ". . . the key to all Newman's writings" and as that which explains ". . . the fundamental unity of all his work."[113] Boekraad declares: "All problems were in their interrelation related to this central theme and from this unity of his vision he threw light on whatever problem came his way."[114] Boekraad describes the unity as one of an "inward system" and of a "spiritual vision" and of its external expression as ". . . a garb with which the inward thought ought to be clothed to bring it out and hand it over to others."[115] Boekraad does note that concentration on this theme alone is misleading. He also argues for the importance of authorities and traditions as well as of the testimony of conscience in analyzing Newman. Nevertheless, his analysis suggests a centrality to the testimony of conscience and to the personal character of thinking which this study will argue is misconceived. These matters have a centrality for Newman in certain contexts and for certain purposes; it is dangerous, however, to make them the keystone of a systematic position.

Zeno. In his study, <u>John Henry Newman</u>: <u>Our Way to Certitude</u>, Father Zeno states that Newman's central purpose in the <u>Grammar of Assent</u> is ". . . to show the psychological basis of an act of faith--in other words, the natural element of belief to the exclusion of the element of grace or supernatural influences."[116] Since Zeno concludes that the basis of an act of faith for Newman was the illative sense, he proposes

". . . to investigate the very central notion of the Grammar: the illative sense, as the last explanation of all rational belief in concrete matters."[117] In that respect, Zeno does an admirably thorough and careful job and renders a most helpful service to Newman scholarship. Nevertheless, one must keep in mind Zeno's own emphasis on Newman's "theory of aspects" in evaluating Zeno's treatment of the illative sense and, more broadly, of Newman's view of the nature of belief. Zeno notes that this theory implies that one cannot adequately comprehend a given thing by viewing it under one aspect alone, i.e., from only one point of view.

The following question can be raised about Zeno's analysis: Does he treat the illative sense under one aspect only while it must be understood in other ways if one is to understand it properly? Or, rephrasing the same question, does he suppose that the function of the illative sense, though actually confined to a given context, serves to explain Newman's view of religious faith? Perhaps the first step in deciding this issue is to discover whether Zeno understands the illative sense to be one among other mental faculties or a designation for human reasoning in general. Zeno does write:

> The operation of the illative sense must be called reasoning, but it is reasoning without the formal application of the rules of logic and without a clear insight into the road taken by the mind.[118]

In this sense, "illative sense" is a designation for the ordinary process of reasoning. On the other hand, Zeno can speak of the illative sense as if it were a kind of mysterious faculty supplying insight to make up for the deficiencies of language. Zeno suggests that according to Newman, there is something inherently faulty and insufficient about words that is not faulty with the illative sense.[119] But, as I shall argue later, Newman used the term "illative sense" as a descriptive designation for the character of the reasoning process rather than for one element within that process. The illative sense is not a recondite faculty, but the character of reasoning in its peculiarity from one discipline to another and from one person to another.

In addition, the peculiar complexity and subtlety of the reasoning process is, in no way, to be interpreted as disallowing the need for rules to guide that process. Yet Zeno

not only implies the absence of rules by the mysterious quality
that he gives to the illative sense; he also explicitly states
that opinion in claiming that ". . . the processes of reasoning
leading to assent, to action, and to certitude, are actually
too multiform, subtle, omnigenous, and implicit to admit of
being measured by rules."[120] What Zeno's analysis overlooks is
that his claim might be true for certain contexts and for certain purposes, but that it cannot possibly fit all of Newman's
work. For Newman, reasoning was not a uniform process subject
to one set of rules (in that sense, Zeno is certainly right),
but a whole network of processes diverse and complex yet each
with its own rules. Is that not the reason for a "grammar"
of assent? Though the process of coming to assent is not fixed
in nature, there are definite features of religious inquiry.
Likewise there are also rules which fit other contexts of religious interest beside that of coming to believe, such as contexts
in which one actually exercises his faith and in which one
asserts what one believes. Each of these contexts operates
according to certain rules. Newman's claim that there is no
ultimate test of truth beside the testimony given to the truth
by the mind itself does not imply an absence of standards but
a complexity and diversity of standards discernible and stateable
only by a given person for a given purpose.

Insofar as Zeno's analysis omits attention to the limits
in which his analysis operates it is faulty; insofar as it does
not give attention to how those limitations were understood by
Newman, whether Zeno admits those limitations or not, Zeno does
not grapple with the question which is central to this study.
It would seem that Zeno does not take the ruled use of the
illative sense seriously enough; certainly he does not investigate the various contexts and rules which operate to make up
Newman's basic reflections on the nature of Christian faith.

Jan Walgrave. In Newman the Theologian, Walgrave proposes to set Newman's theory of the development of doctrine
". . . in its proper framework, viewing it as a section of a
complete psychology and apologetic."[121] This framework can be
characterized, believes Walgrave, as ". . . a philosophy of
human nature."[122] Walgrave's conviction is that Newman's writings imply an "integral concept of man."[123] Thus, Walgrave

proposes to pay attention to the thought of Newman as a whole rather than simply to one or two works. In that respect, Walgrave's book represents a marked advance over those of many other interpreters. He shows a respect for the profound complexity of Newman's point of view, yet his systematizing efforts are often at odds with this appreciation of complexity. This basic conflict accounts for other instances of divided judgment and results from a failure to distinguish separate elements in Newman.

Walgrave takes Newman's "integral concept of man" to be rooted in the Cardinal's understanding of the reality and role of the conscience. Newman's starting point, he asserts, was the contrast between the conscience and the alien and hostile world. This contrast also accounts for the differences between the religious man and the "man of the world." The essential difference is that the former remains attuned to the testimony of his conscience while the latter follows only opinion and reason.[124] Thus, says Walgrave, Newman considered the conscience to be the ". . . sole instrument which enables us to perceive what pertains to religion and morals, and to judge those first principles which follow accordingly."[125] Walgrave goes so far as to claim that, for Newman, the moral experience of the conscience was the sole source of the knowledge of God.[126]

Parallel to his concentration on the testimony of conscience, claims Walgrave, was Newman's valuing of personal over scientific and argumentative thought. It is this valuation which Walgrave terms Newman's "practical psychologism."[127] Walgrave describes this "practical psychologism" as Newman's holding that ". . . the thought can never be viewed in isolation from the thinker" and asserting that the ". . . thinking by which we work out our idea of the world and of life is an expression of what we ourselves are."[128] The upshot of this position is that Newman justified the validity of thoughts on the basis that they are a function of our natures as human beings and not, therefore, subject to question. Newman was not guilty of theoretical psychologism, says Walgrave, because he did not rule out the possibility of epistemological and metaphysical solutions of the same problem; he simply did not employ them himself.

Walgrave understands Newman to have argued for the

existence of God and for the necessity of revelation on the
basis of this interpretation of human nature. The dialectic
of conscience is taken to be such that one is unable to satisfy
its dictates in himself or to see in the world the evidence
of the moral providence which it suggests. In that sense,
Christian revelation as authoritatively interpreted by the
Church offers the only solution for the problems which man
encounters in the world.[129] Walgrave tends, then, to see
ecclesiastical authority as a kind of compensation for the
defects of logic, as a safeguard against the misuse of reason,
and as the aim of conscience. While I can agree with Walgrave
that Newman's goal was to show that there is a religious factor
involved in any truly complete description of man's nature, I
am not so sure that Walgrave has given this view its proper
place in Newman's thought as a whole. For Walgrave, the concept
of "conscience" and all that it involves provide the interpretative clue for understanding all elements of Newman's thought.
On the one hand, conscience is made the source and dialectic of
religious belief. In addition, conscience, or what may more
properly be called a personal mode of thinking, is the source
of the dogmatic impulse. Small wonder that Walgrave finds
Newman to be guilty of "practical psychologism." He has interpreted what Newman had to say in terms of a psychology of moral
obligation and a phenomenology of personalist thinking. I must
agree with J.G. Lawler who finds that Walgrave has a bias for
the affective and non-rational which disregards Newman's constant conjunction of the moral and intellectual life.[130] By
accurately noting this conjunction, one overcomes the need to
accuse Newman of either theoretical or practical psychologism.

Walgrave does recognize certain distinctions in Newman
that seem very important to me. For example, Walgrave notes
that Newman used the word "object" in at least four ways:
one, to mean "end;" two, to mean an "intentional object" or
object of consciousness; three, to mean a "thing" or existing
reality; four, to mean objects or realities independent of the
subject but considered in relation to the subject as deter-
mining the content of the act of knowing.[131] Walgrave considers
the last sense, a combination of the second and third, to be
basic in Newman. He makes no allowance for Newman ever addres-
sing reality in the third mode apart from the second. Walgrave

does implicitly recognize this matter in Newman in noting that Newman held truth to be objective or transcendent to man's mode of knowledge, with external motives and external authority.[132] Thus, while the word "objective" is very often a pejorative term for Newman, indicating a "notional" or rationalistic religion, the word "subjective" can also be used pejoratively. In understanding faith as a state of mind or as a process of implicit reasoning which brings man to faith, one must not separate it from faith as the object or content of belief, i.e., the Creed.[133]

Although Walgrave can state that conscience is the only source of the knowledge of God, he can also write that:

> . . . the intuition of faith has to reach us through the the study of Scripture and of dogmatic theology. We have no direct, independent intuition of faith. In contrast with the process of natural knowledge, we normally require to obtain contact with the realities of faith, a certain verbal expression, as an indispensable condition.[134]

In this sense, however, Scripture and creed are simply "occasions," in the Kierkegaardian use of that word, indispensable in that sense but in that sense only. Although Walgrave accepts the idea that Newman was ". . . no extreme advocate of the method of immanence which seeks to uphold the truth of Christianity and the Church by the sole testimony of religious experience" he also argues that notional or creedal elements do not function as notional for the individual.[135] These elements are not ". . . made use of as notional."[136] That is to say, the description of facts and deeds in Scripture stir one up to an act of the religious imagination by which these elements are assembled into a concrete synthesis.

The content of faith seems, in Walgrave's view, only to count when it is appropriated faith, real assent. This valuing of real assent is, however, most misleading in understanding Newman. Walgrave should have taken his lucid and helpful insights regarding the different uses of the word "object" more seriously. If he had done so, he might not have concentrated so exclusively on the personalist mode of thinking and might not have made the phenomenon of conscience basic to all aspects of Newman's thought. Scripture and creed certainly would have had some other character than that of "occasions," or correctives against fideism and subjectivism. They could have been seen in their rightful place as another entirely different aspect of Newman's thought, deserving separate attention and development.

Walgrave shows, therefore, an awareness of the kinds of distinctions that are necessary for understanding the complex unity of Newman's thought. He notes the problem ". . . of whether it is spiritual insight or theology that is the guiding principle of the life of doctrine in the Church."[137] And Walgrave answers that it is ". . . neither one nor the other, but both together. One balances the other, and each has precedence, but in a different relationship."[138] Walgrave should have been more careful to note that balance and those different relationships. He would have been more faithful to the subject of his study if he had been.

David A. Pailin. As I noted in the introduction of this study, David Pailin, in his study of the Grammar of Assent entitled The Way to Faith, points out that Newman was greatly concerned with the problem of how one could be certain about that which was a matter of faith and not of knowledge.[139] Pailin perceptively comments that Newman's efforts to solve this problem involved essentially the same ideas throughout his career, but he fails to develop adequately several important distinctions which are also present through Newman's whole career. Pailin does see that Newman understood human faith to be an act of the will made on the basis of presumptions and probabilities, but divine faith to be the gracious gift of absolute certainty from God Himself.[140] Certain aspects of these distinctions are not developed, however, in a way that seems satisfactory to me.

In describing the act of assent, Pailin distinguishes between those "conditions" which make the act possible although they do not necessarily cause it and those "antecedents" which are directly responsible for the actualization of the assent.[141] Apprehension of the object of assent or discernment of the meaning of the proposition to which one is assenting was the sine qua non condition of assent for Newman.[142] As Pailin points out: "The reason for this restriction is that assent is never a blind commitment to an inapprehensible assertion but the deliberate avowal of the truth of a particular proposition."[143] None of the critics that we have considered in this section heretofore have seen so clearly the importance of the notion of apprehension to Newman.

Pailin does object to the way in which Newman developed the idea of apprehension. Pailin wants to argue that the apprehension of a proposition must involve a comparison of the description which a proposition makes with the object of that description. He is unwilling to allow any proposition that has an argument from authority as its basis to be apprehensible. According to Pailin, such an argument is based on the assumption that no comparison between description and object is possible. Specifically he rejects Newman's claim that one is able to assent indirectly to an inapprehensible proposition by assenting either to the truth of the inapprehensible proposition or to the veracity of the authority which asserts it. In this way, Newman sought to explain how a Catholic can assent to propositions which he does not understand on the basis of his faith in the word of the Church. Since assent is given only to the authority in this case and not to the proposition, Pailin will not allow that the solution is helpful. He maintains still the necessity to apprehend the object of one's assent.

> For us to be able to hold that a statement 'is true,' we must be able to understand its meaning and to determine whether or not it is correct. In attempting to distinguish between assent to a proposition and assent to the truth of what it asserts, Newman has failed to recognize the purely formal character of the predicate 'is true.'[144]

What is most misleading about Pailin's criticism is that he makes no adequate analysis of the way in which the Church was an authority for Newman or of the notion of authority and what it involved for Newman. Obviously Pailin feels that his logical distinctions regarding propositions and their apprehension make further attention to the problem unimportant. Perhaps his criticism is well-founded; but his failure to develop Newman's understanding of authority renders the soundness of the criticism uncertain.

His treatment of the place of theology in Newman is similarly inadequate. Pailin sees notional and real apprehension as essentially antithetical except for allowing notional reasoning or theology to have a regulative function in serving to curb excesses of real assent. In no way can theology, says Pailin, be informative since ". . . the notional is totally dependent upon the real . . . "[145] And, he goes further to say that a real apprehension is possible for man, in Newman's mind, only on the basis of experiences of conscience.[146] Never does Pailin consider in what way revelation, authority, or theology could be basic to faith. Pailin only looks at Newman's thought from the perspective of its urging a movement from assent to theological notions to a real assent to the referents of these notions. While that attention may reveal a significant amount concerning the nature of conversion, it leaves other matters, such as Newman's concentration on theological notions in and for themselves, unattended altogether.

In connection with the nature of religious inquiry that leads to conversion, Pailin argues that the role of reasoning was one of persuasion for Newman. He notes: "The strength of the antecedent reasoning does not affect the strength of our assent but our willingness to assent. The function of this reasoning is to induce us to give our assent."[147] What is troublesome is that he adds: "There is, however, no objective standard by which a piece of antecedent reasoning can be judged strong or weak. Such an evaluation depends upon the individual concerned."[148] While I must grant with Pailin that there is a logical type-jump between antecedent reasoning and assent, I cannot agree that the value of the process of reasoning is that limited and the role of the will that exclusive. It is in this regard that Pailin makes his most significant errors.

In describing the understanding of faith enunciated in the *Grammar* as one of personal commitment, Pailin writes of Newman:

> He implicitly rejects the view that our conscience may have been determined by what we have been taught about God. He believes rather that our knowledge of God is dependent upon the dictates of our conscience.[149]

Pailin asserts that Newman offered no external criteria by which one is able to distinguish truth from error in the reports of conscience. This does not make Pailin unhappy. He judges that personal commitment implies that, in relation to faith, ". . . objective validity can never be rationally deduced."[150] In fact, he is disappointed that Newman did not always seem to write as if he understood that faith was a distinct act of personal commitment rather than a reasoned conclusion. In other words, according to Pailin, Newman did not always adhere to a distinction between subjective certainty and objective certainty, i.e., between a state of the mind and the actual state of things apart from any recognition of them.[151] Pailin concludes that Newman failed to distinguish psychological and logical certitude and failed to recognize that ". . . the certainty which is required for a living religion is not the logical certainty of its objective truth."[152]

What I shall argue is that Pailin himself fails to distinguish between separate concerns which Newman had for both psychological and logical questions. Newman did indeed recognize that logical certitude was not necessary for faith in a given individual, but he did feel that concern with the objective truth of Christianity was a legitimate and necessary element in understanding the full reality of that religion. If Newman did seem to confuse these matters to Pailin, just so much the more reason for ascertaining to what degree he confused them and in what way he felt the matter of "personal commitment" to be an inadequate description of faith. Those very factors which seem a fault to Pailin raise interesting questions and suggest courses of investigation for this study. While Pailin is right in noting that the "language of objectivity" is not the "language of personal commitment," it also may be that Newman understood neither by itself to be an adequate representation of Christian discourse. While valuing highly Newman's understanding of the necessity of apprehension, Pailin gives little or no consideration to the objective language which apprehension entails.

Near the conclusion of this book, Pailin casually notes that, for Newman, faith statements were ". . . a combination of factual descriptions, normative attitudes, and personal commitments."[153] If this insight had guided Pailin's analysis, we would then have had a much more significant interpretation of the unity of Newman's understanding of the nature of faith and of the language of faith. That statement suggests a different kind of interpretation than Pailin has given us.

<u>Edward J. Sillem.</u> Edward Sillem characterizes the manner of Newman's philosophy as personal thinking in his recent general introduction to the study of the Cardinal's philosophy.[154] According to Newman, says Sillem:

> Knowing is an activity of individual minds which admits
> of many degrees of perfection varying according to the
> intimacy of the individual possession of, or mental hold
> on, the real extramental objects which he knows.[155]

To know, then, is to have assimilated or made a part of oneself what one knows. Sillem concludes: "His philosophy is thus the quest for a consciously 'realized' personal metaphysics based on as clear a vision of existent realities as the mind can reach from its own lived experience."[156]

According to Sillem, Newman opposed the idea that reason is a self-contained principle, the same for all men and the source of knowledge for all men.[157] Rather he argued that thinking is a personal activity and, as such, different in different persons. The accepted notion of reason Newman took to involve the conviction that rational demonstration was necessary to attaining truth and the denial that ". . . any personal or non-scientific way of arriving at the truth. . . " was possible.[158]

> In brief, then, the whole Liberal vision of the exaltation of man without submission to God on any terms, to be wrought by the free and independent Reason of mankind, was in Newman's eyes one enormous illusion, an illusion of the imagination. The illusion did not lie in the claim of Reason to develop on its own lines in the scientific investigation of nature, for in itself this is genuine progress bringing needed light to man about the things of this world. It lay in the claim of philosophers, first, to be able to adopt a technical, scientific method of thinking and set it up as the one and only method of thinking proper to man, and, secondly, to exalt a fictitious impersonal Reason of Mankind to the level of a universal norm of human thinking, denying the rights of the individual to think for himself outside the control of Reason.[159]

To this impersonal Reason of liberalism, says Sillem, Newman opposed a "personal liberalism" or the liberation of individuals from the sovereign rule of philosophical systems and abstract reasoning.[160] In this sense, authority in thinking is a personal and not an impersonal matter in Sillem's judgment. ". . . all authority is invested in persons who guide and assist others to see the truth for themselves."[161] For example, the individual submits his mind to the authority of God as his trusted teacher concerning matters of faith. Although we have the right to differ from others in case we find them in error, we cannot reserve such a right in relation to the authority of One with whom man, by the nature of the case, has no right to differ.[162] Thus, concludes Sillem:

> Personal independence of mind cannot be an absolute, but
> only a relative independence, that is to say, such as
> will assure the individual person's freedom from unreli-
> able and fictitious authorities and safeguard his own
> responsibilities for the control of his mind.[163]

Thus, though thinking is personal in its character, the notion of authority cannot be dismissed. Sillem recognizes this fact. Yet it is the issue of the proper understanding of authority which renders Sillem's following judgment suspect:

> . . . the abstract is not an independent, self-contained
> order that we can isolate from the concrete and treat on
> its own as though it alone gave us knowledge; it is always
> subordinate to and to be found functioning within, two
> stages of concrete thinking, those of our initial real
> apprehension of things and of the final 'realization' of
> our ideas in things. Our knowledge begins with, and devel-
> ops in the perpetual contact we keep with, real things
> in our real, lived apprehensions of each individual one.
> Such apprehension is enlivened by the particular images
> of the imagination private to each individual person,
> reflecting his personal experience of things.[164]

Is it actually the case that abstract or notional thinking was always subordinate to concrete or real thinking in Newman's view? Is it not more to the point to speak of subordination in given contexts and according to given purposes? Sillem does note that Newman held that ". . . the normal experience of men ruled out the right of a philosopher to opt for one kind of apprehension to the exclusion of the other."[165] Nevertheless, Sillem limits the role of notional thinking to its power of enabling conversation between persons as they abstract from their real apprehensions and to its creativity in taking one beyond his present thinking. But I shall argue that neither of these roles by itself nor both together adequately accounts for all that Newman had to say concerning the priority of notional thinking in some contexts. In particular, it does not account for the givenness of a common authoritative Christian discourse external to any individual's apprehension of it or for the universality of that discourse apart from the abstractive powers of individuals.

Sillem's use of the concept of "mystery" does not produce any further clarification of the role of notional thinking and of authority. Sillem understands Newman to have used the word to indicate man's inadequate grasp of his world. That definition implies that mysteries are mainly a matter of what one does not know rather than of what one does know. For example, in relation to the doctrine of the Trinity, the application of this definition would seem to indicate that the mystery in the matter is one's inability to understand how something that is triune could also be one. But such puzzlement is not the only nor even the prime characteristic of mystery in Christian discourse. The mystery of the Trinity is God's manifestation that He is triune and yet one. In other words, for Newman, the mystery is as much a result of what one knows as of what one is not able to understand.[166]

Sillem recognizes the conjunction which Newman made between manifestation and mystery, but he gives no attention to the role that authority played in Newman's understanding of that conjunction and of the positive evaluation of mystery as opposed to its negative definition. For Newman, the factor of authoritative revelation of mystery explained how residual notional assent can be quite normal to the state of Christian faith and not a sign of illegitimiate abstraction; in some cases the Christian holds fast to the mystery with no promise of progress to real assent or realization.[167] Sillem notes this kind of residual lack of fulfillment in a complete synthesis of all knowledge, but he does not seem to recognize its proper place within Christian discourse itself. The concept of authority must be explored more carefully if this matter is to be clarified.

Sillem's lack of treatment of the question of authority perhaps also explains his concentration on the roles of the imagination and of the conscience in faith. Sillem notes correctly that:

> . . . intellect and imagination, distinct in nature as they are, co-operate in the one complex activity of our thinking. It is not reason which thinks; it is I who think, and when I think I use all my cognitive powers in a whole system of interconnected activities, and if any one power fails or is gagged so as to render it inoperative, my thinking is partially paralyzed.[168]

Yet Sillem himself concentrates on the argument that Newman made personal belief in God dependent on an image of God formed from conscience and imagination. Thus, Sillem emphasizes spontaneous experience of particulars as the basis of knowledge for Newman and disparages the "laws and rules" by which other philosophers sought to regulate thinking. Sillem calls Newman's understanding of the character of thinking "moral personalism."

He describes that personal thinking in the following way:

> We become wedded to ideas and to fundamental principles through experience, from the habit of thinking under the influence of the special impressions things make on the mind; we reflect on these ideas and principles in our efforts to express to ourselves and to other people what we at first know only confusedly about things. In time certain 'real' ideas settle down deeply in the mind to become first metaphysical principles, or lived premises from which we reason about everything that concerns us in life.[169]

This emphasis on "moral personalism" or real thinking cannot, however, substitute for an understanding of the role of authority as Newman saw it. While Sillem's analysis is quite helpful in describing the dynamic of the life of faith, his interpretation does not adequately reveal the way in which Newman understood the faith to which one is committed and the relationship of one's life to that faith. The language of the Christian is not always that of "moral personalism" or of imaginative realization.[170] Christian discourse was more complex for Newman than Sillem's analysis seems to suggest.

Conclusions. In this discussion of recent interpretations of Newman's theological and philosophical contributions, we have found a concentration on Newman's understanding of the nature of religious inquiry to be central to their concerns. Two general remarks seem accurate regarding these studies as a body. First, each writer shows an awareness of reductive tendencies in interpretations of Newman and a desire to avoid such reductions in his own study. Second, in each case, the desire to reveal the analysis of religious inquiry as Newman's supreme contribution leads to a misleading concentration on certain aspects of Christian faith that does not account for some other concerns that were of equal importance for Newman.

V. GENERAL CONCLUSIONS

In this chapter I have isolated and described by example the kinds of reductive interpretations that have been made of Newman's work. In some cases, these analyses were crudely vindictive in their portrayal of Newman's purposes. Sometimes they were only misleading in their excessive emphasis on a certain aspect of Newman's thought. In each case, however, whether deliberately reductive or not, the critic proposed a unifying principle or "leading idea" which he supposed offered the most helpful clue to understanding Newman. By contrast to these proposals, the purpose of this study is to show that any kind of reductive analysis of Newman is an inadequate interpretation of his work. I must agree with C.F. Harrold: "The key to the problem of Newman's integrity is his complexity."[171] I am not referring to a psychological complexity but to the complexity of his thought as evidenced in his writings. The psychological reductionists tried to explain that complexity of thought in terms of contradictory elements in Newman's personality.[172] This study assumes that the study of a man's thought does not necessitate a consideration of his life and travail of soul.[173]

My purpose then is to seek the unity of Newman's thought in his literature. Some have evaluated the unity of that literature in terms of its adequacy as a systematic philosophical position.[174] My suggestion is that such an endeavor is self-defeating, ultimately making impossible the clarification of Newman that is its goal. What is more helpful is the attempt to describe the integrity that Newman's literature displays in itself apart from any systematic philosophical or theological position external to it. The implication of the proposed method is not that Newman had no important philosophical and theological opinions, for he certainly did. The implication is that the character of these opinions is such that they are not best described in the kind of investigation that the Thomist defenders of Newman made. I shall argue that Newman's central philosophical, more specifically his central metatheological, proposals are not systematic in the sense that they involve a consistency of relationships between central concepts and a consistency of meaning for those concepts.

The most obvious parallel to Newman in the matter of interpretation is Søren Kierkegaard, or, to be more precise, the authorship of Kierkegaard as he himself interprets it in his _The Point of View for My Work as an Author_. Kierkegaard has also suffered from the kinds of reductive interpretation that have characterized Newman research. In _The Point of View_, however, Kierkegaard claimed that the unity of his work was his authorship of a given body of literature. In other words, the unity was not to be found in some abstraction from the literature which could then be imposed upon it or in some one portion of the literature; Kierkegaard asked his readers to grasp his literature as a whole. He designated his literature as making plain what it was and was not to become a Christian, which aim he took to involve "deceptive" literary methods and life style.[175] Unlike Kierkegaard, Newman never devoted a full essay to a discussion of his literature and the nature of its unity.[176] What Newman and Kierkegaard share in common, nevertheless, seems apparent. Each has a constant sphere of intention in which they operate despite the diversity of their literary modes. For Kierkegaard, his ". . . whole literary activity turns upon the problem of becoming a Christian in Christendom. . . ."[177] For Newman, his entire corpus reveals a dedication to the cause of revealed religion.[178] In neither case, however, does the constancy of their aim necessarily involve the reductive conclusions drawn by some interpreters.

Newman's devotion to revealed religion at least was not exercised solely for apologetic purposes nor for any other single purpose. Apologetic concerns are central in some places, but other concerns are clearly dominant elsewhere. The reductive analysts have been unable to understand that the various elements within Newman's literature refuse a simple description. Reference to the constancy of Newman's dedication to revealed truth is simply a way of describing the concern which permeates his work and not the determination of the proper modes of reflection to be found in his work. Reductive analysis of his work is as misleading as assuming that the purpose of Kierkegaard's literary activity is exercised in his aesthetic and ethical writings in the same way as in his religious works. I shall argue that any adequate interpretation of Newman must recognize the "comprehensiveness" of his thought by which he refuses to allow one set of truths or one mode of reflection to displace another set or mode.[179]

It would seem that the only corrective for the kind of criticism found in studies of Newman is a reconsideration of his literature. If the unity of Newman's thought is its complexity, then only a complete investigation of his literature will suffice to display that unity. My reading of the critics of Newman suggests certain principles that should

characterize one's reading of that literature. Edmond D. Benard
delineates three such principles: first, always judge a work
of Newman according to the phase of his life in which it was
written; second, always judge each work in light of the precise
purpose for which it was written; third, never judge Newman's
works as systematic theology or in the light of scholastic
terminology or with a meaning not given by Newman himself.[180]
Perhaps John J. Toohey summarizes these principles adequately
by simply suggesting that, in any study of Newman, a regard
for the context is absolutely essential.[181] If this warning be
kept in mind, Benard's claim seems warranted: "Newman's
works . . . should need no elaborate defense. If studied carefully and with attention to their background, they are their
own best witnesses."[182]

    What such a study of Newman's literature reveals is the
subject of the next three chapters. In these chapters I shall
develop a case for the integrity of Newman's literature in
terms of its complex unity of reflection on the Christian faith.
In other words, I shall show how his dedication to revealed
truth is exercised in diverse ways and according to various
purposes in different contexts. His literature reveals Newman
as being, as he described it, in ". . . the position of a man,
who, from various circumstances, has been obliged through so
many years to think aloud."[183] I shall attend to the diversity
of that thought, hoping to reveal the kind of integrity there
that does not depend on a simple unity. For the purpose of
this study, I shall isolate three uses of Christian discourse
that regularly appear throughout the course of Newman's literature. Those three uses appear in contexts of the movement to
faith, of the life of faith, and of the explication of the
content of one's faith. In each context, Christian discourse
and its concepts function, relate, and take their meanings in
different ways. Mapping this diversity is what I have referred
to as one of the tasks of metatheology. I shall argue that
Newman's metatheological principles do not prejudice the essential integrity of his thought since that integrity does not
reside in some systematic view which he offers but in the rich
diversity of his reflection on the Christian faith.

    Newman's metatheology does not consist in the reduction
of the various uses of Christian discourse to some one

systematic description or "essence" but in the recognition and description of diverse uses, their differences, and patterns of relationship. In that regard, I find myself following Edwin Burgum's understanding of the complexity of reflection in Newman as consisting not ". . . in any one generalization, not even in the whole body of them, but in the whole body of relationships among them," without overlooking the wisdom of Charles Stephen Dessain's reminder that the Cardinal was in all that richness of reflection seeking to point to revealed truth in as accurate and complete a way as possible. His thought had a definite orientation that prescribed his field of concern; but he found that the object of that concern--revealed truth-- demanded a diversity of perspectives to be taken if one were to grasp its essential integrity.

NOTES TO CHAPTER II

[1]Samuel Parkes Cadman, "John Henry Newman and the Oxford Movement of 1833-1845," The Three Religious Leaders of Oxford and Their Movements: John Wycliffe, John Wesley, John Henry Newman (New York: The Macmillan Company, 1916), p. 435.

[2]The following sources represent the most helpful bibliographical references for the critical literature concerning Newman: Werner Becker, "Newman's Influence in Germany," The Rediscovery of Newman: An Oxford Symposium, John Coulson and Arthur Macdonald Allchin, editors (London: Sheed and Ward, 1967), pp. 174-189; Adrian J. Boekraad, "Newman in the Low Countries: A Note," The Rediscovery of Newman, op. cit., pp. 190-194; Louis Bouyer, "Newman's Influence in France," The Dublin Review, 217 (October, 1945), 182-188; John Francis Cronin, "An Evaluation of Newman's Epistemology," Cardinal Newman: His Theory of Knowledge (Washington, D. C.: The Catholic University of America Press, 1935), pp. 72-113; H. Cunliffe-Jones, "Notes on the Free Church Attitude to Newman," The Rediscovery of Newman, op. cit., pp. 213-215; H. Francis Davis, "The Catholicism of Cardinal Newman," John Henry Newman: Centenary Essays (London: Burnes, Oates, and Washbourne, Ltd., 1945), pp. 36-54; H. Francis Davis, "Newman's Influence in England," The Rediscovery of Newman, op. cit., pp. 147-173; L. Gougaud, "Le Prétendu Modernisme de Newman," Revue du Clergé Francais, LVII (1909), 560-565; Mary Benoit Holahan, "Newman in France," an abstract of a Ph.D. dissertation, the University of Illinois, 1943; Christopher Hollis, "Newman and the Modernists," Newman and the Modern World (Garden City, New York: Doubleday and Co., 1968), pp. 190-206; J. F. Leddy, "Newman and His Critics, A Chapter in the History of Ideas," Report of the Canadian Catholic Historical Association (1943), 25-38; Gordon Rupp, "Newman through Nonconformist Eyes," The Rediscovery of Newman, op. cit., pp. 195-212; Paul Simon "Newman and German Catholicism," The Dublin Review, 219 (July 1946), 75-84. By far the most useful bibliographical source, however, is the Newman-Studien, seven volumes, Heinrich Fries and Werner Becker, editors (Nürnberg: Glock und Lutz, 1948-1967).

[3]Ernest Baudin, "La Philosophie de la Foi chez Newman," Revue de Philosophie, VIII (January-July, 1906), 573.

[4]Francis William Newman, Contributions Chiefly to the Early History of the Late Cardinal Newman (London: Kegan Paul Trench, Trubner and Co., Ltd., 1891).

[5]Ibid., p. 141.

[6]Edwin Abbott Abbott, The Anglican Career of Cardinal Newman (London: Macmillan and Co., 1892), I, 318.

[7]Edwin Abbott Abbott, Philomythus: An Antidote Against Credulity; A Discussion of Cardinal Newman's Essay on Ecclesiastical Miracles (second edition; London: Macmillan and Co., 1891), p. ix.

51

[8] Abbott, *The Anglican Career of Cardinal Newman*, op. cit., II, 110-128, 178, 221, 405, 407.

[9] Walter K. Firminger, an Anglican sympathetic to Newman, attacked Abbott's *Philomythus* in *Some Thoughts on the Recent Criticism of the Life and Works of John Henry Cardinal Newman* (printed for private circulation; Oxford: James Parker and Co., 1892), defending Newman against its unreasonable charges.

[10] A contemporary of Abbott, Arthur W. Hutton, made an interpretation similar to Abbott's in his "Personal Reminiscences of Cardinal Newman," *The Expositor*, II (1890), 223-240, 304-320, 336-348. In these essays, Hutton claimed that Newman was a man with a superstitious habit of mind and that his theology was based on feeling and personal experience (cf. especially *ibid*., 228, 309-310). In addition, he claimed that Newman displayed a lack of concern for the poor (*ibid*., 239-240); an extravagant devotion to Mary (*ibid*., 235-236); and favoritism and grudge-bearing (*ibid*., 305-306). Two famous personalities followed Abbott's interpretation. Lord Acton saw Newman as a "sophist, the manipulator, and not the servant of truth." This judgment can be found in *Letters of Lord Acton to Mary Gladstone*, Herbert Paul, editor (New York: The Macmillan Company, 1904), p. 70. John Morley, in his *Critical Miscellanies* (London: The Macmillan Company, 1908), IV, 163, claimed that "Newman made mere siren style do duty for exact, penetrating and coherent thought . . . ."

[11] Alfred Fawkes, "Newman," *Studies in Modernism* (London: Smith, Elder and Co., 1913), p. 217.

[12] One should add, however, that there usually is some implication of a weakness or deficiency in Newman's character or personality.

[13] Charles Sarolea, *Cardinal Newman and His Influence on Religious Life and Thought* (The World's Epoch Makers, Oliphant Smeaton, editor; New York: Charles Scribner's Sons, 1908), pp. 61-62.

[14] Gaius Glenn Atkins, *Life of Cardinal Newman* (Creative Lives, Harold E. B. Speight, editor; New York: Harper and Brothers Publishers, 1931), pp. 288-289.

[15] Gwilyn Oswald Griffith, "Newman," *Interpreters of Man* (London: Lutterworth Press, 1943), pp. 59-74.

[16] Francis Vincent Reade, "The Sentimental Myth," *John Henry Newman: Centenary Essays*, op. cit., pp. 139-154.

[17] This portrait is reproduced in Meriol Trevor, *Newman: Light in Winter* (Vol. II of *Newman*. 2 vols.; Garden City, New York: Doubleday and Company, Inc., 1962), p. 595.

[18] Edwin Berry Burgum, "Cardinal Newman and the Complexity of Truth," *The Sewanee Review*, XXXVIII (July, 1930), 310. One can find examples of this sentimental interpretation or at least portions of it in the following works: J. H. Rigg, *Oxford High Anglicanism* (London: C. H. Kelly, 1895); Lytton Strachey, *Eminent Victorians* (London: Chatto and Windus, 1918); Geoffrey C. Faber, *Oxford Apostles: A Character Study of the Oxford Movement* (New York: Charles Scribner's Sons, 1934); Paul Elmer More, "Cardinal Newman," *The Drift of Romanticism* (Shelburne Essays, Eighth Series; New York: Houghton Mifflin Company,

1913), pp. 37-79. Contrary to the prevailing tendencies in biography since World War II, Emmeline Garnet's life of Newman suggests in its title, method and content this romanticized view of the Cardinal. Cf. her *Tormented Angel: A Life of John Henry Newman* (New York: Farrar, Strauss and Giroux, Ariel Books, 1966).

[19]This testimony includes: R. W. Church, "Cardinal Newman's Naturalness," *Occasional Papers* (London: Macmillan and Co., Ltd., 1897), II, 479-482; James Anthony Froude, "The Oxford Counter-Reformation," *Short Studies on Great Subjects* (London: Longmans, Green, and Co., 1917), IV, 231-360; Richard H. Hutton, "Cardinal Newman," *Essays on Some of the Modern Guides to English Thought in the Matter of Faith* (London: Macmillan and Co., 1888), pp. 49-101, and *Cardinal Newman* (New York: Houghton, Mifflin and Company, 1890). Church, Froude and Hutton claimed a freedom from pretence and an honest belief for Newman, though none shared Newman's beliefs completely.

[20]At least two studies have appeared that argue for the intellectual character of Newman's conversions in opposition to the widely held opinion that they could be explained in affective or psychological terms. These two articles are: Charles Stephen Dessain, "Newman's First Conversion," *Studies: An Irish Quarterly Review*, XLVI (Spring, 1957), 44-59; and Daniel J. Saunders, "The Psychology of a Conversion," *American Essays for the Newman Centennial*, John K. Ryan and Edmond Darvil Benard, editors (Washington, D. C.: The Catholic University of America Press, 1947), pp. 39-64. Louis Bouyer's *Newman: His Life and Spirituality*, trans. J. Lewis May (London: Burns and Oates, 1958) pictures Newman as a saint, concentrating on his interior and moral life rather than on his literature. Meriol Trevor's authoritative biography has replaced that of Wilfrid Ward, *The Life of John Henry Cardinal Newman* (two volumes; London: Longmans, Green, and Co., 1912), as the authoritative source although Ward's work remains quite helpful. Trevor's *Newman* (two volumes; Garden City, New York: Doubleday and Company, Inc., 1962) gives extensive treatment to exonerations of Newman from charges like those made by Francis Newman and Abbott. Invaluable for biographical purposes has been the appearance of *John Henry Newman: Autobiographical Writings*, Henry Tristram, editor (New York: Sheed and Ward, 1957).

[21]Vincent Francis Blehl, "The Sanctity of Cardinal Newman," *America*, XCIX (June 14, 1958), 328-330, outlines the steps taken up to that time in the process necessary for canonization. The sermon by which F. J. Grimshaw, archbishop of Birmingham, inaugurated the diocesan process in this matter is "The Holiness of Newman," *The Tablet*, 211 (June 21, 1958), 578. The further history of this process can be found in a series of articles entitled "The Cause of John Henry Newman," *The Tablet*, 211 (June 21, 1958), 579; *The Tablet*, 213 (October 24, 1959), 904; *The Tablet*, 215 (January 21, 1961), 69. This writer has been able to find only one further reference to the process itself in the last decade. *Newman-Studien*, op. cit., VII, 312, enters the following work in a bibliography: H. ten Kortenaar, *A Newman Calendar 1965* (printed on behalf of the American Secretariat for the Cause of Beatification of Cardinal Newman; Pittsburgh). There is considerable evidence of interest and controversy surrounding the cause in the years between 1958 and 1960. Robert I. Gannon, "Note on Newman,"

America, XCIX (June 28, 1958), 361, questions Blehl's claim that there is any enthusiasm for Newman's canonization. Joseph Clifford Fenton directly calls Newman's sanctity into question in "Some Newman Autobiographical Sketches and the Newman Legend," *The American Ecclesiastical Review*, CXXXVI (June, 1957), 394-410; "Newman's Complaints Examined in the Light of Priestly Spirituality," *The American Ecclesiastical Review*, CXXXVIII (January, 1958), 49-65; "The Newman Legend and Newman's Complaints," *The American Ecclesiastical Review*, CXXXIX (August, 1958), 101-121. In these articles, Fenton claims that Newman was justly criticized by ecclesiastical leaders of his day since, in certain matters, he meant to go beyond Catholic teaching. Fenton believes that Newman sometimes forgot in his rancor that a priest's role is delegated by the bishop and not chosen by the priest himself. A less negative appraisal that also questions whether Newman merits canonization is D. J. Dooley's "The Newman Question," *Culture*, XX (March, 1959), 41-47. Fenton's views have been disputed by Joseph F. Beckmann, "Another View of Newman," *The American Ecclesiastical Review*, CXXXVIII (January, 1958), 37-48; and by E. Leo McMannus, "Newman and the Newman Legend," *The American Ecclesiastical Review*, CXXXIX (August, 1958), 93-100. Jonathan Robinson, "Did Newman 'Fit In'?: Reply to a Critic," *The Dublin Review*, 232 (Autumn, 1958), 245-259, also answers criticisms of Newman and his sanctity raised by D. J. B. Hawkins, "Newman the Man: An Approach to Pere Bouyer's Study," *The Dublin Review*, 232 (Spring, 1958), 81-88. Throughout these years of debate, Blehl has maintained his advocacy of canonization in a series of articles: "The Sanctity of Newman," *op. cit.*; "The Holiness of John Henry Newman," *The Month*, XIX (June, 1958), 325-334; "Newman and the Missing Miter," *Thought*, XXXV (Spring, 1960), 111-123.

[22] One of the most important modern studies of Newman, A. Dwight Culler's *The Imperial Intellect*, has been charged with psychological reductionism. J. G. Lawler critizes Culler for having written "psychography rather than biography in making secondary unpublished materials from Newman's hand more important than his published writings." Cf. Justus George Lawler, "Newman: Biography or Psychography?" *Renascence*, XIV (Autumn, 1961), 46-47. In effect Lawler claims that Culler interprets Newman's writings--in this case, in particular, *The Idea of a University*--in terms of Newman's personal life history alone rather than at their face value; and that charge fits what I have called reductionism. Culler's central thesis is that Newman's life focuses in an oscillation between intellectual liberalism and a religious submissiveness that reveals itself most dramatically in the five illnesses of Newman's adolescence and early manhood. Culler also finds a conflict between the religious and humanistic elements of Newman's educational ideal. He reports that his first thought was that this intellectual conflict was a reproduction of the conflict which was the "central pattern of his entire life" in *The Imperial Intellect: A Study of Cardinal Newman's Educational Ideal* (New Haven: Yale University Press, 1965), p. xii. In other words, the intellectual conflict was based on a "controversy in Newman's own nature between his intellectual aspirations . . . and his sense that this knowledge was somehow forbidden." (*Ibid.*, p. 228.) Culler then imagines that it might be helpful in interpreting aspects of *The Idea of a University* which seem contradictory to

posit a kind of schizophrenic author. ". . . by a kind of exaggeration one might say that these two persons were respectively the author of the humanistic and the religious discourses in The Idea of a University." (Ibid.) Newman was able to achieve the measure of balance which he did, reasons Culler, as a result of his having moved from the evangelical piety with its distrust of the intellect to a religious position which was not distrustful of intellectual achievement. Culler's conclusion is that: "Newman achieved in his writings a kind of reconciliation of opposites which he had already achieved in his own person and which gives to his cultural ideal a rich and interesting ambivalence." (Ibid., p. 229).

Hints of a kind of psychological reductionism can be found in Culler's interpretation. Of course, it is not the crude reductionism of Abbott; it is a variety of that interpretation which suggests that Newman's intellectual conclusions follow upon personal experience and need. Or is it? Culler is careful to limit the purpose and importance of his study. He is offering no full scale biography and no complete treatment of Newman's thought. He is limiting his study to an evaluation of Newman's educational development and to his lectures on university education. In addition, he attempts to lessen the significance of the correlation between the resolution of a personal problem and the content of the university lectures. He states that the correlation is only a "first thought" and a "kind of exaggeration." Nevertheless, he does make the connection. The important observation to be made is that his refusal to allow what he thinks is an important psychological and biographical insight to substitute for a careful study of Newman's views on university education is not a characteristic of psychological reductionism. His conclusion may or may not adequately account for Newman's views—it is not my concern to make a judgment on that question. It is only important, for my purposes, that he does not fail to take those views seriously in and for themselves. The latter and not the former failure characterizes psychological reductionism.

[23] Joseph William Blakesley, "Dr. Newman's Grammar of Assent," English Catholics and English Ultramontanism: Three Reviews (reprinted for private circulation only from The Times of April 21, 1870; London: Macmillan and Co., 1874), 69. Cf. an anonymous article, "Newman's Grammar of Assent," The London Quarterly Review, 35 (January, 1871), 364, 389, and Cadman, op. cit., 584, for similar views.

[24] John Locke, An Essay Concerning Human Understanding, A. S. Pringle-Pattison, editor (Oxford: Oxford University Press, 1934), Book IV, chapter xix. A principal spokesman for this morality of knowledge was William Kingdon Clifford in his Lectures and Essays, Leslie Stephen and Frederick Pollock, editors (two volumes; London: Macmillan and Co., 1879). Elements of the discussion have been revived recently by Van A. Harvey, "Is There an Ethics of Belief?" The Journal of Religion, XLIX (January, 1969), 41-58.

[25] Fitzjames Stephen, "Dr. Newman's Apologia," Frasers Magazine, LXX (September, 1864), 266.

[26] Ibid., 274-280.

[27] Leslie Stephen, "Cardinal Newman's Scepticism," The

Nineteenth Century, XXIX (February, 1891), 179.

[28]Leslie Stephen, "Dr. Newman's Theory of Belief," The Fortnightly Review, XXVIII (November, 1877), 685.

[29]Ibid., 686-687.

[30]Stephen, "Cardinal Newman's Scepticism," op. cit., 193. Cf. Stephen's "Dr. Newman's Theory of Belief," The Fortnightly Review, XXVIII (December, 1877), 809.

[31]Stephen, "Cardinal Newman's Scepticism," op. cit., 201.

[32]Cf. anonymous, "Dr. Newman's Grammar of Assent," The Edinburgh Review, 132 (October, 1870), 382-414; Thomas Henry Huxley, "Agnosticism and Christianity," The Nineteenth Century, XXV (June, 1889), 937-964; and Andrew M. Fairbairn, "Catholicism and Modern Thought," The Contemporary Review, XLVII (May, 1885), 652-674; "Catholicism and Apologetics," The Contemporary Review, XLVII (February, 1885), 164-184; "Catholicism and Historical Criticism," The Contemporary Review, XLVIII (July, 1885), 36-64. These essays are collected in Fairbairn's Catholicism: Roman and Anglican (New York: Charles Scribner's Sons, 1899).

[33]A charge seemingly first made by Bishop J. C. Hedley in "Dr. Barry on Newman," The Ampleforth Journal, X (July, 1904), 1-12.

[34]Cf. Alec R. Vidler, The Modernist Movement in the Roman Church: Its Origins and Outcome (Cambridge: Cambridge University Press, 1934).

[35]B. D. Dupuy, "Newman's Influence in France," The Rediscovery of Newman, op. cit., pp. 166-167.

[36]Vidler, op. cit., p. 187.

[37]George Tyrell, "The Prospects of Modernism," The Hibbert Journal, VI (January, 1908), 243.

[38]George Tyrell, "Introduction," The Mystery of Newman, by Henri Bremond, trans. H. C. Corrance (London: Williams and Norgate, 1907), p. xvii. In that same essay, ibid., p. xv, he claimed that "Newman's incontestable abhorrence of doctrinal liberalism does not at once prove that he may not be the progenitor of it."

[39]George Tyrell, "The Limits of the Development Theory," The Catholic World, LXXXI (September, 1905), 735.

[40]Ibid., 732, 739. It is difficult to find the dramatic difference that Tyrell professed to find, and one wonders if he falls under the warning which Newman set forth in "The Theory of Developments in Religious Doctrines," Fifteen Sermons Preached before the University of Oxford (London: Rivingtons, 1887), p. 351, where he criticized " . . . the ambition of being wiser than what is written."

[41]Note an anonymous article "The Pope and Modernism," The Manchester Guardian, November 20, 1907, p. 4, which cites Tyrell's essay on "The Condemnation of Newman" that appeared in the November, 1907, edition of the "Church" Guardian. This writer has been unable to find the original article.

[42]Ernest Dimnet, "Quelques aspects du Cardinal Newman," La Pensée Catholique dans l'Angleterre Contemporaine (Paris: Victor

Lecoffre, 1906), pp. 73-129.

⁴³Cf. "Le Développement Chrétien d'après le Cardinal Newman," *Revue du Clergé Francais*, XVII (1899), 5-20, for his specific interpretation of Newman that accords closely with his own views as evident in "Les Preuves et l'Economie de la Révélation," *Revue du Clergé Francais*, XXI (1900), 126-153.

⁴⁴J. C. Hedley, "Dr. Barry on Newman," *op. cit.*, pp. 1-12.

⁴⁵Henri Bremond, *Newman: Essai de Biographie Psychologique* (Paris: Librairie Bloud et Cie, 1906). The English version is *The Mystery of Newman*, trans. H. C. Corrance (London: Williams and Norgate, 1907). Bremond's selections from and translations of Newman's work also aided in fostering this image. A similar view can be found in Raoul Gout, *Du Protestantisme au Catholicisme: John Henry Newman. Notes Psychologiques* (Geneve: Librairie J. H. Jeheber, 1906).

⁴⁶Bremond, *op. cit.*, p. 129.

⁴⁷Leonce de Grandmaison, "John Henry Newman considerée comme Maitre," *Etudes*, CIX (December, 1906), 721-750; and *Etudes*, CX (January, 1907), 39-69.

⁴⁸This view was not successfully challenged until the appearance of Francis Joseph Bacchus and Henry Tristram's "Newman," *Dictionnaire de Theologie Catholique*, commencée sous la direction de A. Vacant et E. Maugenot et continue sous selle de E. Amann (Paris: Librarie Letouzey et Ané, 1931), tome onzième, premièr partie, columns 327-398.

⁴⁹Bremond and Dimnet did so in response to articles by Jules Lebreton, editor of the *Revue de Practique d'Apologetique* at that time, in which Lebreton attacked certain "Newmanists" and their views of Newman as a religious pragmatist for whom the subjective conscience is supreme and for whom apologetics is a matter of provoking an experience with the object of faith rather than of showing the truth of religion. Lebreton argued that the conscience was supreme for Newman only in natural religion and not in revealed. Newman, he claimed, always combated private judgment and held to the heteronomy of Catholic doctrine. Cf. Jules Lebreton, "Autour de Newman," *Revue de Practique d'Apologetique*, III (January 15, 1907), 488-504, and "Le Primat de la Conscience d'aprés Newman," *Revue de Practique d'Apologetique*, III (March 1, 1907), 667-675. Bremond conceded that he had drawn out the logical direction of Newman's thought to a point at which Newman well may not have agreed in his "Nouvelle Communication," *Revue de Practique d'Apologetique*, III (March, 1907), 676-677; and Dimnet denied that he ever implied that Newman was a pragmatist or a fideist since Newman placed such importance on giving reasons in his "Letter to the Editor," *Revue de Practique d'Apologetique*, III (February 15, 1907), 616-618. Nevertheless, Bremond asserted that he still held that the conscience is the ultimate sanction of religion and that the illative sense is a form of private judgment. Dimnet also qualified the emphasis on reasons in Newman by claiming that more basic than reasons was the fact of the soul, his life, his person itself.

⁵⁰Dupuy, *op. cit.*, 169. On the one hand were those who continued to view Newman as a modernist including Charles Sarolea, *op. cit.*, p. 173, but who also concluded that Newman

". . . was only unwittingly a father of modernism." An anonymous writer shared this opinion in "Cardinal Newman," The Edinburgh Review, 215 (April, 1912), 263-290. Others continued more absolute identifications of Newman with modernism; one such writer included an anonymous reviewer of Wilfrid Ward's biography of Newman in Current Literature, 52 (June, 1912), 678-681, who claimed that Newman was the "encouraging originator of modernism." Perhaps the most confused judgment from the period was that of Algernon Cecil who denied that Newman was a modernist but claimed that Newman ". . . had never, any more than his Master, made religion primarily dogmatic. He had rested it always on experiences--experiences felt and experiences desired." Cf. Algernon Cecil, "J. H. Newman," Six Oxford Thinkers (London: John Murray, 1909), pp. 44-122. On the other hand, there were those who unequivocally denied that Newman was a modernist. They include an anonymous writer who signed an article "Theologus"; in the article, "Letter to the Editor: Cardinal Newman and the Mere Probability of Supernatural Revelation," The Tablet, LXXIX (January 11, 1908), 59-60, he quoted Newman as having told him in a private conversation that ". . . it [Christianity] can be proved, even to demonstration." Others who denied Newman's modernism include H. P. Russell, "A Lesson from Newman," The American Ecclesiastical Review, XXXVIII (May, 1908), 514-528, Sylvester P. Juergens, Newman on the Psychology of Faith in the Individual (New York: The Macmillan Company, 1928), and John Francis Cronin, op. cit. By far the best article from this period was that by William Henry Allison, "Was Newman a Modernist?" American Journal for Theology, 14 (October, 1910), 552-571. He offered a catalogue of differences between Newman and the modernists.

[51] Tyrell, "The Condemnation of Newman," as cited in "The Pope and Modernism," op. cit.

[52] Pope Pius X, "Newman et le Modernisme: Lettre a Mgr. O'Dwyer, Évêque de Limerick (10 Mars 1908)," Nouvelle Revue Theologique, XL (1908), 419-420. Bishop O'Dwyer offered his own defense of Newman in his essay, Cardinal Newman and the Encyclical (London: Longmans, 1908).

[53] Frederick Denison Maurice, "Dr. Newman's Grammar of Assent," The Contemporary Review, 14 (May, 1870), 151-172.

[54] Thomas Harper, "Dr. Newman's Essay in Aid of a Grammar of Assent," The Month, XII (May, 1870), 599-611, and XII (June, 1870), 667-692. Harper wrote three other articles in this series but I have been unable to locate volume XIII of The Month in which they appear.

[55] A. Bellesheim, "Newman," Wetzer und Welte's Kirchenlexikon (zweite auflage; Freiburg im Breisgau: Herder'sche Verlagshandlung, 1895), IX, 219-226. Sharing this somewhat modified approval of Newman were Francis Aveling, "Universals and the Illative Sense," The Dublin Review, 137 (October, 1905), 236-271, and George Lee, "Newman's Probabilities," The American Ecclesiastical Review, XXXVIII (May, 1908), 528-541. Both of these writers criticized Newman for what he omitted from his presentation rather than for what he explicitly claimed. Their verdict was that Newman shows the weakness of any system that is not thoroughly and rigorously scholastic. What they denied was that Newman in any way contradicted scholastic teaching.

⁵⁶John Joseph Toohey, "Newman and Modernism," The Tablet, LXXIX (January 4, 1908), 7-9; "Newman and Modernism, II," The Tablet, LXXIX (January 11, 1908), 47-48; "Newman and Modernism, III," The Tablet, LXXIX (January 18, 1908), 86-88; "Newman and Modernism, IV--Conclusion," The Tablet, LXXIX (January 25, 1908), 122-125; "The Grammar of Assent and the Old Philosophy," The Irish Theological Quarterly, II (October, 1907), 466-484; and "Newman on the Criterion of Certitude," The Irish Theological Quarterly, V (October, 1910), 444-453. Thomas J. Gerrard found Newman ". . . in complete harmony with the scholastics" in "Bergson, Newman, and Aquinas," The Catholic World, XCVI (March, 1913), 758. Cf. also Gerrard's "The 'Grammar of Assent' and the Sure Future," The Dublin Review, 137 (October, 1905), 113-128; "Dichotomy: A Study in Newman and Aquinas," The New York Review, III (January-April, 1908), 381-390; and "Newman and Conceptualism," The New York Review, II (January-February, 1907), 430-441. In these articles, Gerrard enunciated what has become a familiar claim, i.e., that Newman and Aquinas are complementary in their thought, the latter offering an objective basis for theology and the former, a subjective apologetics that gives that base life. Others who affirmed Newman's agreement with the scholastics include: Sydney F. Smith, "The 'Edinburgh Review' on Cardinal Newman," The Month, CXIX (June, 1912), 561-578, and "Newman's Relation to Modernism," The Month, CXX (July, 1912), 1-15; Alfred G. Brickel, "Cardinal Newman's Theory of Knowledge," The American Catholic Quarterly Review, XLIII (July, 1918), 507-518 and XLIII (October, 1918), 645-653; John Francis Cronin, op. cit.; and Borghild Gundersen, Cardinal Newman and Apologetics (Oslo: I Kommisjon hos Jacob Dybwad, 1952). A recent article turns the usual procedure in reverse, attempting to show that St. Thomas Aquinas can be given an interpretation more in line with the subjective emphases of Newman although the writer essentially shares the polarity view. Cf. Martin Versfeld, "St. Thomas, Newman, and the Existence of God," New Scholasticism, XLI (Winter, 1967), 3-30.

⁵⁷Martin Cyril D'Arcy, The Nature of Belief (London: Sheed and Ward, 1931), 148-149.

⁵⁸Erich Przywara, Gottgeheimnis der Welt: Drei Vorträge über die Geistige Krisis der Gegenwart (Munchen: Theatiner Verlag, 1923), p. 176. Przywara's opinion is shared by Father Zeno in John Henry Newman: Our Way to Certitude, an Introduction to Newman's Psychological Discovery: The Illative Sense, and His Grammar of Assent (Leiden: E. J. Brill, 1957), p. 13. In his book, Newman, Faith and the Believer (London: Sands and Co., Ltd., 1946), pp. 168-170, Philip Flanagan characterizes the value of Newman's work as primarily "practical" or helpful in understanding the process of conversion but in no way of comprehensive theological significance.

⁵⁹Gerrard, "Newman and Conceptualism," op. cit., 430-431, 436.

⁶⁰George P. Klubertanz, "Where is the Evidence for Thomistic Metaphysics?" Revue Philosophie de Louvain, 56 (May, 1958), 294-315.

⁶¹Henri Bremond, "Letter to the Editor," The Tablet, LXXIX (January 18, 1908), 100.

⁶²Cf. Franz Michel Willam, "Aristotelische Bausteine der

Entwicklungstheorie Newman," <u>Newman-Studien</u>, herausgeben von Heinrich Fries und Werner Becker (sechste folge; Nürnberg: Glock und Lutz, 1964), pp. 193-226; <u>Aristotelische Erkenntnislehre bei Whately und Newman und Ihre Bezüge zur Gegenwart</u> (Freiburg: Herder, 1960); "Bezeichnungen und Characterisierungen des Probabilitätes, Beweises bei Newman, " <u>Newman-Studien</u>, herausgegeben von Heinrich Fries und Werner Becker (fünfte folge; Nürnberg: Glock und Lutz, 1962), pp. 229-250; "Die Vorgeschichte des Begriffes 'Konvergierende Probabilitäten'," <u>Newman-Studien</u>, herausgegeben von Heinrich Fries und Werner Becker (vierte folge; Nürnberg: Glock und Lutz, 1960), pp. 138-143.

[63]Adrian J. Boekraad, "Critical Notice: <u>Aristotelische Erkenntnislehre bei Whately und Newman</u>," <u>Philosophical Studies</u> [Maynooth], XI (1961-1962), 175. Boekraad makes similar criticisms of Father Zeno in "Continental Newman Literature," <u>Philosophical Studies</u> [Maynooth], VII (December, 1957), 110-116.

[64]Adrian J. Boekraad, "Critical Notice: Cardinal <u>Newman Studien III</u>," <u>Philosophical Studies</u> [Maynooth], VIII (December, 1958), 142.

[65]Boekraad, "Critical Notice: <u>Aristotelische Erkenntnislehre bei Whately und Newman</u>," <u>op</u>. <u>cit</u>., p. 175.

[66]Cf. Johannes Artz, "Newman's Contribution to Theory of Knowledge," <u>Philosophy Today</u>, IV (Spring, 1960), 12-25. Among those having influence on Newman, he mentions the Stoics, Augustine, Pascal, Locke, Butler, and Reid.

[67]Quoted in an anonymous article, "The Month and John Henry Newman," <u>The Month</u>, CI (April, 1903), 344. In a letter written to Pope Leo XIII, though perhaps not sent, Newman congratulated the Pope for the encyclical as an attempt to rectify the deplorable lack of recognition, on the part of many Catholics, of their appropriate philosophical tradition. Such a tradition, he claimed ". . . should not start from a novel and simply original tradition, but should be substantially one with the teaching of St. Athanasius, St. Augustine, St. Anselm and St. Thomas, as those great doctors in turn are one with each other." Thomas received, therefore, no individual recognition but was included among those of a whole tradition, the tradition seemingly given more importance than the individual. Cf. Ward, <u>Life</u>, <u>op</u>. <u>cit</u>., II, 501-502.

[68]Anonymous, "<u>The Month</u> and John Henry Newman," <u>op</u>. <u>cit</u>., p. 238. The letter was written to Father Coleridge and dated April 30, 1870.

[69]Ward, <u>Life</u>, <u>op</u>. <u>cit</u>., II, 269. This letter was written to Father Coleridge and dated February 5, 1871.

[70]Ernest Baudin, "La Philosophie de la Foi chez Newman," <u>Revue de Philosophie</u>, VIII (January-July, 1906), 571-598; and IX (July-December, 1906), 20-55, 253-285, 373-390. His opinions were shared by Albert Farges, <u>La Crise de la Certitude</u> (Paris: Berche et Tralin, 1907).

[71]Baudin, <u>op</u>. <u>cit</u>., IX, 25.

[72]Ibid., 270-277.   [73]Ibid., 281.

[74]Ibid., 374-376. A modern example of this same type of critique--though leveled against religious belief as such and

not directly against Newman--is the highly influential article by Alasdair MacIntyre, "Is Understanding Religion Compatible with Believing?" Faith and the Philosophers, John Hick, editor (New York: St. Martin's Press, 1964), pp. 115-133.

[75]Eric Michael Zale, "The Defenses of John Henry Newman" (microfilmed Ph.D. dissertation, University of Michigan, 1962), interprets Newman's entire career as a ceaseless effort to defend his religious views. In that sense, says Zale, ibid., p. 1, ". . . a majority of his works constitute a series of apologias." Even Henry Tristram describes Newman's works as parts of ". . . a magnificent Summa Apologetica" in John Henry Newman: Autobiographical Writings, Henry Tristram, editor (New York: Sheed and Ward, 1957), p. 18. Tristram's usually balanced judgment seems one-sided on this point.

[76]Lawrence F. Barmann, "The Spiritual Teaching of Newman's Early Sermons," Downside Review, 80 (1962), 228.

[77]R. W. Church, "Newman's 'Apologia'," Occasional Papers (London: Macmillan and Co., Ltd., 1897), II, 388. This essay was originally published in the Guardian for June 22, 1864. Cf. also Church, "Cardinal Newman's Course," Occasional Papers, op. cit., II, 470-472.

[78]Philip Hughes, "Newman and His Age," The Dublin Review, 217 (October, 1945), 115-116, 123, 134-135. For a similar view see "Editorial: The Conversion of Mr. Newman," The Tablet, CLXXXVI (October 6, 1945), 159-160, and Joseph J. Reilly, "The Tone of the Centre," American Essays for the Newman Centennial, op. cit., pp. 65-70.

[79]H. Francis Davis, "Newman on Educational Method," The Dublin Review, 230 (Winter, 1956), 109.

[80]Ibid., 111.

[81]James Munro Cameron, "The Night Battle: Newman and Empiricism," Victorian Studies [Indiana], IV (1960), 99-117, sees an even more thoroughly sceptical description of our talk about the world in Newman. Following Hume, says Cameron, Newman concluded that our faith must be in our personal natures rather than in what we can prove that we know about the world.

[82]H. Francis Davis, "Newman and the Theology of the Living Word," Newman-Studien, herausgegeben von Heinrich Fries und Werner Becker (sechste folge; Nürnberg: Glock und Lutz, 1964), 167.

[83]Ibid., 171.

[84]Francis Davis, "Newman on Faith and Personal Certitude," The Journal of Theological Studies, XII (October, 1961), 254-283.

[85]H. Francis Davis, "Newman and the Psychology of the Development of Doctrine," The Dublin Review, 216 (April, 1945), 97.

[86]Wilfrid Philip Ward, "The True Nature of Newman's Genius: A Criticism of Popular Misconceptions," Last Lectures (London: Longmans, Green, and Co., 1918), pp. 1-149. These lectures were the Lowell Lectures of 1914.

[87]Ibid., pp. 7, 10, 23, 44, et passim.

[88]Ibid., pp. 10-11.

[89] Ibid., p. 104.   [90] Ibid., pp. 104-105.

[91] Ibid., pp. 108-109, 123.

[92] Maurice Nédoncelle, *La Philosophie Religeuse de John Henry Newman* (Strasbourg: Société Strasbourgeoisie de Libraire, 1946), p. 29.

[93] Ibid., pp. 32-55.   [94] Ibid., pp. 98-101, 108.

[95] Ibid., p. 213.   [96] Ibid., p. 268.

[97] Ibid., pp. 287-288.   [98] Ibid., p. 21.

[99] Ibid., p. 22.

[100] Ibid., p. 188.   [101] Ibid., pp. 134-135.

[102] Cf. ibid., pp. 21-22, 74, 152, 188, 268.

[103] Ibid., p. 200.

[104] Adrian J. Boekraad, *The Personal Conquest of Truth according to J. H. Newman* (Louvain: Editions Nauwelaerts, 1955), p. 9.

[105] Ibid., p. 11. Cf. pp. 37-40 for a discussion of Newman's insistence on the "objectivity of truth."

[106] Ibid., pp. 50, 56.   [107] Ibid., pp. 58-59.

[108] Ibid., p. 134.   [109] Ibid., pp. 149, 154-155.

[110] Ibid., pp. 180, 205.   [111] Ibid., p. 251.

[112] Ibid., p. 303. Cf. Boekraad, "Newman's Argument to the Existence of God," *Philosophical Studies* [Maynooth], VI (December, 1956), pp. 50, 54-55.

[113] Adrian J. Boekraad and Henry Tristram, *The Argument from Conscience to the Existence of God* (Louvain: Editions Nauwelaerts, 1961), p. 49. Note the preface, ibid., pp. 5-6, where Boekraad explains what portions of the book are his work.

[114] Ibid., p. 49.   [115] Ibid.

[116] Dr. Zeno, *John Henry Newman: Our Way to Certitude, An Introduction to Newman's Psychological Discovery: The Illative Sense, and His Grammar of Assent* (Leiden: E. J. Brill, 1957), p. 13.

[117] Ibid., p. 31.   [118] Ibid., p. 136.

[119] Cf. ibid., p. 11, where Zeno describes one of Newman's purposes in writing the book as being to show even educated people that their faith was ultimately based not on syllogisms but ". . . on personal reasonings and implicit workings of the mind, which cannot be adequately put into words." Also see ibid., p. 40, where he describes a word as ". . . a poor symbol of the idea . . ." and, thus, ". . . a very imperfect equivalent of the thing itself."

[120] Ibid., p. 195.

[121] Jan Hendrik Walgrave, *Newman the Theologian: The Nature of Belief and Doctrine as Exemplified in His Life and Works*, trans. A. V. Littledale (New York: Sheed and Ward, 1960). The book was originally published as *Newman, le Development du Dogme* (Paris: Casterman, 1957).

[122] Ibid., pp. 4-5.

[123] Cf. ibid., pp. 4, 9.

[124] Ibid., pp. 24, 27; cf. pp. 148-163.

[125] Ibid., p. 34.

[126] Ibid., p. 76. Cf. ibid., p. 206, where Walgrave urges that, for Newman, "Conscience alone gives us the key to the mystery of the universe."

[127] Ibid., pp. 89, 334-341.

[128] Ibid., p. 77.

[129] Ibid., pp. 220, 232.

[130] Justus George Lawler, "Both-And," *Renascence*, XV (Fall, 1962), 50-53.

[131] Walgrave, op. cit., p. 48.

[132] Ibid., p. 54.   [133] Ibid., p. 124.

[134] Ibid., pp. 132-133. Cf. ibid., p. 180, where he writes that ". . . the faith is a product, not of any natural experience, but of a revelation . . . ."

[135] Ibid., p. 226.   [136] Ibid., p. 135.

[137] Ibid., p. 137.   [138] Ibid.

[139] David A. Pailin, *The Way to Faith: An Examination of Newman's Grammar of Assent as a Response to the Search for Certainty in Faith* (London: Epworth Press, 1969), p. 60, says: "Newman sought to demonstrate how a person could justifiably be certain of what he believed."

[140] Ibid., pp. 78-79.   [141] Ibid., p. 97.

[142] Ibid., p. 189.   [143] Ibid., p. 100.

[144] Ibid., p. 108.   [145] Ibid., p. 116.

[146] Ibid., pp. 161-169.   [147] Ibid., p. 127.

[148] Ibid.   [149] Ibid., p. 165.

[150] Ibid., p. 172.   [151] Ibid., pp. 178, 181.

[152] Ibid., p. 183.   [153] Ibid., p. 195.

[154] Edward J. Sillem, *General Introduction to the Study of Newman's Philosophy* (Vol. I of *The Philosophical Notebook of John Henry Newman*. 2 vols.; New York: Humanities Press, 1969).

[155] Ibid., p. 11.   [156] Ibid., p. 13.

[157] Ibid., pp. 26, 61.   [158] Ibid., p. 62.

[159] Ibid., p. 65.   [160] Ibid., p. 87.

[161] Ibid.   [162] Ibid., p. 88.

[163] Ibid., p. 87.   [164] Ibid., p. 105.

[165] Ibid., p. 106.

[166] Cf. the section on "Belief in the Holy Trinity" in Newman's *An Essay in Aid of a Grammar of Assent*, Charles Frederick Harrold, editor (new edition; New York: Longmans, Green and Co., 1947), pp. 92-107.

[167] Sillem, op. cit., pp. 110ff.

[168] Ibid., p. 123.   [169] Ibid., p. 131.

[170] Ibid., p. 85. Sillem makes the point that men embrace truth as their own ". . . by following ways of thinking which are personal or largely independent of logical control." Presumably Sillem had formal logic in mind. He nowhere gives any attention to material rules guiding the use of discourse in given contexts.

[171] Charles Frederick Harrold, John Henry Newman: An Expository and Critical Study of His Mind, Thought and Art (Hamden, Connecticut: Archon Books, 1966), p. 377.

[172] Contradictions judged to be so great by one critic that he could consider Newman to be ". . . both outspoken and disingenuous, an apostle and a sophist." Cf. Griffith, op. cit., p. 69.

[173] This conclusion is influenced by the work of the "new critics" in literary criticism. In particular, I should cite René Wellek and Austin Warren, Theory of Literature (third edition; New York: Harcourt, Brace and World, Inc., 1956) and William K. Wimsatt, Jr., The Verbal Icon: Studies in the Meaning of Poetry (New York: The Noonday Press, 1966). In following these principles, I have rejected the suggestions of Werner Becker in his article "Zum Problem der Einheit von Leben und Werk bei John Henry Newman," Miscellanea Erfordiana, herausgegeben von Erich Kleineidam und Heinz Schurmann (Leipzig: St. Benno-Verlag GMBH, 1962), pp. 291-313. Within the context of a biographical study, Becker's suggestions regarding the unity of Newman's life and work certainly would have value, but they seem to be misleading in relation to the purposes of this study. The closest to a successful use of this kind of study that Becker suggests is Thomas L. Sheridan's Newman on Justification: A Theological Biography (Staten Island, New York: Alba House, Division of the Society of St. Paul, 1967).

[174] Both M. J. Ryan, "The Philosophy of Newman," The American Quarterly Review, 33 (1908), 77-86, and John Tucker, "Newman as Philosopher and Littérateur," The Catholic World, CXXV (May, 1927), 155-163, argue that Newman has a systematic philosophical view of classical thoroughness even though it is not formalized in one work but must be pieced together from all his works. Curiously enough neither Ryan nor Tucker discuss even the rudiments of that philosophy. M. C. D'Arcy, on the other hand, faults Newman for the incompleteness of his system and seeks to develop a more rigorous philosophical theory of knowledge in which the intellect is central in its capacity for interpretation. Cf. D'Arcy, op. cit., 201, 314.

[175] Søren Kierkegaard, The Point of View for My Work as an Author: A Report to History, trans. Walter Lowrie (New York: Harper and Row, Publishers, Torchbooks, 1962), pp. 5-6, claimed: ". . . I am and was a religious author. . . . the whole of my work as an author is related to Christianity, to the problem of 'becoming a Christian,' with a direct or indirect polemic against the monstrous illusion we call Christendom." Cf. ibid., p. 22 (note), where Kierkegaard noted that ". . . the thought behind the whole work is: what it means to become a Christian."

[176] Kierkegaard did discuss his literature in The Point of

View for My Work as an Author, op. cit. It is also true that Newman wrote the Apologia pro vita sua as a defense against misunderstandings of his life and thought, but the scope of Newman's effort is limited. Newman also edited most of his writings before his death, adding notes to passages that seemed out of harmony with his profession of Catholicism. In neither case, however, does one find evidence of the seeming design that Kierkegaard described as his "authorship."

[177] Kierkegaard, op. cit., p. 92. Cf. ibid., pp. 143, 151, 153-154.

[178] Charles Stephen Dessain, "Newman's First Conversion," op. cit., 51; and John Henry Newman (London: Thomas Nelson and Sons, Ltd., 1966), p. xii. Dessain gives priority to Newman's allegiance to the object of faith rather than to his defense of the faith. Many others have recognized the importance of these two concerns in Newman but have usually given the most emphasis to the apologetic motif. Cf., for example, "Editorial: The Conversion of Mr. Newman," op. cit., and Wilfrid Ward, "The True Nature of Newman's Genius . . .," op. cit.

[179] Reade, "The Sentimental Myth," op. cit., 146. This factor was also recognized by Allison, "Was Newman a Modernist?" op. cit., 55; by Cecil Chesterton, "The Art of Controversy: Macauley, Huxley, and Newman," The Catholic World, CV (July, 1917), 453; by Edwin Berry Burgum, "Cardinal Newman and the Complexity of Truth," op. cit., 323; and by J. F. Leddy, "Newman and Modern Educational Thought," American Essays for the Newman Centennial, op. cit., p. 115.

[180] Edmond Darvil Benard, A Preface to Newman's Theology (London: B. Herder Book Co., 1945), pp. 47-74. Benard lists a fourth principle: Judge any particular work in light of the two doctrines which form the foundation of his thought, the principle of dogma and the principle of the existence of the visible church. This last principle seems unsuitable for the purpose of this study, as it reveals the difficulty which faces even the most astute critic of Newman. Benard has called for an openness to Newman's works apart from prejudiced conclusions; his fourth principle, however, militates against this openness by its material content. While these two principles are very important in Newman's thought, they are not present in all contexts in the same way or, even, with the same prominence.

[181] Toohey, "Newman and Modernism," op. cit., 47.

[182] Benard, A Preface to Newman's Theology, op. cit., pp. xi-xii.

[183] John Henry Newman, "Advertissement," Essays Critical and Historical (new edition; London: Longmans, Green, and Co., 1891), I, viii.

CHAPTER III

THREE USES OF CHRISTIAN DISCOURSE:
A DESCRIPTIVE ANALYSIS

In the second chapter of this study, I set forth evidence for a history of reductive analysis in the study of Newman. I also argued that a fresh consideration of the unity characterizing the Cardinal's work is the necessary antidote to this history. Many excellent studies of individual aspects of Newman's thought have appeared in recent years, but only one significant thesis concerning that unity has been developed at length. Critics who espouse this thesis propose that the unity of Newman's thought resides in his understanding of the rationality of religious inquiry and the nature of personal faith. I dealt with that thesis in the last section of the second chapter and concluded that the thesis, however helpful in other respects, was limited and misleading as an interpretation of the unity of Newman's reflections on the relationship of faith and reason. The thesis which I defend has been hinted at most directly by C. Stephen Dessain and Wilfrid Ward. Ward tied his helpful insights, however, to a proposal that identifies Newman's work too completely with apologetic purposes. Dessain simply has not developed his case; yet his basic insight is sound: The unity of Newman's thought consists in his dedication to revealed truth. What Dessain has failed to point out is how that dedication made reductive proposals impossible for Newman. He has not shown how Newman's dedication to revealed truth led him to use Christian discourse in diverse ways in different contexts.

In the present chapter, I examine Newman's writings, both published and unpublished, in order to make the metatheological distinctions which are necessary to the development of Dessain's suggestion. In the fourth and fifth chapters, I shall use these distinctions in order to defend my own thesis regarding the unity of Newman's thought. In this chapter, however, my task is primarily descriptive. My method of procedure is only partially chronological in character since

Newman's writings do not lend themselves to any easy chronological division. For that reason, I have found thematic treatment to be the most helpful course of action. Nevertheless, I shall begin with a case study of Newman's earliest essays since they allow one to grasp the basic elements in Newman's attention to metatheological distinctions; those elements do not change though they are refined.

The principal elements in these metatheological distinctions are three uses of Christian discourse and the relation of reason and faith which each involves for Newman. Concern for revealed truth is present in each context but evidences itself in different ways. In what is presently an enigmatic statement of Newman's manner of dedication to revealed truth through diverse modes of reflection, one can claim that the realities of the faith are basic to each context but that their roles as concepts differ from one context to another. In order to clarify this proposal, I shall isolate the distinctions which Newman makes through the case study of his early essays and, then, consider the development of the separate distinctions in the course of his literature. In the present chapter, basic descriptive analyses of the distinctions are made, while the resolution of interpretative difficulties that raise doubts regarding my thesis is left to the fourth and fifth chapters.

I. A CASE STUDY: EARLY ESSAYS AND THEOLOGICAL PAPERS, 1816-1834

Newman displayed an early interest in issues related to the problem of the relation of faith and reason. In an essay written at the age of twenty on the difference between mathematics and religion, he argued that one's lack of knowledge regarding God should discourage objections to revelation and the *a priori* conviction that, by the nature of the case, mysteries are not to be admitted as possible. Just as in mathematics so in religion, argued Newman, we should be humbled by a recognition of the "contracted range of our imagination and judgment by showing us how little we can comprehend, and how erroneous oftentimes are the conclusions to which *a priori* speculations would lead us."[1] Thus, Newman showed some suspicion of reason and argued for its limited powers. But one should note here as elsewhere that the "reason" which he attacked is a reason of particular mold, one which stands in opposition to revelation on the basis of certain a priori commitments. Newman did not oppose reason as such (supposing, for the moment, that Newman even held there to be such a thing) but reason exercised in a certain way.

Other essays published during this period suggest that Newman was willing to bring rational criteria to bear on revelation, if those criteria were such that they did not rule out the possibility of revelation before one ever investigated the matter. Especially important in this regard is his "Essay on the Miracles of Scripture," published in 1826 in the Encyclopaedea Metropolitana. He argued there that the very nature of revelation is miraculous and, thus, that any reasoned study of that revelation must not do away with the possibility of miracle from the outset. The possibility of miracle is made real by the agency of God; thus, a miracle is not a violation of the given nature of things but "the interposition of an external cause."[2] Therefore, while miracles may be ". . . exceptions to the laws of one system, they may coincide with those of another."[3]

The system of which miracles are a part--a revealed system--is known only by the medium of testimony. Newman proposed to answer antecedent objections to the reliability of the testimony by an appeal to man's sense of moral obligation and need of a guide beyond himself. Newman concluded that ". . . the moral system points to an interference with the course of nature."[4] In addition, miracles are in harmony with God's providence and His moral attributes. These antecedent tests, however, cannot prove the case; they can only indicate why certain miracles could not have taken place. Only the quality of direct testimony can substantiate the fact of the miracle.[5] The credibility of such testimony is based on the character and competency of eye-witnesses.[6] Thus, Newman argued, the authority for the miracles is the testimony in which they are narrated and not a priori considerations, however important these considerations are for disqualifying certain alleged miracles.[7] The Christian narrative, in fact, can only be understood if miracles are granted--to exempt them is to misunderstand Christianity. Newman did note, on the other hand, that the proof of miracles is only one kind of evidence for the truth of Christianity.[8]

In these two essays Newman was concerned to replace a certain notion of reason with another. The most prejudicial error of those who avow that reason tells against revelation is their assumption that reason has a structure and rules transferable from one context to another without alteration. Newman introduced the thesis which he would develop more fully in time: Except for a very few formal rules, reason is always material, i.e., reason acting in a given province with given rules, and never formal reason alone or reason acting with the same rules no matter the context. Part of the material character of reason in the case of Christianity is an openness to the veracity of testimony regarding miracles.

In another essay from this period, "Poetry with reference to Aristotle's *Poetics*," Newman discussed the dynamics of understanding a given narrative or piece of testimony materially. He accused Aristotle of telling his reader what Greek tragedy should be rather than what it in fact is. Against that position, Newman argued that Greek tragedy has its own distinct structure and should be allowed to exhibit itself as it is.[9] In an essay published in 1833, "The Church of the Fathers," Newman applied these critical principles to Christianity. He asserted that ". . . our business is not to speculate about possible Dispensations of Religion, but to resign and devote ourselves to that in which we are actually placed."[10] That dispensation in which we are placed is, for Newman, that one to which the early Fathers of the Church testify. These Fathers are reporters of what was believed, so that not they but the times about which they wrote are authoritative.[11] It is this material conception of Christian reason which Newman opposed to an *a priori* conception of the nature of rationality.

In his essay on Aristotle's *Poetics*, Newman was also concerned to display what he calls the "poetical" nature of Christian faith. Newman described that poetical nature this way:

> Revealed Religion should be especially poetical--and it is so in fact. While its disclosures have an originality in them to engage the intellect, they have a beauty to satisfy the moral nature. It presents us with those ideal forms of excellence in which a poetical mind delights, and with which all grace and harmony are associated. It brings

>   us into a new world—a world of overpowering interest, of
>   the sublimest views, and the tenderest and purest feelings
>   . . . With Christians, a poetical view of things is a duty,—
>   we are bid to colour all things with hues of faith, to
>   see a Divine meaning in every event, and a superhuman
>   tendency.[12]

As he understood poetry to be the "gift of moving the affections through the imagination," so faith here is seen as involving such a capacity of the imagination that one's view of the world is imbued with a Christian interpretation and one's affections moved by that view to action in accordance with it.[13]

Certain manuscripts on theological subjects written by Newman during this early Anglican period provide evidence of a third area of the exploration of faith in addition to the material rationality suggested by the character of Christian testimony and the poetic quality of faith with its emphasis on the imagination. These papers are concerned with the nature and process of conversion.[14] Some date from a period in which, by Newman's own confession, he was very much an "Evangelical."[15] He was concerned to show that for any man to assent to the mysterious doctrine of Christianity without a "full conviction of the naturally depraved condition of mankind" is impossible.[16] He was convinced that this doctrine is the keystone of the arch which holds all other doctrines in their proper place and insures to them their proper vitality. He claimed that all objections to the Christian faith are a necessary consequence of the rejection of this doctrine. At one point, he said that there may be twenty thousand other reasons for disbelief but that he was only concerned with this one; and, yet, in another place, he maintained that the rejection of this doctrine is the "great barrier, perhaps the _only_ barrier."[17]

It is interesting that, in a private memorandum for July 6, 1826, he evidenced a significant change in his views on this subject. Newman explained that, in 1821, he had been concerned to give ". . . a _description_ of the ordinary _process_ of conversion, (i.e., the hopes, fears, despair, joy. . . of the person under conversion) which I thought almost necessary to a true Christian."[18] By 1828, Newman was making an important distinction between regeneration as a work of God and as a work of man. As a work of God it is indeed instantaneous and complete, but as a work of man it is a work of time. More importantly Newman argued that the process of conversion is such that:

> Individual instances of course present every diversity of spiritual history and experience--still viewing the Christian body as a whole, baptism is the one time to be assigned for the commencement of spiritual influence upon its members. . . .[19]

In a subsequent paper on "Holy Baptism," Newman argued that to give up belief in baptismal regeneration is to be forced to measure God's grace by the sensible effects which it has on the life of the person and leads to the false identification of the spiritual life with a sort of religious ecstasy or impassioned thought.[20] Thus, Newman moved from an early emphasis on some inward principle as the evidence of conversion to an emphasis on the objective character of the sacrament of baptism. In that earlier emphasis he wrote of the state of conversion as a "certain state of the heart and affections--including indeed good works and religious observances, but only as external signs or evidences of an inward principle . . . ."[21] In the later emphasis, Newman understood the process and state of conversion to be so variable as to defy one description or one model. He attacked all "grand views, which are to settle all questions, and to which all phenomena are to be reduced."[22] He rejected the identification of Christian faith either with feeling or with practice. In the first case, holiness would become identifiable with passion, which would be prejudicial to the truth claims of religion. In the second place, tying doctrines to a rule of expediency or to their practical influence would have the same effect. In either case, the danger is that one will give up important elements of the creeds because faith has become a habit of mind directed toward an essence of religion rather than faith in the Gospel.[23] Newman's concern with "objective religion" became the dominating interest of the period in which the Tracts for the Times (1834-1841) appeared and in which Newman made his transition to the Roman Catholic Church.

In these early essays, Newman already displayed tendencies and interests which one finds to be characteristic. First, he demanded that one give attention to revelation as providing its own structure by its own testimony, establishing rules, defining concepts, and suggesting evidence. Against this material shape of reasoned faith, he opposed and rejected a formal reason supposed to have its own criteria and central concepts apart from any object of investigation. Second, he gave attention to another characteristic of revealed religion, namely its "poetical" quality. While the concept of reason is central in some contexts, the concept of imagination is paramount in others. In the context of one, a person seeks evidence and makes arguments; in the context of the other, one constantly encounters evidence of God in all things and in every event. Third, he was concerned to argue for the variety of individual life histories in coming to faith, rejecting the notion that there is some one pattern. The constant element in coming to faith shifted from certain personal aspects of appropriation to identifiable objective factors such as the sacraments. We shall see that his need for subjective guarantees of conversion lessened and finally disappeared as he gained confidence that there is a depositum fidei and an authoritative source of instruction in the faith. At the same time, he did evidence a concern to differentiate, rather than to equate, the spheres of authority and theology and the sum total of significant aspects of the life of faith.

In order to clarify the ways in which these distinctions function for Newman, I shall consider each of the three uses in turn and, in the fifth chapter, Newman's own remarks concerning the kind of unity characterizing the conjunction of these diverse uses. These distinctions and the understanding of their relationships to one another were not limited to Newman's early essays but continue essentially the same throughout his corpus though, to be sure, they undergo refinement.

II. CONTINUITY AND DIVERSITY IN COMING TO FAITH

In his book on the Arian controversy, The Arians of the Fourth Century, Newman offered his understanding of the disciplina arcani as it was practiced by teachers in the catechetical school at Alexandria. He described the mode of this instruction as "economical," a term which indicates an accommodation of the elements of the Christian doctrine to the feelings and prejudices of the hearer. By teaching in this way, the instructor hopes to lead the catechumen to accept what he might otherwise find objectionable.[24] Newman argued in this way for the method:

> . . . those who are strangers to the tone of thought and principles of the speaker, cannot at once be initiated into his system . . . and therefore, if he is to teach them at all, he must put before them large propositions, which he has afterwards to modify, or make assertions which are but parallel or analogous to the truth, rather than coincident with it.[25]

In short, Christian teachers should not prematurely insist on difficulties and should address themselves to their hearers in such a way as to show an understanding for the peculiar capacities and personalities of the individual.[26]

The practice of "economy" in teaching can easily be mistaken for intentional lying. In fact, Newman's primary concern in his Apologia pro vita sua was to defend himself against Charles Kingsley's charge that he sanctioned lying in the cause of the Church. In making this defense, he clarified the nature of "economy" and its relation to the truth. In the Apologia, he noted that

> . . . the rule of the Economy, at least as I have explained and recommended it, did not go beyond (1) the concealing the truth when we could do so without deceit, (2) stating it only partially, and (3) representing it under the nearest form possible to a learner or inquirer, when he could not possibly understand it exactly.[27]

Economy was, for Newman, a mode of prudence which follows this basic principle:

> . . . out of various courses, in religious conduct or statement, all and each _allowable_ _antecedently_ and _in themselves_, that ought to be taken which is most expedient and most suitable at the time for the object in hand.[28]

Economy, in this sense, is distinguished clearly from lying. The principle of economy on the human level is merely an analogy of God's gradual preparation of men for the advent of the Gospel. This principle of economy is basic to Newman's understanding of the way in which God brings men to faith. The principle allowed Newman to maintain the definite content of the faith without the dictation of a stereotyped mode of propagation and appropriation.

The Problem: The Relation of Continuity and Diversity in Paths to Faith

Several sermons in Newman's collection of _Parochial and Plain Sermons_ contain his early reflections on the relationship between the content and the appropriation of the faith.

Two sermons preached in 1839, "Unreal Words" and "Sacred Privileges," contain the earliest instances of Newman's famous distinction between "real" and "notional" assent. Newman's essential claim was that one's reasoning in religious matters is not guided by a formal set of rules of argument but by a reliance on the testimony of the Christian witnesses and the informal rules that the testimony involves.[29] Newman held that a certain disposition of the mind is necessary for an openness to that testimony and its informal rules of evidence and meaning. This disposition was taken to involve the need for the renewal of one's life. In short, said Newman, men believe because religion has the power to renew their lives.[30] Newman described man's recognition of the truth as characterized by edification as well as knowledge.[31] Love or the desire for knowledge and obedience is the condition without which reason could not begin to function. He described the condition which love establishes as a desire for something which one cannot do without--in the case of faith, the next world. Such a desire makes one open to evidence other than that attainable by sight, as in the case of the testimony of the Apostles.[32]

Thus, the principle of economy allowed for the diversity of paths to faith while Newman's isolation of a disposition of the mind prerequisite to faith suggested a continuity and universality in the appropriation of the faith. The attempt to develop an intelligible resolution of these two factors was a focus of reflection for Newman throughout most of his life. He gave consideration to certain important questions again and again. Is the process of faith as variegated as the rejection of Evangelicalism led one to believe? Does the existence of a necessary disposition of mind argue for a single description of the process of coming to faith being possible? Does the reliance on the priority of personal reasons for believing and on the power of religion to renew a person's life seem to indicate that the concerns of rational reflection are limited in faith? These questions were basic for Newman's own reflections and for my investigation.

The Problem Under Discussion: The Oxford University Sermons

The sermons usually referred to as the <u>Oxford University Sermons</u> are the first published materials in which Newman addressed himself in extended fashion to the relation of faith and reason as dimensions of religious inquiry. These sermons can be read apart from the notes which Newman appended as a Catholic in 1871, but they are not so helpful to understanding Newman if read in that way. Without these notes, one is left in confusion about his estimate of reason, the relation of intellectual and moral concerns, and the nature of the content of revelation. For instance, his sermon "The Usurpation of Reason," preached late in 1831, seems to indicate a totally negative view of the use of reason in relation to revealed doctrine. The notes appended to the sermon, however, indicate that he was using the word "reason" in a very specific and limited sense.

One might sceptically conclude that Newman had simply misread his own mind, reflecting later understandings back upon his earlier work. But I have found, on the contrary, that his notes only reflect uses of the word "reason" which I had already discovered in the earliest of his essays. One finds again the rejection of certain schema of rational criteria that deny, at the outset, the possibility of revelation. One finds the distinction between an informal, implicit mode of reflection that is present, though unanalyzed, in all men of faith and an explicit analysis of modes of reflection in order to ascertain their meaning and validity. My conclusion, therefore, is that the notes clarify rather than distort Newman's actual position at the time that the sermons were written.

Uses of the word "reason." In the preface to the third edition of the sermons, Newman offered a summary clarification of the ways in which he used the word "reason" in the collection.[33] In the initial sermons, noted Newman, there is no precise definition of the terms "faith" and "reason" but an acceptance of the popular understanding of the words.[34] In that sense, faith is a kind of feeling or sentiment convinced by little evidence, and satisfied with presumptions. Reason, on the other hand, is an exercise of common sense demanding rigid grounds and concerned with proof.[35] More precisely defined, reason is a process by which one moves from knowing one thing on to knowing another, a process which may be either explicit or implicit.[36] In the case of implicit reason there is no direct recognition of the process of coming to a given conclusion. However, such direct recognition can be a property of reason. Although reason is a process complete in itself apart from giving an explicit account of it, such an account can be given.

> The exercise of analysis is not necessary to the integrity of the process analyzed. The process of reasoning is complete in itself, and independent. The analysis is but an account of it; it does not make the conclusion correct; it does not make the inference rational. It does not cause a given individual to reason better.[37]

In this preface, Newman tended to identify implicit reasoning with probabilities and explicit reasoning with what he calls "the method of evidence," or a priori versus a posteriori evidence.[38] Such an identification seems most misleading since an analysis should provide no new evidence and certainly not a different kind of evidence but only a description of the logic of a given discourse. Newman clarified this distinction in the Grammar.

Newman's principal conclusions in the Oxford sermons involved the isolation of three senses of the word "reason": explicit reason or the ability to analyze; evidential reason or a posteriori arguments from evidence; secular reason or an abuse of reason by which rational criteria are generalized without attention to the peculiarity of a subject matter and its first principles.[39] The importance of attention to the peculiarity of a subject matter involves Newman's recognition that reasoning well in one subject matter does not necessarily mean that one will be able to do the same in another. The reason for this diversity is that any given subject matter involves separate rules and principles.[40] Newman argued, for instance, that faith is rational in none of the three general senses that he had isolated. Faith, he contended, is a rational process in that it gives knowledge on the basis of grounds offered though these grounds are implicit and probable in character.[41] A fourth sense of the word "reason" in the sermons is, then, identifiable with implicit reason.

Thus, in the clearest sense, the sermons are attempts to distinguish the way in which faith as involving a peculiar subject matter is rational in contrast to false notions of how that is or is not the case. The understanding of reason which Newman opposed is that conception which seeks to impose

principles foreign to religion on that subject matter with
". . . its own principles, homogeneous with itself, and necessary for reasoning justly in it."[42]

Rational inquiry and the testimony of the conscience.
Many have argued that the Oxford sermons identify the principles of judgment in religion with those gained through exercise of the conscience. According to this identification, men are said to find the evidence of the moral life adequate to lead them to faith. Conscience implies a relation between the soul and something external and superior to the soul.[43] Included in the dictates of this natural religion, according to Newman, are a sense of right and wrong, of failure and fear of judgment, of future life with its rewards and punishments for conduct in this world. One should be conscious, at the same time, of several provisos which Newman made regarding such an identification if he is to understand the role of conscience and the role of reason in faith. He understood natural religion to be inadequate in the information which it provides regarding the divine personality.[44] In one sermon, Newman also allowed that at least some men are brought to Christian faith by means of a consideration of the evidences for its truth.[45]

One must be careful then of understanding Newman's description of natural religion as a description of the process of conversion. He told his listeners that the conversion process admits of something other than a sense of sin as the initiation of the movement to faith.[46] The memorandum of 1826 which I noted above should be sufficient evidence that it was not his intention to provide such a description. What he did suggest is that the dictates of conscience found in natural religion have a kind of fittingness with the doctrines of revelation--there is a natural process of movement from one to the other not present between secular reason and faith. In some sense, then, the description of the dictates of conscience provided Newman a way in which to differentiate between faith, reasoned faith, and secular reason.

Newman opposed the contention that one must come to faith by means of explicitly reasoned argument even though he did not deny the possibility that one may come by means of such argument. On the other hand, he did hold that the doctrines of faith must be approvable by reason or shown to be true if they are to be regarded as true. Newman made the distinction in this way:

> . . . undeniable though it be, that Reason has a power of analysis and criticism in all opinion and conduct, and that nothing is true or right but what may be justified and, in a certain sense, proved by it, and undeniable, in consequence, that, unless the doctrines received by Faith are approvable by Reason, they have no claim to be regarded as true, it does not therefore follow that Faith is actually grounded on Reason in the believing mind itself . . . . Reason need not be the origin of Faith, as Faith exists in the very persons believing, though it does test and verify it.[47]

Newman offered two reasons for faith being of this nature. On the one hand, the confusion and hurried activity of the world prevents excessive dependence on evidence for resolving many questions and decisions.[48] Also, claimed Newman, revelation itself demands that faith be understood in this way; God has ordained in His providence that evidence shall not be the simple foundation on which faith is based.[49] Faith also involves "prejudices" or what Newman called "antecedent considerations" or "antecedent probabilities" in the Grammar of Assent. These antecedent considerations or prejudices involve the hopes, fears, and existing opinions of the believer as well as the evidence for the matter.[50] Newman argued that this bias of mind lessens the need for conclusive evidence. Love of the object of faith gives one a readiness to believe and fosters an attention to phenomena as evidence that would not ordinarily be taken as evidence.[51] Religious persons embrace the Gospel as having a suitableness to their needs.[52] In a kind of summary statement, Newman concluded:

> . . . Reason, weighing evidence only, or arguing from external experience, is counter to Faith: but, admitting the legitimate influence and logical import of the moral feelings, it concurs with it.[53]

Newman's Continued Exploration of the Problem: His Catholic Period

Those who identify coming to faith with the awakening of the voice of conscience do not, however, adequately account for Newman's emphasis on the positive uses of explicit reason, his suspicion of the promptings of conscience, and his continued efforts to relate the diversity and continuity of paths to faith in his Catholic period. Regarding the matter of diversity in religious pilgrimages and the mode of inquiry related to them, Newman continued to note:

> God deals with us very differently; conviction comes slowly to some men, quickly to others; in some it is the result of much thought and many reasonings, in others of a sudden illumination . . . . Some men are converted merely by entering a Catholic Church; others are converted by reading one book; others by one doctrine. They feel the weight of their sins, and they see that that religion must come from God which alone has the means of forgiving them. Or they are touched and overcome by the evident sanctity, beauty, and (as I may say) fragrance of the Catholic Religion. Or they long for a guide amid the strife of tongues; and the very doctrine of the Church about faith, which is so hard to many, is conviction to them. Others, again, hear many objections to the Church, and follow out the whole subject far and wide; conviction can scarcely come to them except as at the end of a long inquiry . . . so Holy Church presents herself very differently to different minds who are contemplating her from without. God deals with them differently; but, if they are faithful to their light, at last, in their own time, though it may be a different time to each, He brings them to that one and the same state of mind, very definite and not to be mistaken, which we call conviction.[54]

Newman concluded: ". . . men are convinced in very various ways,--what convinces one does not convince another; but this is an accident . . . ."[55]

At the same time that he recognized this diversity, however, he was still attempting to isolate factors common to all paths to faith. Basic to those common factors, for Newman, was the fact that one encounters a mystery of one kind or another which he cannot solve or dissolve and which leads him to the belief that a revelation that will resolve the problem is not unlikely.[56] For example, conscience can convict one of the existence of a Being, a Judge external and superior to man. What is problematic is the separation of what the Being says from what one's own self-love and pride counsel. In that problem, said Newman, is the basis for asserting that ". . . the gift of conscience raises a desire for what it does not itself fully supply."[57]

In short, Newman offered, a religious man is one who is on the "look out" for the infallible teaching of revelation. The non-religious man is falsely contented with himself and with his ability to obey a code of morals which he has framed for himself.[58] The religious man and the non-religious man differ sharply in relation to their inquiry into truth:

> The one is active, and the other passive, when Christ
> is preached as the Saviour of the world. The one goes
> to meet the truth; the other thinks that the Truth ought
> to come to him.[59]

The active inquirer examines the faith and its credentials out of personal interest rather than waiting for God to prove Himself. He makes the most of his knowledge, cumulating facts and arguments and actively working to overcome difficulties. "To be easy in believing is nothing more or less than to have been ready to inquire; to be hard of belief is nothing else but to have been loth and reluctant to inquire."[60] Or, as he elsewhere phrased it, ". . . the difference between one whose heart is hard, and one whose heart is softened" is that one ". . . man has often thought about religion, another never."[61]

<u>Correspondence with the Froudes.</u> Given his recognition of diversity and continuity in the ways in which men come to faith, Newman continued his more rigorous analyses of the peculiar subject matter and informal rules attending Christian discourse. His efforts at analysis were conducted in an era in which the scientific model for arriving at truth was in its ascendancy and beginning to assume a kind of hegemony in the pursuit of truth. For this reason, one can understand Newman's attack on the proposal that reason is applicable in the same way and according to the same rules in every context. The proper exercise of reason, he suggested, calls for attention to the context in which one operates. His effort to make this distinction was refined through his correspondence with his good friends William Froude and his wife.[62]

Froude's friendship was of great intellectual as well as personal value to Newman, as Froude, a scientist himself, was an able representative of the scientifically oriented epistemology prominent in intellectual circles of that day. Like those whom I described in the first chapter as espousing a rigid set of rational criteria, Froude held two tenets inviolable: one, the moral obligation to doubt every proposition and conclusion; two, the lack of any permanent certainty.[63]

To this rigid notion of verification, Newman opposed another description of attaining truth by means of faith:

> I wish you would consider whether you have a right notion
> how to gain faith. It is, we know, the Gift of God,
> but I am speaking of it as a human process and attained

by human means. Faith then is not a conclusion from
premises, but the result of an act of the <u>will</u>, following upon a <u>conviction</u> that to believe is a duty . . . .
For directly you have a conviction that you ought to
believe, reason has done its part, and what is wanted for
faith is, not proof, but will.[64]

Or again, in opposition to strict verification, he said:

I think it a fallacy--but I don't think it easy to show it
to be so . . . . In truth I think there is a far deeper
philosophy on the subject than yours, if I could develop it,
much lies in the meaning of the words certainty and doubt,
much again in our duties to a <u>person</u>, as e.g. a friend.
Religion is not merely a science but a devotion . . . .[65]

Thus, for Newman, there was a personal and informal way of
arriving at certainty in Christian faith which is as logical
as other ways. On the other hand, he also claimed that

. . . assuming <u>duty</u> proved, still you cannot believe without
1. a <u>creed</u> 2. <u>an authority</u> which will not mislead you.[66]

The existence of a creed and an authoritative teacher, then, is
not a practical rule but a sovereign principle demanded by the
theological system itself.[67] If one trusts and loves God and
His Church, he cannot doubt.[68]

Froude urged that such a demand for firm assent, for
unwavering faith demanded the existence of a faculty which
enables one to perceive with certainty matters of supernatural
consequence.[69] Newman responded to that objection by asserting
that he and Froude differed on the meaning of the word "certain."
Newman noted that he used the word in reference to minds while
Froude used it in relation to propositions. Newman granted
that all propositions are uncertain in Froude's sense of the
word, but he maintained that minds or individuals may be certain
in themselves:

. . . a recognition and judgment that the proof is not
wholly complete, attaches to all propositions; this I
would maintain as well as you. But if you mean that the
laws of the human mind do not command and force it to
accept as true and to assent absolutely to propositions
which are not logically demonstrated, this I take to be so
great a paradox, that all the scientific philosophers
in Europe would be unable by their united testimony to
make me believe it.[70]

Newman called the faculty by which one makes such judgments of
certainty the "inductive sense" in these letters. He identifies it here as he does the "illative sense" in the <u>Grammar</u>
with Aristotle's <u>phronesis</u> or prudent judgment.

"Lectures on the Theory of Faith." Newman's unpublished manuscripts from this period of reflection on the issues dealt with in the Grammar also reflect his concentration on the relation of faith and reason and the consequent attempt to describe the elements of continuity in religious inquiry. In a series of notes entitled "Lectures on the Theory of Faith" dating from 1848, Newman gave early expression to his notion of faith as producing a moral certainty or a certainty of mind.[71] Such a certainty, he said, results from the conclusion that we *ought* to believe a certain thing. Such a conclusion is not reached by logical proof of a rigorous nature but by a proof that convinces one that he ought to believe some thing. A person is not certain only when he pronounces a conclusion logically certain but also when he can claim that it is credible. The other aspect in a case of credibility is the imposition of the will by which one comes to believe. Needless to say such an analysis left Newman with several problems. He made initial analyses of these problems in the 1848 papers.

First, he described the conditions which made an assent credible. He dubbed this aspect of faith *fides acquisita* or the means of proposing and recommending the object of faith to the mind as credible on the basis of certain pieces of evidence and as a result of a certain logical process. These conditions or *credibilia* do not necessarily lead to conviction; thus, the actual cause of faith is not any constraint upon the reason by means of evidence or by means of the laws of reasoning. Nevertheless, these *credibilia* are an important element in one's coming to faith. Newman asserted that the objective evidence for revelation is "most abundant, varied, and consistent." By a cumulation of probabilities, that is, by the conjunction of many separate pieces of evidence, one can gain certainty of mind. No one person will be able to make use of all parts of the evidence for revealed truth; different minds will be convinced by different parts of it in accordance with their differing capacities or accidental circumstances. This sort of certitude was a law of the mind for arriving at truth and certitude regarding that truth. Or speaking more religiously, as Newman put it, this constitution of the mind was the will of God.

> Accordingly, I considered that He, by His superintending providence took man by man, each in his own way, a way

which cannot be analyzed or generalized by science, and supplied the means of certitude to each; that He blessed and completed the probabilities afforded to each, giving in each case a perfection, to a process in itself imperfect. . . .[72]

Just as surely, then, as these <u>credibilia</u> precede faith as conditions of certainty, they do not themselves cause certainty. The real cause of faith is not these <u>motiva credibilitas</u> but the will which commands the intellect to accept the object of this evidence with certainty. Thus, assent or faith is not really dependent upon these <u>motiva</u> in any direct way; faith is not discursive, i.e., resolvable into these pieces of credible evidence and cogent argument. Rather such an assent is, by its very nature, a supernatural, a divine gift. Such faith holds to the propositions to which it assents not as conclusions from a series of premises but as revealed truths believed on the basis of God's veracity.

The object of faith is thus twofold. The material object of faith consists of the <u>res revelata</u> or the things revealed. The formal object of faith is God Himself both as that which faith directly contemplates and which gives the various elements of the <u>res revelata</u> their meaning and as that which makes faith possible. Newman concluded in this regard that the certainty of faith is based on the truthfulness of God and, thus, is itself a matter of faith or trust in God. Newman proposes two ways in which one might analyze this characteristic of faith. On the one hand, one could assume that the things revealed and the formal object of faith are accepted in one act of faith. In this way, one argues in a circle. As an example, Newman described an argument to the effect that the Catholic faith is true because God has given it and His having given it as certain because the Church declares it to be from Him. The Church so declares because Scripture says it is from God and is to be received; Scripture is to be received, for the Church declares it. On the other hand, one might argue that the <u>res revelata</u> are facts and do not need to be proved. The proof of God's speaking in the Church is impressed on one by means of such visible informants or notes as miracles and saints. Newman summarized this argument as follows: This is true for God says it. He says it, for the Church says it from Him. The Church says it from Him, for it has notes of being His voice. And these notes bring their own evidence with them.[73]

Newman followed Thomas, however, in arguing that, though revealed truth is never against reason, it may be above reason. In other words, there are no objections against Christianity which cannot be "repelled," even though there are many questions about it which cannot be solved or explained.[74] If all such questions could be answered, then there would be nothing in revelation above reason. Newman believed that this residual suprarational element results from the imperfection of the human intellect in relation to those truths made known.

> In other words the fact of that ignorance accounts for the questions not being solved; and an appeal to that ignorance is the proof that the objections are refuted.[75]

There is another sense in which Newman spoke of faith as beyond human possibility. In this sense, the witness to God is not on a priori grounds, not even solely by means of man's moral nature, but witnessed externally by the testimony of mankind and by his experience of the course of things.[76] Newman wrote:

> We must consider Him, not on a priori grounds, but as one who lives and acts independent of us, whether we will or no--as an existing fact, witnessed indeed by our moral nature, but disclosing Himself objectively by the testimony of mankind and our experience of the course of the world.[77]

Even more importantly, the independent, objective existence of a system parallel to the one that man knows in his daily life has God as its first cause; the possibility of miracles is based on the existence of a miraculous system.[78]

Thus, revelation is above reason in two senses. On the one hand, its very externality and objectivity, its separate existence means that it is not discernible except as it makes itself known. Revealed truth is not given within us but from without man and to him. In addition, revealed truth is beyond reason in that it is beyond full comprehension by man's limited intellect. Revelation is above reason or man's rational control in that it has its own separate existence and in that its structure does not correspond directly to man's apprehension of reality. This supernatural quality often produces confusion in man, for his own nature is closer to him than this supernatural realm.

> Sight is closer than faith; reason is closer than authority; and human affection is closer to us than devotion, and passion than mortification.[79]

Therefore, though a process of reasoning precedes faith, the imagination of man can lead him to take up objections even against sound and convincing reasons. Because of the invincible irrationality of the imagination, grace alone is sufficient to subdue these objections.[80] Grace itself operates upon the imagination and not so much upon the reason. One can contemplate the facts of the faith apart from the process by which one comes to accept them as the case.[81]

These papers suggest a further sophistication of Newman's understanding of the relation of faith and reason. And this further development is an additional indication that the kinds of distinctions made by Newman between real and notional assent in the Grammar characterize his work as a whole. First, there is the initial distinction between faith and a certain kind of reason. The determinate character of this reason is here largely understood in terms of the scientific method. Faith is predominantly viewed as an act of the will. Second, however, faith and reason of another kind are found to be quite compatible, even necessarily related. The evidence for faith must be credible if one is to be able to give any kind of assent to it--either notional (of the reason) or real (of the will). These credibilia amass themselves as a cumulation of probable arguments for the truth of revelation. Third, faith is not to be equated with these pieces of evidence. In the first place, man's imagination can lead him to oppose even the most probable masses of evidence. Reason is not sufficient by itself to turn man's imagination from the readily accessible life of the world. In the second place, moreover, elements of the revelation itself go beyond man's natural capacity. These elements demand the gift of faith by grace if one is to believe and the voice of tradition and of the Church if error is to be avoided. The concept of authority is important for this aspect of faith. Faith is not to be equated with an inherent possibility of man; faith is a gift that comes from beyond man. Though some aspects of that reality can be understood to be absolutely substantiated by facts as man finds them, others only avoid a lack of consistency with the facts.[82] One is aware of these truths and able to believe them only on the basis of their authoritative and gracious revelation.[83]

The peculiar character of religious inquiry involves

not only a certain state of mind and heart but also a distinctive form of evidence. In a tract "On the Controversy with the Romanists," Newman noted the importance of being able ". . . to analyze and to state formally our own reasons for believing what we do believe. . . ."[84] The arguments offered are not, however, rationalistic in character; rather they appeal to the practice and doctrine of the early Church.[85] Newman reiterated his view that the authority of the early church is her witness to the fact that certain doctrines were then received and believed by Christians.[86] Thus, the creed has one authoritative sense and that sense is determined by the belief of the Catholic Church.[87]

Conclusions

Newman gave the most complete expression to his concern with the relation of the formal continuity between modes of religious inquiry and the diversity of individual paths to faith in his famous Essay in Aid of a Grammar of Assent of 1870 and in certain philosophical papers dating from the same general period. Because of their importance in interpreting Newman's final perspective on the issue, I shall consider them in the next chapter in which I seek to defend my thesis regarding the unity of Newman's thought. My investigation of his work apart from the Grammar and these papers suggests certain general conclusions that must be supported and amplified in his mature work if my thesis regarding the complex unity of his thought is to be shown to be accurate.

First, this study reveals Newman's sense of the basic problem in describing the movement of a person from unfaith to faith. He asked himself certain very important questions. Can one describe the transition implied by the fact of conversion? Can one make any general remarks regarding the nature of inquiry preceding conversion that hold for all examples of a person's coming to faith? Second, the study displays that Newman, in response to these questions, became suspicious of the attempt to give a description of the process of conversion while maintaining the effort to offer some description of the nature of religious inquiry as a human enterprise.

Third, the investigation of his writings reveals that, in exploring the nature of religious inquiry, Newman gave a prominent role to the testimony of the conscience and to its function in natural religion. The testimony of conscience tended to assume a centrality in Newman's analysis of religious inquiry that threatened to obscure his awareness of the diversity of life histories and of pilgrimages to faith. In that sense, his formal description of the characteristics of religious inquiry tended to become a material description of the prerequisite steps of appropriation necessary to one's coming to faith. A more careful analysis is needed to reveal whether he avoided this kind of reductionism. I shall make this analysis in the next chapter in investigating the Grammar and related writings. Before doing that, however, I should like to describe two additional uses of Christian discourse apart from its role in relation to religious inquiry. They constitute two other functions of Christian discourse in that complex unity which Newman understood to characterize an appropriate understanding of the Christian faith. Newman dealt with elements of the third function--which I shall discuss in more detail below--in the "Lectures on the Theory of Faith" in describing the res revelata and their relation to fides acquisita. First, however, I shall note Newman's understanding of another function of Christian discourse, namely, its "poetical" quality.

III. THE "POETICAL" QUALITY OF CHRISTIAN FAITH

Newman had very little to say directly regarding the nature of the "poetical" quality of faith by which the Christian colors ". . . all things with hues of faith . . . " and sees ". . . a Divine meaning in every event . . . ."[88] This poetical quality is described in terms of the role of the imagination in faith when the subject does receive direct attention. As Thomas Vargish points out in his recent book Newman: The Contemplation of Mind, Newman held the imagination to be a conserver of forms or a reservoir which stores up sense impressions in the forms of images or pictures.[89] For instance, in one of the Tracts for the Times which he authored, Newman noted the great consolation that the visible church along with its visible creed, ordinances and hierarchy provides the Christian. This visibility is a consolation ". . . because it is an appeal to a fact, which no one can deny. . . ."[90]

For Newman, facts act directly on the imagination while argumentative proof moves one less directly. Though the imagination does not create these images or pictures, it does act as a powerful stimulus on the affections and on actions through them.

Newman often opposed this immediate power of the imagination to the scientific notion of "reason" prominent among his contemporaries. One of the most interesting essays in which this opposition appears is his "Tamworth Reading Room," an essay attacking Robert Peel's hope for a community established on scientific knowledge. Newman sought to displace this hope for enlightenment through scientific reason with what he considered to be man's only firm possibility for a meaningful grasp of reality.

In the essay against Peel's proposal, Newman described Christianity as being constituted by the facts and events of revelation, the testimony to which reaches man through his imagination rather than through his reason initially. According to this thesis, direct impressions of the dogmas of faith and not arguments first reach the hearts of men. Newman wrote:

> Many a man will live and die upon a dogma: no man will be a martyr for a conclusion. A conclusion is but an opinion; it is not a thing which <u>is</u>, but which we are '<u>certain about</u>,' and it has often been observed, that we never say we are certain without implying that we doubt. To say that a thing must be, is to admit that it <u>may not</u> be. No one, I say, will die for his own calculations; he dies for realities.[91]

And, for Newman, realities are such that they capture the imagination in the form of pictures. Christianity is a message, a testimony, a revelation which faith assumes as its first principle. The hold of that message on the imagination through the powerful images which it imprints there forms the affections and actions of the believer.[92] Peel and others, said Newman, overlook the fact that man cannot be defined as a reasoning animal; man is a ". . . seeing, feeling, contemplating animal."[93] The religious mind is one so imbued with faith in all its dimensions that the world is seen in a way not accountable for in terms of reason alone.

Newman did not always make such a sharp dichotomy between reason and imagination as he did in this essay on the "Tamworth Reading Room." One should keep in mind, therefore, the context in which the essay appeared. The disagreement with

Peel is simply a concrete instance of Newman's effort to distinguish between a formal reason that seeks to impose itself in all contexts and forms of material reason shaped by the objects of their investigation. He also opposed any effort which sought to isolate reasoned reflection from the equally important function of the imagination. If one keeps these contextual matters in mind, he realizes that the antagonists, for Newman, were not faith and reason but the exclusive reliance of Peel on scientific method and the reality of the seemingly contradictory aspects of Christianity in which reason, on the one hand, and imagination, on the other, predominate in various contexts.

In relation to the impact of these images or pictures on the believer, Newman urged that one make his professions, creeds, prayers, dealings, conversations, arguments, and teaching sincere or "real"[94] In this way, Newman described the need to make one's faith more and more a part of oneself. To use the language of faith in an insincere fashion is a dangerous matter according to Newman since the true meaning of the language always constitutes a judgment on an insincere use.[95] Newman was careful to point out that one's profession of the creed and, thus, one's use of Christian language, does often outstrip one's own feelings and beliefs; he did not understand that to constitute insincerity. Insincerity involves professing when one need not do so and failing to feel when one might have done so.[96] Newman was aware that ". . . it takes a long time to apprehend what we confess."[97]

> We ever promise things greater than we master, and we wait on God to enable us to perform them. Our promising involves a prayer for light and strength. And so again we all say the Creed, but who comprehends it fully? All we can hope is, that we are all in the way to understand it; that we partly understand it; that we desire, pray, and strive to understand it more and more. Our creed becomes a sort of prayer.[98]

This process of being on one's way to understanding was called "realizing" by Newman.[99] The ultimate goal of this process is that the man of faith see the world as God sees it. To do so is to learn the ". . . new language which Christ has brought us" and by which He has interpreted all things in a new way.[100] This notion of a new vision and the role of the imagination in grasping and employing that vision are central to Newman's description of the Christian life in his sermons. Understanding that this concern for describing the Christian life is central in the sermons will eliminate the tendency to identify this concern as Newman's only purpose as a writer; he had other purposes in other contexts. His concern with the practical aspect of revelation is natural to a pastoral context, while his concern with objective religion always is at least a reminder that one should not take the analysis of the practical element as the only aspect of Christian faith.

IV. NEWMAN'S CONCERN FOR OBJECTIVE RELIGION

Newman's emphasis on testimony and tradition made historical inquiry an extremely important part of the theological task. In fact, the primary responsibility of the theologian is to give attention to the primitive and transmitted witness of the church, her "received opinions."[101] It is not surprising, therefore, that Newman made use of this mode of inquiry early in his career. With the possible exception of the "Essay on the Miracles of Scriptures," the earliest example of this interest is Newman's study of The Arians of the Fourth Century, published in 1833. The book delineated diverse, sometimes heretical, parties in the church of the fourth century and the triumph, within that diversity, of the orthodox Trinitarian Christianity.

Newman identified the cause of heresy with the application of the wrong logic or tools of interpretation to revelation.[102] In these cases, men are ". . . impatient of ignorance, and loth to confess that the laws of truth and falsehood which their experience of the world furnished, could not at once be applied to measure and determine the facts of another."[103] The notion of criticizing the doctrines of the faith never occurred to early Christians who accepted them as facts.[104] Revealed religion was simply received as ". . . the doctrine taught in the Mosaic and Christian dispensations, and contained in the Holy Scripture, and . . . from God in a sense in which no other doctrine can be said to be from Him."[105] Because of the speculations of those unwilling to accept this dispensation, the Church gradually developed authoritative forms or creeds that left no room for investigation of certain matters.[106] Newman did point out a more positive cause for creedal formulation as the result of one's inclination with maturity to ask what is the nature of the ground of his affections and conduct.

> As the mind is cultivated and expanded, it cannot refrain
> from the attempt to analyze the vision which influences
> the heart . . . nor does it stop till it has, in some
> sort, succeeded in expressing in words, what has all along
> been a principle both of its affections and obedience.[107]

Theological reflection on the objective grounds for one's coming to faith and for the legitimacy of the picture which shapes one's imagination has a positive as well as a negative stimulus.

In his attempt to describe the nature of "objective religion," Newman was concerned with issues of the relation of scripture and creedal tradition, of apostolicity and unity. In his view,

> The essence of religion is the submission of the reason
> and heart to a positive system, the acquiescence in doc-
> trines which cannot be proved or explained. A realized
> system is pre-supposed as the primary essential, from the
> nature of the case.[108]

For that reason, Newman opposed any tendency to disregard the necessity to accept what God has given and the Church has received and preserved. Newman criticized the fact that

> . . . we have accounted that belief alone to be manly
> which commenced in doubt, that inquiry alone philosophical
> which assumed no first principles, that religion alone
> rational which we have created for ourselves.[109]

Some of Newman's remarks regarding the nature of objective religion seem to suggest a confusion in the use of the word "system." He used the word positively in the case of distinguishing the Christian revelation from self-creation or argumentative conclusion. In this sense, the Gospel is a system insofar as it is something given or "positive" rather than something to be discovered. The Gospel is a system in that it has been revealed by God, delivered by the Apostles, and preserved in the Church as a definite and separate doctrine. On the other hand, the Gospel is not to be considered a "system" in one very definite sense. The doctrines of Christianity are not to be assigned positions of relative importance or "systematized" according to man's own reasonings; this can be done only if the revelation itself makes such distinctions and connections. The danger of reducing all the parts of the Christian revelation to a system is that one will come to substitute something of his own making for that which God has disclosed.[110]

Objective Religion and Rationalistic Principles

One of the most significant themes in the <u>Tracts for the Times</u> written by Newman is his attack on this tendency to reduction or to ". . . the introduction of rationalistic principles into revealed religion."[111] He noted that a "taste for criticism" can grow upon the mind in such a way that one's judgments become perplexed and one's feelings unsettled.[112] He asserted that the Reformation doctrine of the primacy of Scripture led to the ascendancy of intellectual gifts and ultimately to a dissatisfaction with anything less than certainty.[113] In each of these cases, Newman felt that there was an abuse of reason. The abuse consisted for him in assuming that reason can be the standard and measure of revelation, that reason is a purely formal matter that subjects revelation to its impartial scrutiny. Rather, said Newman, faith and reasoned reflection on faith follow on the acceptance of what can be known only by testimony.[114] In the case of an illegitimate exercise of reason, the inquirer refuses to allow the revelation to speak for itself and makes the revelation acceptable to himself by proposing a hypothesis about it which puts aside what is obscure to him and which ascribes to God what are one's own motives and understanding.[115] It is in this sense that "system" is a negative term for Newman. The man of faith realizes that such a systematization does not account for revelation. Newman held:

> Revelation . . . is not a revealed <u>system</u>, but consists of a number of detached and incomplete truths belonging to a vast system unrevealed, of doctrines and injunctions mysteriously connected together; that is, connected by unknown media, and bearing upon unknown portions of the system.[116]

Just as reason could not discover the content of revelation before the fact of revelation, it cannot now ". . . account for it, or reconcile it to experience, or explain the manner of it: the utmost it does is by some faint analogies to show that it is not inconceivable."[117]

Newman's conclusions from these considerations were:

> . . . first, that we should be very reverent in dealing with Revealed Truth; next, that we should avoid all rash theorizing and systematizing as relates to it . . . and lastly, which is implied in all these, that we should religiously adhere to the form of the words and the ordinances under which it comes to us, through which it is revealed to us, and apart from which the Revelation does not exist, there being nothing else given us by which to ascertain or enter into it.[118]

Internal and external means for understanding the Christian faith. This reverence for the received revelation through Scripture and tradition is that basis of what Newman meant by "objective religion." Newman carefully considered the relation of this objective religion to that illegitimate exercise of reason which he often called "private judgment." "Private judgment" consists in an exclusive reliance on certain internal means for understanding and evaluating the Gospel--common sense, conscience, the sympathy of the affections, and imagination. External means included, for Newman, Scripture, tradition, antiquity, and Church.[119]

"Objective religion" involves the primacy of these external means over the internal means without the exclusion of those internal means from consideration in understanding the nature of Christian faith. Newman established the following principles:

> (1) That Scripture, Antiquity, and Catholicity cannot really contradict one another:
>
> (2) That when the Moral Sense or the Reason of the individual seems to be on one side, and Scripture on the other, we must follow Scripture, except Scripture anywhere contained contradictions in terms, or prescribed undeniable crimes, which it never does:
>
> (3) That when the sense of Scripture, as interpreted by the Reason of the individual, is contrary to the sense given to it by Catholic Antiquity, we ought to side with the latter:
>
> (4) That when Antiquity runs counter to the present Church in important matters, we must follow Antiquity; when in unimportant matters, we must follow the present Church:
>
> (5) That when the present Church speaks contrary to our private notions, and Antiquity is silent, or its decisions unknown to us, it is pious to sacrifice our own opinion to that of the Church:
>
> (6) That if, in spite of our efforts to agree with the Church, we still differ from it, Antiquity being silent, we must avoid causing any disturbance, recollecting that the Church, and not individuals, 'has authority in controversies of faith.'[120]

Thus, the appropriate attitude of the individual is to begin by faith and not by controversy, taking for granted what he is taught and cannot prove. The Christian begins in obedience to the external means, to objective religion, to the Catholic Church.[121] Since the Church is the keeper and interpreter of

Scripture, she is the authority in matters of faith and indefectible in that authority. As such, the Church is also an object of our obedience.[122] Of course, Newman did not understand the Church and her authority in exactly the same way throughout his life, but the differences are far fewer than one might be inclined to think. What is certainly constant, however, is the logical priority of external over internal factors in faith. This principle is a major element in Newman's delineation of the rational criteria appropriate to an explication of the Christian dispensation.

According to Newman,

> Christianity is faith, faith implies a doctrine; a doctrine propositions; propositions yes or no; yes or no differences. Differences, then, are the natural attendants on Christianity, and you cannot have Christianity, and not have differences.[123]

In Newman's view, Christianity is synonomous with revelation, never a deduction from what one knows but always an assertion of what one is to believe. "It has never lived in a conclusion; it has ever been a message, or a history, or a vision . . . it tells us what its Author is, by telling us what He has done."[124] A diversity of opinions regarding the content of faith suggests by itself that there is no religious truth. Newman argued that such diversity is a <u>reductio</u> <u>ad</u> <u>absurdum</u> of the attempt to find the truth and is intolerable to those who honestly and diligently seek the truth. More importantly, urged Newman, diverse opinions cannot be equally pleasing to God.[125] For Newman, there is an authoritative, objective truth in religion.

Newman opposed, consequently, any identification of Christian faith with a peculiar feeling different in kind from those feelings which normally influence and affect a person. In many cases, such an identification, said Newman, involves the claim that Christian faith is irrational, a mere fancy or feeling.[126] Newman argued that faith itself is not such a strange principle of action for man since he acts on trust in many ways every day. One example which Newman characteristically offered is that of reliance on ourselves and our faculties—e.g., memory, sense, reason. But, in the case of the Christian faith, it is ". . . the things believed, not the act of believing them, which is peculiar to them."[127] For Newman, the peculiar and distinctive factor in a religion, certainly in Christianity, is not the element of trust but the content of the belief, what one believes.

Practical knowledge and the content of revelation.

The content of revelation involved two basic descriptions for Newman. The first involved the description of revelation as imparting practical knowledge, i.e., knowledge given to influence, guide, and strengthen one in performing his duty toward God and man.[128] This knowledge provides one with a set of first principles, a vision of things that influences the way in which one sees the world, other people, and oneself.[129] This knowledge forms the affections and guides action, giving a peculiar shape to the Christian character. And yet, warned Newman, to understand revelation only in this way is in fact to misunderstand it.

> . . . the very revelation that brings us <u>practical</u> and <u>useful knowledge</u> about our souls, in the <u>very act of doing</u> so, nay (as it would seem), in <u>consequence of</u> doing so, brings us mysteries. We gain <u>spiritual light</u> at the price of intellectual perplexity. . . .[130]

Newman's reflections on this dual nature of revelation seemed at times to be contradictory. On the one hand, he could claim that revelation was not given to satisfy men's doubts but to make them better persons.[131] He warned that reasoning and proving can lead one away from faith and obedience.[132] In short, he could describe the nature of revelation in such a way as to suggest that its practical side is its only side. On the other hand, he made an effort to emphasize the external, objective character of revelation and to note, in that regard, that the content of that revelation goes beyond ". . . the real belief and frame of mind of even the best Christians."[133] It is this characteristic of revelation which Newman designated as its quality of mystery, the quality of not being against reason but that of being above it. The effect of this emphasis on mystery is to safeguard revelation from an identification with its practical influence or benefits.

To identify the purpose of revelation with its effect on the heart is, claimed Newman, to concentrate on the work of Christ to the virtual exclusion of concern with His person.[134] Newman understood Christian faith, in this sense, to be ". . . some definite doctrine; not a mere temper of mind or principle of action, much less, vaguely, the Christian cause. . . ."[135]

In this context, Newman returned to his theme of "objective religion," emphasizing that the Gospel is a definite deposit in set words and not a matter of opinion or deduction. He understood revelation to be the limit of one's inquiries, the fact beyond which one could not go.[136]

Faith and the Exercise of Legitimate Rational Reflection

Although the use of reason has its abuses and the exercise of explicit reasoning or analysis is not necessarily a part of the act of faith, Newman did allow, that rational reflection is a legitimate aspect of the act of faith. Newman claimed that

> . . . the mind may be allowably, nay, religiously engaged, in reflecting upon its own Faith; investigating the grounds and the Object of it, bringing it out into words, whether to defend, or recommend, or teach it to others.[137]

Newman continued:

> Nothing could be more theoretical and unreal than to suppose that true Faith cannot exist except when moulded upon a Creed, and based upon Evidence; yet nothing would indicate a more shallow philosophy than to say that it ought carefully to be disjoined from dogmatic and argumentative statements. To assert the latter is to discard the science of theology from the service of Religion; to assert the former, is to maintain that every child, every peasant, must be a theologian. Faith cannot exist without grounds or without an object; but it does not follow that all who have faith should recognize, and be able to state what they believe, and why. Nor, on the other hand, because it is not identical with its grounds, and its object, does it therefore cease to be true Faith, on its recognizing them. In proportion as the mind reflects upon itself, it will be able to give an account of what it believes and hopes; as far as it has not thus reflected, it will not be able. Such knowledge cannot be wrong, yet cannot be necessary, as long as reflection is at once a natural faculty of our souls, yet not an initial faculty.[138]

In this way, Newman distinguished between an implicit reasoning that is a collection of various processes by which all men move spontaneously from one point to another and an explicit reasoning or an analysis and ordering of these implicit processes.

> Faith, then, though in all cases a reasonable process, is not necessarily founded on investigation, argument, or proof; these processes being but the explicit form which the reasoning takes in the case of particular minds.[139]

Faith, either in the form of implicit or of explicit reasoning, is ". . . assenting to a doctrine as true, which we do not see, which we cannot prove, because God says it is true, who cannot lie."[140] Christian doctrine is based in the

Word of God as commissioned to be delivered by a messenger of God. Divine faith is held, therefore, by one

> . . . who believes that God is true, and that this is His word, which He has committed to man. . . . He is as certain that the doctrine taught is true, as that God is true; and he is certain, <u>because</u> God is true, <u>because</u> God has spoken, not because he sees its truth or can prove its truth.[141]

The early Christians went to the Church as their teacher, not as someone with whom to argue or to examine, but as one whose word was to be accepted. Newman remarked: "In the Apostle's days the peculiarity of faith was submission to a living authority. . . . "[142]

Once a Catholic, one can never, claimed Newman, inquire again into the truth of the Church's doctrines, i.e., one can never doubt their truth. The Church cannot allow this kind of doubt of what is external; for Newman, there could be no possible merit in such freedom.[143] The man who believes cannot imagine ever discovering reasons which could lead him not to believe; his loving trust of God does not allow him to anticipate the possibility of doubting or denying Him.[144] One may legitimately investigate the grounds of his faith, however, for it is not a case of doubt to consider arguments for and against the faith; what is denied is a "wanton entertainment of objections."[145] Newman suggested, therefore, that ". . . it seems allowable too, to look back at length on what has been occupying the heart, and to reason upon it."[146] In fact, he contended, the nature of revelation requires this reflection.

> The great truths of Revelation are all connected together and form a whole. Every one can see this in a measure even at a glance, but to understand the full consistency and harmony of Catholic teaching requires study and meditation.[147]

Nevertheless, the elements of revelation are not always capable of systematic treatment by rational analysis. For example, the Church teaches both that the grace of God is sovereign and that man has freedom of will. But the Church does not teach how one is to reconcile these two truths.[148] It simply notes that both are true. Or, as another example, general notations of the attributes of God do not dispel their infinite transcendence of man's comprehension of them.[149] Or, again, no doctrine of the Church is capable of conclusive historical proof or disproof.[150] Such restrictions constitute warnings against "vain curiosity" or excessive desire for knowledge.[151] The exercise of man's rational powers are praiseworthy only if exercised in subjection to God's revelation, not in passing judgment on that revelation or in seeking to go beyond it.

> We can enjoy it, if we take it as presented to us; but if we attempt to outstep those bounds, if we attempt by our own skill, or our own wit, to know more about it, or to come to conclusions about it, over or beyond what Almighty God has told us by revelation, we are as if we dazed and blinded ourselves with the sun.[152]

Newman distinguished sharply, therefore, between legitimate reflection on the faith and the exercise of private judgment. The Gospel, in his view, is a message distinct, special, and separate from what the world is able to offer or to analyze. The Church is the organ and oracle of a supernatural doctrine, independent of individuals and their appropriation or lack thereof: ". . . a sacred deposit and tradition, a mystery or secret, as Scripture calls it, sufficient to arrest and occupy the whole intellect, and unlike anything else. . . ."[153]

<u>Prejudices and first principles.</u> The tradition or testimony of the Church, then, comprises the "first principles" of Newman's understanding of the Christian faith. Newman designated first principles as presumptions but not prejudices. A prejudice, claimed Newman, is a prejudgment formed prior to any particular question which comes to one and is made to bear on all such questions without appealing to evidence.[154] In this sense, prejudices are "habitual and invariable modes of judging and believing" which are nevertheless false. They become impressed on the mind by repetition without an appeal to evidence and are held by will even in the face of counter evidence. Prejudices cannot be overcome by arguments or evidence. Newman explained that:

> Arguments are the fit weapon with which to assail an erroneous judgment, but assertions and actions must be brought to bear upon a false imagination. The mind in that case has been misled by representations; it must be set right by representations.[155]

His <u>Apologia</u> is an illustration of this principle. Deciding that the atmosphere of suspicion against himself could not be met simply by an answer to Kingsley's separate objections, he proposed to change the atmosphere by replacing an erroneous with a true "representation" of the history of his religious development. In a sermon preached in 1880, which serves as another example, Newman asserted that the appropriate weapon for opposing modern infidelity is not controversy but a good life and a thorough knowledge of the consistency and completeness of Catholic theology. One does not use the elements of Catholic doctrine so much as arguments but more as instances of definiteness over against the doubts, confusions, and inconsistencies of the world.[156] Prejudices, then, can only be dissolved if there is a fundamental change of one's imagination, that is, of one's way of viewing a given thing.

Presumptions, on the other hand, argued Newman, rest on argumentative grounds and are given up when those grounds fail to support those presumptions. Yet first principles do not depend on such previous grounds, proceeding immediately from the mind as a part of the person himself. Newman noted that:

> He holds them and continues to hold them, whatever is urged against him to the contrary; and thus these opinions and beliefs look like prejudices, though they are not. They are not prejudices, because prejudices are opinions formed upon grounds, which grounds the prejudiced person refuses to examine; whereas these opinions which I am speaking of have from the first no grounds at all, but are simple persuasions or sentiments, which came to the holder he cannot tell how, and which apparently he cannot help holding, and they are in consequence commonly called First Principles.[157]

First principles are, therefore, the basis of all one's reasoning, the final court of appeal beyond which a request for proof is out of place. They are the means by which one proves, but not themselves proved. They are the conditions of man's intellectual life and constitute the difference in shape and content in that regard between one man and another.[158] Of course, Newman recognized, some first principles are false. ". . . they are absolute monarchs, and if they are true, they act like the best and wisest of fathers to us; but, if they are false, they are the most cruel and baneful of tyrants."[159] In this regard, Newman was particularly anxious that Christianity be judged according to its own first principles and not by principles from another point of view or discipline.[160] He was particularly sceptical of the assumption on the part of some spokesmen that their own first principles are to be taken for granted and that those of Christianity are to be quietly and easily dismissed.[161] Against this "wisdom of the world,"

Newman urged: "For our First Principle is our reason, in the same sense in which theirs is their reason, and it is quite as good a reason."[162] In being clear about one's first principles, one can be clear about the ways in which one differs from those who hold to other first principles.

The first principles of Christianity are made available by tradition. Tradition is the initial means of gaining information about historical facts. Newman held that one acts properly and naturally in trusting tradition as <u>prima facie</u> evidence. A solitary tradition is not sufficiently trustworthy to offer evidence; only two or three independent witnesses are adequate.[163] The tradition of the Catholic Church is the "whole system of faith and ordinances" which has been passed from one generation to the next since their foundation in Jesus Christ and His Apostles. ". . . the whole Catholic truth has ever lived, and only lived, in the hearts and on the tongues of the Catholic people. . . ."[164] Thus, tradition tells what Catholic doctrines are, how Catholics think and speak, what are their principles of judgment.[165]

> Every Catholic holds that the Christian dogmas were in the Church from the time of the Apostles; that they were ever in their substance what they are now; that they existed before the formulas were publicly adopted, in which, as time went on, they were defined and recorded, and that such formulas, when sanctioned by the due ecclesiastical acts, are binding on the faith of Catholics, and have a dogmatic authority.[166]

In an unpublished paper from this period, written in 1868, Newman explained that these doctrines were present from the inception of Christianity in the sense that what the Church has subsequently defined would have seemed the natural response to an Apostle if he were responding to the same question which led to the definition. That such definitions were not made earlier is to be explained by the fact that the occasion for certain questions did not arise until a later time.[167]

Theology, said Newman, is a science which seeks to ascertain the rules guiding authoritative texts and definitions. He takes theology to be a science of a special kind with its own modes of expression and manner of reasoning. Theology is ". . . the fundamental and regulating principle of the whole Church system. It is commensurate with Revelation, and Revelation is the initial and essential ideal of Christianity."[168]

Religious faith as knowledge. One central purpose of Newman's lectures on university education was the defense of the notion that religious doctrine is knowledge in as full a sense as other claims to knowledge. The omission of theology from the program of the university, claimed Newman, suggests one of two things: either, that religion is devoid of any real knowledge content, or, that the university is overlooking one important branch of knowledge. He suggested that the idea that religion is without any claim to knowledge has been aided by developments within Christianity itself, e.g., in Protestantism and in the evangelical movement. While the old Catholic notion was that ". . . faith was an intellectual act, its object truth, and its result knowledge," it became fashionable to speak of faith as a feeling or affection rather than as an acceptance of revealed doctrine and as an act of the intellect.[169] In this way, Newman complained, religion has become a matter of taste and sentiment rather than of truth and knowledge. Men ". . . learned to believe and to take it for granted that religion was nothing beyond a supply of the wants of human nature, not an external fact and a work of God."[170] In this case, of course, Newman admitted that it would be as senseless to have a chair of religion in the university as to have one of fine feeling, maternal affection, or good companionship.[171]

Newman understood that to identify religion with needs or affections is to give up its place in the field of knowledge.

> What we contemplate, then, what we aim at, when we give a religious education, is, it seems, not to impart any knowledge, whatever, but to satisfy anyhow desires after the Unseen which will arise in our minds in spite of ourselves, to provide the mind with a means of self command, to impress on it, the beautiful ideas which saints and sages have struck out, to embellish it with the bright hue of a celestial piety, to teach it the poetry of devotion, the music of well-ordered affections, and the luxury of doing good.[172]

In an essay which I did not discuss in the preceding section but which dates from 1846, Newman described such poetic concerns as

> . . . the refuge of those who have not the Catholic Church to flee to and repose upon, for the Church herself is the most sacred and august of poets. . . . Now what is the Catholic Church, viewed in her human aspect, but a discipline of the affections and passions? . . . She is the poet of her children; full of music to soothe the

> sad and control the wayward,--wonderful in story for the
> imagination of the romantic; rich in symbol and imagery,
> so that gentle and delicate feelings, which will not bear
> words, may in silence intimate their presence or commune
> with themselves.173

Newman warned in that 1846 essay that this kind of poetic faith demands the control exercised by a more intellectual grasp of the Gospel. What Newman was describing in his university lectures was a view of religion that had eliminated any place for such reasoned reflection, describing the nature of faith only in terms of the imagination and the affections. For Newman, only an infallible authority can finally resist the tendency of excess and error that results from private judgment.174

Clearly the dangers of the use of the imagination in faith are those of excess and reductionism and not inherent in the role of the imagination itself. For Newman, the imagination was not to be excluded from consideration in describing the nature of faith; that consideration is, however, to be made in conjunction with others, e.g., certain intellectual matters and questions of authority. While Newman was not altogether happy about the loss of certain "lovely superstitions" and their poetic influence, he was fully convinced that the growth of sober and reasoned reflection is beneficial to man and, in no way, detrimental to the mission of the Church.175 That is not to say, for Newman, that he favored secular culture's tendency to make knowledge of God coincident with the laws of nature. This tendency is characterized by making language about God into a kind of poetry which suggests the beauty and sublimity of nature. In this sense, said Newman, ". . . divine truth is not something separate from nature, but it is nature with a divine glow upon it."176

The error commanding Newman's attention results from a refusal to allow that religious matters are at all related to the issue of truth and falsity. The end of that kind of prejudice is the suggestion that nothing can be known about God with certainty which, according to Newman, is not much different from denying that He exists.177 As a counter proposal, Newman offered a certain view of truth in his university lectures. Newman stated that

> All that exists, as contemplated by the human mind, forms
> one large system or complex fact, and this of course
> resolves itself into an indefinite number of particular
> facts, which, as being portions of a whole, have countless

> relations of every kind, one toward another. Knowledge
> is the apprehension of these facts, whether in themselves
> or in their mutual positions and bearings.[178]

The human mind, being unable to comprehend the whole complex fact in one glance, takes various partial views of it which are called "sciences." As abstractions from the fact or "aspects," sciences deal with the relations of things to one another rather than with the things themselves. Sciences arrange and classify; ". . . they reduce separate phenomena under a common law. . . ."[179] Only when held in conjunction do these aspects or sciences approximate to a "representation or subjective reflection of the objective truth. . . ."[180] The omission of any one science, therefore, argued Newman, leads to the inaccuracy and incompleteness of knowledge; they each complete, correct, and balance one another. As a science, theology is ". . . the truths we know about God put into system. . . ."[181] To withdraw theology as a subject within the university is to impair the completeness of knowledge.

The most dangerous result of leaving the subject of theology out of the university curriculum is the likelihood that some other discipline will settle its questions.

> . . . any secular science cultivated exclusively may become
> dangerous to religion, and I account for it on this broad
> principle, that no science whatever, however comprehensive
> it may be, but will fall largely into error if it be con-
> stituted the sole exponent of all things in heaven and
> earth, and that, for the simple reason that it is encroaching
> on territory not its own, and undertaking problems which
> it has no instruments to solve.[182]

Newman warned that expertise in one science or method of thought gives one no right to generalize from it beyond its scope. The absence of any given science from the curriculum does, however, give rise to the natural tendency of the human mind to speculate and systematize through the usurpation of the legitimate role of that science by means of another. Theology must be allowed to answer the questions which fall in its legitimate domain if false speculation regarding the nature of faith is to be avoided.

As in regard to other instances of knowledge, Newman took theology and its study to be an end in itself. In that sense, the aim of any science is the pursuit of knowledge for its own sake. The aim of a university education is not, therefore, the passive acquisition of ideas and facts but the

attainment of a connected view of all things as one whole
and as having a certain place in that whole.[183] Nor is knowledge to be measured according to its usefulness in some art,
business, or profession. It is rather ". . . an acquired faculty of judgment . . . of philosophical reach of mind. . . ."[184]
Just so theology should be cultivated for itself and not made
only to serve the purposes of the preacher and the catechist.
In such a case theology loses its reality as knowledge and is
seen in terms of ". . . an art or a business making use of
theology."[185] Prior to being a power and an instrument, knowledge, in this case theology, is a good and an end in itself.

> To open the mind, to correct it, to refine it, to enable
> it to know, and to digest, master, rule, and use its knowledge, to give it power over its own faculties, application,
> flexibility, method, critical exactness, sagacity, resource,
> address, eloquent expression, is an object as intelligible
> (for here we are inquiring, not what the object of a liberal
> education is worth, nor what the Church makes of it, but
> what it is in itself), I say, an object as intelligible
> as the cultivation of virtue, while, at the same time,
> it is absolutely distinct from it.[186]

Newman was mindful that the cultivation of liberal knowledge tends to substitute a religion of civilization, a mere
philosophical theory, for revelation.[187] This solely intellectual religion transforms the command of duty from God into
the self-reproach of a moral sense as an offense against one's
human nature.[188] The former characterizes the religion of the
Christian; the latter, the religion of the gentleman. The
religion of the gentleman is totally subjective, a matter of
the imagination and sentiment alone; in this religion, a perception of the beautiful becomes a substitute for faith.[189]
The Christian, on the other hand, is obedient to revelation as
given by a divine act and as independent of man and incapable
of increase in itself. ". . . God Himself is the author as
well as the subject of theology."[190]

The fact that revelation presents a totally different
aspect of the world from that presented to man by the sciences
suggests to man's imagination that reason (usually interpreted
in its scientific sense alone) and revelation are essentially
distinct and opposed.[191] Rather, suggested Newman, there are
simply distinct kinds of sciences with their own rules and
subject-matter. Knowledge of one does not necessarily qualify
one for adequate judgments in the other. While some sciences

admit of new facts, theology reflects on just that which has been revealed and nothing more. No new truth can be added to revelation or to that which has been delivered by the Apostles and kept by the Church.[192] The true philosopher, said Newman, knows that discrimination and not simplification or reduction is the true method in understanding the relation of the sciences to one another and to the truth.

> His watchword is, Live and let live. He takes things as they are; he submits to them all, as far as they go; he recognizes the insuperable lines of demarcation which run between subject and subject; he observes how separate truths lie relatively to each other, where they concur, where they part company, and where, being carried too far, they cease to be truth at all . . . . If he has one cardinal maxim in his philosophy, it is that truth cannot be contrary to truth; if he has a second, it is that truth often seems contrary to truth; and, if a third, it is the practical conclusion that we must be patient with such appearances, and not be hasty to pronounce them to be really of a more formidable character.[193]

One burden of the lectures contained in the Idea of a University was this delineation of the appropriate scientific character of theology and of its legitimate claim to be concerned with issues that can be resolved in terms of their truth or falsity. In particular, Newman warned against the identification of theology with aesthetic or ethical concerns and the delegation of its legitimate scientific concerns to some other discipline supposedly more capable of resolving such questions. As an "objective religion" with its own subject-matter, Christianity, claimed Newman, has its own criteria of meaning and truth.

V. CONCLUSIONS

In chapter two of my study, I concluded that Newman's understanding of the unity of the Christian faith had not been adequately analyzed by his interpreters. I found them to be always insisting on some one aspect of Newman's work as the systematic principle by which to judge all other elements. In this chapter, I have sought to describe some of Newman's own reflections on the complex richness of the Christian faith and of man's reflection on it. I have sought to isolate the kinds of observations and distinctions which this kind of dedication to complex unity led Newman to make. I have chosen to describe those distinctions as representing diverse functions of

Christian discourse and, consequently, as relating to diverse contexts of use.

Particularly important to my investigation has been the description of the set of rules peculiar to each function. First, I noted Newman's efforts to delineate the nature of religious inquiry, giving equal attention to its variable and its constant elements. Likewise I have described the important role of the imagination in relation to the life of faith--its interpretative and behavioral influence. And, finally, I have given attention to Newman's awareness of the content of the faith itself, i.e., to the nature of "objective religion."

In describing the context of coming to faith or the nature of religious inquiry, Newman, while retaining his characteristic awareness of the concrete differences between various ways to faith, did attempt to map out more clearly what he believed are certain general characteristics of that inquiry. Forsaking his early desire to describe the path to conversion in a material way, Newman decided that only certain very general and formal observations regarding the nature of religious inquiry could be made. He found that the inception of such inquiry involves a felt problem in the form of a mystery and the resulting openness to revelation as a means for alleviating the problem. A second formal factor in inquiry into the Christian faith is its termination in the gift of grace that produces divine faith and willing submission to God and His Church.

In making the shift from a material to a formal description, Newman secured two vital objectives. One, he was able to give full notice to the infinite variety of the paths to faith. Two, he was able to distinguish religious inquiry as a rational enterprise from understandings of rationality essentially out of harmony with religious concerns. The inclusion of the testimony of conscience, the influence of moral dispositions, and the importance of the will provide the elements for Newman's description of the personal involvement of the religious inquirer in his search. They also provide Newman with the means by which he can account for the fact that demonstration is not a necessary prerequisite to faith. On the other hand, as his discussion of <u>credibilia</u> suggests, rational considerations can and do enter the inquiry for many persons and rightfully do so far as the content of revelation itself is concerned. Finally, however, the element of will is a safeguard against the equation of _fides acquisita_ and _fides divina_ or that faith which is the gift of God. For Newman, the categories of religious inquiry do not adequately account for the latter.

Although the will has a certain precedence in Newman's description of religious inquiry and its completion in conversion, the concept of imagination is central to his discussion of the Christian life which follows upon conversion. If grace enables the will to put away the objections to revealed truth which the imagination entertains, grace also imbues the imagination with a new vision. The imagination is turned from a concentration on the things of this immediate world to a contemplation of an essentially unseen world that, nevertheless, impinges upon this one. The picture of that unseen world molds the way in which one sees the world, forms one's passions and affections, and directs one's actions. The Christian has a "new mind" in him.

And thirdly, to account for the way in which grace moves the will and forms the imagination, Newman gave attention to rational reflection on the Christian faith, not in the sense of religious inquiry, but in the sense of a consideration of its peculiar structure as a separate and distinct body of subject-matter. The objectivity of the Church is a figure of the objectivity of the Christian dispensation. Newman accounted for that objectivity in terms of the tradition of the Church. The starting points for all rational explication of that tradition are the concepts, rules, and strata of discourse which characterize the authoritative tradition. These considerations are the first principles which guide one's reflections. To go beyond, or outside of, them is to reason illegitimately. That is not to say that one cannot reflect on those rules and concepts, seeking greater clarification of their meaning and function as well as considering the grounds for their truth. Newman seemed to suggest at times that the question of the truth of first principles could not be raised since they have the character of assumptions. But he did not hold to that conclusion; rather he suggested that there are occasions on which one can ask about the truth of first principles. In theological reflection, one legitimately attends to questions of meaning and truth. The questions of personal appropriation and conversion are put aside not because they are forgotten but simply because they are different strata of Christian discourse or different aspects of Christianity. They must be put aside at times lest concentration on them lead to the exclusion of the sorts of questions which arise in the theological sphere.

The unity of Newman's diverse reflections on the nature of Christian faith lay in a dedication to revealed truth that was at once humble in its awareness of the limitations of human description of divine matters and yet bold in its legitimate concerns. In attempting to grasp faithfully the nature of faith, Newman found it helpful to bring diverse descriptions and concerns into conjunction without feeling the need to find a more basic description that accounted for these separate functions in and by itself. I turn in the next chapter to show how he avoided any such reduction of his reflections on the Christian faith.

NOTES TO CHAPTER III

[1] John Henry Newman, "Scientific and Religious Inquiry," Philosophical Readings in Cardinal Newman, James Collins, editor (Chicago: Henry Regnery Company, 1961), p. 50. The article was originally published in the Christian Observer in 1821 under the title "Mathematics."

[2] John Henry Newman, "Essay on the Miracles of Scripture," Two Essays on Biblical and on Ecclesiastical Miracles (fifth edition; London: Longmans, Green, and Co., 1885), p. 4. Hereafter only Newman's last name will be cited even in initial references to a work.

[3] Ibid., p. 5.   [4] Ibid., p. 20.

[5] Ibid., pp. 46, 70.   [6] Ibid., pp. 72, 79.

[7] He developed his own case against the miracles of Apollonius of Tyana on these grounds. Cf. Newman, "Apollonius of Tyana," Historical Sketches (London: Basil Montagu Pickering, 1873), I, 301-331. This essay was originally published in 1824 in the Encyclopaedea Metropolitana. See also his "Essay on the Miracles of Early Ecclesiastical History," Two Essays on Biblical and on Ecclesiastical Miracles, op. cit., pp. 37-393, for further examples of this method.

[8] He also mentioned marks of design, a system of doctrine, the gradual disclosure of unknown truths which shows the Bible to be the work of one mind, prophecy, the character of Christ, the morality of the Gospel, and the wisdom of its doctrines in "Essay on the Miracles of Scripture," op. cit., p. 94.

[9] Newman, "Poetry with reference to Aristotle's Poetics," Essays Critical and Historical (new edition; London: Longmans, Green, and Co., 1891), I, 1-4.

[10] Newman, "Primitive Christianity," Historical Sketches (London: Basil Montagu Pickering, 1873), I, 340.

[11] Ibid., 386.

[12] Newman, "Poetry with reference to Aristotle's Poetics," op. cit., 23

[13] Ibid., 29.

[14] Newman, "Papers on Theological Subjects from 1816 to 1834" (unpublished manuscript, Birmingham Oratory, England; microfilmed copy, Yale University Beinecke Library, New Haven, reel 7, batch 43, A 9.1). On the first sheet of these manuscripts, Newman affixed a note dated May 12, 1874, in which he judged of these papers: "None of them is worth anything but burning, I leave them as illustrations of the historical fact, what I have been doing with myself all my life."

[15] For a reference to Newman's manuscript note to this effect see "Introduction," Faith and Prejudice and Other Unpublished Sermons of Cardinal Newman, Charles Stephen Dessain and

Fathers of the Birmingham Oratory, editors (New York: Sheed and Ward, 1956), p. 16.

[16]Newman, "Papers on Theological Subjects from 1816 to 1834: On the Necessity of a thorough reception of the doctrines contained in the 9th article and first part of the 10th, to a belief in the rest" (op. cit.). Dated May, 1821.

[17]Ibid.

[18]Newman, "Private Memoranda, 1816-1826" (unpublished manuscript, Birmingham Oratory, England; microfilmed copy, Yale University Beinecke Library, New Haven, reel 8, batch 46, A 10.1). One can find this remark reproduced in John Henry Newman: Autobiographical Writings, Henry Tristram, editor (New York: Sheed and Ward, 1957), p. 172. Cf. Newman, "The Autobiographical Memoir," John Henry Newman: Autobiographical Writings, op. cit., pp. 80-84, for references to his changing opinions. Meriol Trevor, Newman: The Pillar of the Cloud (Garden City, New York: Doubleday and Company, Inc., 1962), p. 58, judges that ". . . it was his parishioners who first shook his confidence in the specifically evangelical doctrines . . . [they] just would not fit into the categories of Saved and Unsaved."

[19]Newman, "Papers on Theological Subjects from 1816 to 1834: Remarks on the Covenant of Grace" (op. cit.). Dated 1828. A paper in this same group from a date perhaps as early as 1822 involves an interesting "Dialogue" between an advocate of the evangelical position and his foe. The dialogue offers no serious handling of the theological issues which were to grip Newman in a few years but does suggest certain lines of criticism that he develops.

[20]Newman, "Papers on Theological Subjects from 1816 to 1834: Holy Baptism" (op. cit.).

[21]Newman, "Papers on Theological Subjects from 1816 to 1834" (op. cit.). Dated 1822 or 1823.

[22]Newman, "Papers on Theological Subjects from 1816 to 1834: Dr. Chalmer's Theology" (op. cit.). Dated 1834.

[23]Thomas L. Sheridan, Newman on Justification: A Theological Biography (Staten Island, New York: Alba House, Division of the Society of St. Paul, 1967) offers an excellent chronicle of the changes in theological conviction involved in this development.

[24]Newman, The Arians of the Fourth Century, their Doctrine, Temper and Conduct, chiefly as exhibited in the Councils of the Church between A.D. 325 and A.D. 381 (new edition; London: Longmans, Green, and Co., 1895), pp. 71-72.

[25]Ibid., p. 72.   [26]Ibid., pp. 51, 53.

[27]Newman, Apologia pro vita sua (New York: The Modern Library, 1950), p. 264. Cf. "Preface," The Via Media of the Anglican Church, illustrated in Lectures, Letters, and Tracts written between 1830 and 1841 (third edition; London: Longmans, Green, and Co., 1901), I, pp. lvi-lxvi.

[28]Newman, Apologia pro vita sua, op. cit., p. 324.

[29]Newman, "Faith without Demonstration," Parochial and Plain Sermons (new edition; London: Rivingtons, 1870), VI, 341;

and "Faith and Experience," <u>Sermons bearing upon Subjects of the Day</u> (new edition; London: Rivingtons, 1869), pp. 64-66. The <u>Parochial and Plain Sermons</u> shall hereafter be cited as <u>PPS</u>.

[30]Cf. Newman, "Grounds for Steadfastness in Our Religious Professions," <u>Sermons bearing upon Subjects of the Day</u>, op. cit., pp. 343-366.

[31]Newman, "Holy Scripture in Its Relation to the Catholic Creed," <u>Discussions and Arguments on Various Subjects</u> (seventh edition; London: Longmans, Green, and Co., 1891), p. 201.

[32]Ibid., pp. 251-252.

[33]Newman, "Preface to the Third Edition," <u>Fifteen Sermons preached before the University of Oxford between A.D. 1826 and 1843</u> (new edition; London: Rivingtons, 1887), pp. ix-xviii. This volume of sermons is hereafter cited as <u>OUS</u>.

[34]Newman, "Faith and Reason, Contrasted as Habits of Mind," <u>OUS</u>, p. 200.

[35]Newman, "Preface to the Third Edition," <u>OUS</u>, pp. x-xi.

[36]Cf. Newman, "The Nature of Faith in Relation to Reason," <u>OUS</u>, p. 202; "Love the Safeguard of Faith against Superstition," <u>OUS</u>, p. 223; "Implicit and Explicit Reason," <u>OUS</u>, pp. 256-259; "Wisdom, as contrasted with Faith and with Bigotry," <u>OUS</u>, p. 290.

[37]Newman, "Implicit and Explicit Reason," <u>OUS</u>, p. 259.

[38]Newman, "Preface to the Third Edition," <u>OUS</u>, p. xii.

[39]Ibid., pp. xiii-xiv.

[40]Ibid., pp. xiv-xv.

[41]Ibid., pp. xvi-xvii.

[42]Newman, "Evangelical Sanctity the Completion of Natural Virtue," <u>OUS</u>, p. 54 (note). Cf. His sermon "Contrast between Faith and Sight," <u>OUS</u>, pp. 120-135, for Newman's understanding of how these principles impose themselves on the imagination.

[43]Newman, "The Influence of Natural and Revealed Religion Respectively," <u>OUS</u>, p. 18.

[44]Ibid., p. 22. Newman's note on this page.

[45]Newman, "The Usurpations of Reason," <u>OUS</u>, pp. 65-66. Cf. "Faith and Reason, contrasted as Habits of Mind," <u>OUS</u>, p. 199, where Newman viewed argument as a test of honesty; as a stay, refuge, and encouragement when confused; and as a means of confirming faith.

[46]Newman, "The Influence of Natural and Revealed Religion Respectively," <u>OUS</u>, p. 34.

[47]Newman, "Faith and Reason, contrasted as Habits of Mind," <u>OUS</u>, pp. 182-183. Cf. "Love the Safeguard of Faith against Superstition," <u>OUS</u>, p. 225.

[48]Newman, "Love the Safeguard of Faith against Superstition," <u>OUS</u>, p. 227.

[49]Ibid., p. 231.

[50]Newman, "Faith and Reason, contrasted as Habits of

Mind," OUS, pp. 187-188.

⁵¹Ibid., pp. 193-194.   ⁵²Ibid., p. 197.

⁵³Ibid., p. 195.

⁵⁴Newman, "Faith and Doubt," Discourses addressed to Mixed Congregations (fifth edition; London: Burns, Oates, and Co., 1876), p. 152. This volume shall hereafter be cited as DMC.

⁵⁵Ibid., p. 236. Cf. Newman, Certain Difficulties felt by Anglicans in Catholic Teaching considered I. in Twelve Lectures addressed in 1850 to the Party of the Religious Movement of 1833 (new impression; London: Longmans, Green, and Co., 1908), I, p. 399. Hereafter this two volume work is cited as CDA.

⁵⁶Newman, "Mysteries of Nature and of Grace," DMC, p. 277.

⁵⁷Newman, "Dispositions for Faith," Sermons Preached on Various Occasions (sixth edition; London: Burns and Oates, Limited, 1887), p. 66. Cf. Newman, "Stewards and also Sons of God," Faith and Prejudice and other Unpublished Sermons of Cardinal Newman, Birmingham Oratory, editors (New York: Sheed and Ward, 1956), p. 64. Faith and Prejudice is hereafter cited as FP and Sermons Preached on Various Occasions, as SVO.

⁵⁸Newman, "The Religion of the Pharisee the Religion of Mankind," SVO, pp. 15-30, and CDA, I, pp. 349-351.

⁵⁹Newman, "Dispositions for Faith," SVO, p. 69.

⁶⁰Ibid., p. 70. Cf. Newman, "The Omnipotence of God the Reason for Faith and Hope," FP, p. 25.

⁶¹Newman, "The Calls of Grace," FP, p. 44.

⁶²Gordon Huntington Harper, Cardinal Newman and William Froude, F.R.S.: A Correspondence (Baltimore: The John Hopkins Press, 1933). I shall make clear in my citations from these letters the addressee and date for each letter.

⁶³Ibid., p. 9. Cf. ibid., pp. 119-122, where Froude develops his views in this regard in a letter to Newman dated December 29, 1859.

⁶⁴Ibid., p. 77. Newman to Mrs. Froude, June 27, 1848.

⁶⁵Ibid., p. 127. Newman to William Froude, January 2, 1860. Cf. Newman, The Text, Edward J. Sillem, editor, revised by A. J. Boekraad (Vol. II of The Philosophical Notebook of John Henry Newman. 2 vols; New York: Humanities Press, 1970), pp. 167-169, where Newman expanded this observation in a note dating from 1867: "In saying the above we are not postponing truth to feeling or experience; for the way in which God wills us to seek truth in religion and blesses and rewards us in seeking and by finding is this devotional and charitable search after it."

⁶⁶G. H. Harper, op. cit., p. 81. Newman to Mrs. Froude, July 3, 1848.

⁶⁷Cf. Newman, "Sundries Continued," The Text, op. cit., pp. 167-169, where he noted that religion is not only a science (theology) and a devotion or passion but also a party adherence. In regard to the latter, one pays deference to superiors and

waits on the consent of the many.

[68] G. H. Harper, op. cit., p. 150. Newman to William Froude, January 2, 1860.

[69] Ibid., p. 181. William Froude to Newman, September 30, 1864.

[70] Ibid., pp. 201-202. Newman to William Froude, April 29, 1879. Cf. also his "Papers on the Grammar of Assent" (unpublished manuscript, Birmingham Oratory, England; microfilmed copy, Yale University Beinecke Library, New Haven, reel 14, batch 78, A 23.1) and a paper dated July 20, 1865 (ibid.).

[71] Newman, "Lectures on the Theory of Faith" (unpublished manuscript, Birmingham Oratory, England; microfilmed copy, Yale University Beinecke Library, New Haven, reel 9, batch 55, A 11).

[72] Newman, "Papers on the Grammar of Assent" (unpublished manuscript, Birmingham Oratory, England: microfilmed copy, Yale University Beinecke Library, New Haven, reel 10, batch 61, A 12.8).

[73] Newman, "Sundries Continued," The Text, op. cit., p. 157, where Newman wrote that: ". . . the notes of the Church are (not proofs) but certain strong and broad prima facie arguments or manifestations in favor of the Church . . . ."

[74] Ibid., p. 101.   [75] Ibid., p. 103.
[76] Ibid., p. 131.   [77] Ibid., p. 143.
[78] Ibid., pp. 145, 148.   [79] Ibid., p. 135.
[80] Ibid., p. 195.

[81] Newman, "Paper dated July 20, 1865" (op. cit.).

[82] A distinction made by Newman in "On Argument, Demonstration" (unpublished manuscript, Birmingham Oratory, England; microfilmed copy, Yale University Beinecke Library, New Haven, reel 9, batch 33, A 11).

[83] Newman, "Theses de Fide," The Expositor, fourth series, II (1890), 349-350, provides a short summary statement of these conclusions regarding the relation of the motiva of fides acquisita and the grace responsible for fides divina.

[84] Newman, "On the Controversy with the Romanists," Tracts for the Times (London: J. G. and F. Rivington, 1839), III, 1. This tract was the seventy-first in the series.

[85] Ibid., 9.

[86] Newman, "The Patristical Idea of Antichrist," Discussions and Arguments on Various Subjects, op. cit., p. 45. This essay appeared as the eighty-third tract of the series in 1838.

[87] Newman, "Letter to a Magazine on the Subject of Dr. Pusey's Tract on Baptism," Tracts for the Times (London: J. G. and F. Rivington, 1839), IV, xxxiii-xxxvi; and Newman, "A Letter addressed to the Rev. R. W. Jelf, D.D., Canon of Christ Church, in Explanation of No. 90, in the Series called The Tracts for the Times" (second edition; Oxford: John Henry Parker, 1841), p. 24. The former essay was published as the eighty-second number in the series of the Tracts.

[88] Newman, "Poetry with Reference to Aristotle's Poetics,"

op. cit., 23.

⁸⁹Thomas Vargish, *Newman: The Contemplation of Mind* (Oxford: The Clarendon Press, 1970), p. 48.

⁹⁰Newman, "The Visible Church," *Tracts for the Times* (London: J. G. and F. Rivington, 1834), I, 2. This tract was the twentieth in the series.

⁹¹Newman, "The Tamworth Reading Room," *Discussions and Arguments on Various Subjects*, op. cit., p. 293.

⁹²Ibid., p. 297.   ⁹³Ibid., p. 294.

⁹⁴Newman, "Unreal Words," *PPS*, V, 31.

⁹⁵Ibid., 33-34.   ⁹⁶Ibid., 43.

⁹⁷Newman, "Sacred Privileges," *PPS*, VI, 99.

⁹⁸Newman, "Unreal Words," *PPS*, V, 43.

⁹⁹Newman, "Subjection of the Reason and Feelings to the Revealed Word," *PPS*, VI, 263.

¹⁰⁰Newman, "Unreal Words," *PPS*, V, 44. Cf. "Waiting for Christ," *PPS*, VI, 237, where Newman wrote that ". . . judging by Scripture you would ever be expecting Christ; judging by the world, you would never expect Him."

¹⁰¹Newman, *The Arians of the Fourth Century*, op. cit., p. 31.

¹⁰²Ibid., p. 31.   ¹⁰³Ibid., pp. 33-34.

¹⁰⁴Ibid., p. 134.   ¹⁰⁵Ibid., p. 79.

¹⁰⁶Ibid., p. 35. Cf. ibid., pp. 147, 163.

¹⁰⁷Ibid., p. 144.

¹⁰⁸Newman, "Lectures on the Prophetical Office of the Church viewed relatively to Romanism and Popular Protestantism," *The Via Media of the Anglican Church* (London: Longmans, Green, and Co., 1901), I, 22.

¹⁰⁹Ibid., 2.   ¹¹⁰Ibid., 98-102.

¹¹¹Newman, "On the Introduction of Rationalistic Principles into Revealed Religion," op. cit., 30-101.

¹¹²Newman, "Thoughts respectfully addressed to the Clergy on Alternatives in the Liturgy," *Tracts for the Times* (London: J. G. and F. Rivington, 1834), I, 2. This tract was published as the third of the series in 1833.

¹¹³Newman, "The Grounds of Our Faith," *Tracts for the Times* (London: J. G. and F. Rivington, 1834), I, 2. This tract was published as the forty-fifth of the series in 1834.

¹¹⁴Newman, "On the Introduction of Rationalistic Principles into Revealed Religion," op. cit., 31.

¹¹⁵Ibid., 32.

¹¹⁶Ibid., 42. Cf. ibid., 45, where Newman wrote in a similar way of the doctrines of the creed: "Each of these doctrines is a Mystery; that is, each stands in a certain degree isolated from the rest, unsystematic, connected with the rest by unknown intermediate truths, and bearing upon subjects

unknown."

[117] Ibid., 43.   [118] Ibid., 47.

[119] Newman, "Lectures on the Prophetical Office of the Church . . .," op. cit., 131.

[120] Ibid., 134-135.   [121] Ibid., 135-136.

[122] Ibid., 190.

[123] Newman, "The Tamworth Reading Room," op. cit., p. 284.

[124] Ibid., p. 296.

[125] Newman, "Private Judgment," Essays Critical and Historical, op. cit., II, 336-337.

[126] Newman, "Religious Faith Rational," PPS, I, 190.

[127] Ibid., 191. Cf. Newman, Lectures on the Doctrine of Justification (fourth edition; London: Rivingtons, 1885), pp. 324-325, 330. One should not assume, however, that Newman identified coming to faith with the development of belief in a set of defined doctrinal propositions. Newman concluded, on the contrary, in his Lectures on the Doctrine of Justification, op. cit., p. 1, that: "No one but God can decide what compass of faith is required of given individuals." Thus, while there is one object of faith, one circle of sacred truths, which are independent and external in relation to the individual, these truths are sometimes clearly, sometimes faintly, sometimes completely, sometimes only partially apprehended. In this way, Newman once again made a clear distinction between two ways of viewing the matter of Christian faith. There are rules of logical priority that apply to concrete cases, but, in no case, is one aspect to displace the other altogether.

[128] Newman, "The Christian Mysteries," PPS, I, 203.

[129] Newman, "Mental Prayer," PPS, VII, 205-206.

[130] Newman, "The Christian Mysteries," PPS, I, 208. Cf. "Faith and Obedience," PPS, III, 77-89.

[131] Newman, "Obedience the Remedy for Religious Perplexity," PPS, I, 229.

[132] Newman, "Ignorance of Evil," PPS, VIII, 264. Cf. "Subjection of the Reason and Feelings to the Revealed Word," PPS, VI, 259.

[133] Newman, "Profession without Hypocrisy," PPS, I, 139. Cf. "The Religion of the Day," PPS, I, 314, where he spoke of ". . . the authority of religion as external to the mind . . . ."

[134] Newman, "Self-Contemplation," PPS, II, 167.

[135] Newman, "The Gospel, a Trust committed to Us," PPS, II, 258.

[136] Newman, "The Mysteriousness of Our Present Being," PPS, IV, 290, 292-293.

[137] Newman, "Implicit and Explicit Reason," OUS, p. 253.

[138] Ibid., pp. 253-254.   [139] Ibid., p. 262.

[140] Newman, "Faith and Private Judgment," DMC, p. 195. Cf. Newman, Sermon Notes, 1849-1878, Fathers of the Birmingham

Oratory, editors (New York: Longmans, Green, and Co., 1913), pp. 15-16.

^{141}Newman, "Faith and Private Judgment," DMC, p. 196.

^{142}Ibid., p. 208.

^{143}Newman, "Faith and Doubt," DMC, pp. 217, 279-280.

^{144}Ibid., p. 219. ^{145}Ibid., p. 228.

^{146}Newman, "Omnipotence in Bonds," SVO, p. 75.

^{147}Newman, "The Glories of Mary for the Sake of Her Son," DMC, p. 344.

^{148}Newman, "Perseverance in Grace," DMC, pp. 125-126.

^{149}Newman, "The Infinitude of the Divine Attributes," DMC p. 319.

^{150}Newman, "A Letter addressed to His Grace the Duke of Norfolk on the Occasion of Mr. Gladstone's Expostulation of 1874," CDA, II, p. 312.

^{151}Newman, "Surrender to God," FP, p. 71. Cf. "The Infidelity of the Future," FP, pp. 122-125, and "A Letter addressed to the Rev. E. B. Pusey, D.D., on Occasion of His Eirenicon," CDA, II, pp. 81-82.

^{152}Newman, "Sermon I--Trinity Sunday Morning," Two Sermons preached in the Church of St. Aloysius, Oxford, on Trinity Sunday, 1880 (printed for private circulation; Oxford: James Parker and Co., 1880), p. 6.

^{153}Newman, CDA, I, p. 218.

^{154}Newman, Lectures on the Present Position of Catholics in England addressed to the Brothers of the Oratory in the Summer of 1851, Daniel M. O'Connell, editor (New York: The America Press, 1942), p. 174. Hereafter cited as LPPC.

^{155}Newman, "Rise and Progress of Universities," Historical Sketches (London: Basil Montagu Pickering, 1873), III, 4.

^{156}Newman, "The Infidelity of the Future," FP, p. 128. Cf. Newman "Speech of Cardinal Newman on Receiving the Biglietto in Rome, May 12, 1879," Catholic University Reports and Other Papers (Part I of My Campaign in Ireland. Two parts; printed for private circulation; Aberdeen: A. King and Co., 1896), p. 395.

^{157}Newman, LPPC, p. 212. ^{158}Ibid., p. 219.

^{159}Ibid., p. 216. ^{160}Cf. ibid., p. 221.

^{161}Newman, "The Development of Religious Error," The Contemporary Review, XLVIII (October, 1885), pp. 459-460, 463. This article was a rebuttal of Principal A. M. Fairbairn's criticism of Newman and, as such, Newman's direct response to allegations of a philosophical kind.

^{162}Newman, LPPC, p. 230. ^{163}Ibid., pp. 35-37.

^{164}Ibid., p. 251. Cf. Newman, On Consulting the Faithful in Matters of Doctrine, John Coulson, editor (New York: Sheed and Ward, 1961) for his understanding of how the laity are ultimately the witnesses to apostolic tradition,

^{165}Newman, LPPC, p. 249.

[166] Newman, "On St. Cyril's Formula, mia phusis sesarkomene," *Tracts Theological and Ecclesiastical* (London: Basil Montagu Pickering, 1874), p. 287. This essay was originally published in July, 1858.

[167] Newman, "An Unpublished Paper by Cardinal Newman on the Development of Doctrine," H. de Achaval, editor, *Gregorianum*, XXXIX (1958), 595.

[168] Newman, "Preface," *The Via Media* . . . , *op. cit.*, I, p. xlviii.

[169] Newman, *The Idea of a University* (Garden City, New York: Doubleday and Company, Inc., Image Books, 1951), p. 68.

[170] *Ibid.*   [171] *Ibid.*, p. 69.

[172] *Ibid.*, p. 72.

[173] Newman, "John Keble, Fellow of Oriel," *Essays Critical and Historical* (new edition; London: Longmans, Green, and Co., 1891), II, 442-443.

[174] *Ibid.*, p. 451.

[175] Cf. Newman, "On the Study of Modern History" (unpublished manuscript, Birmingham Oratory, England; microfilmed copy, Yale University Beinecke Library, New Haven, reels 5 and 6, batch 37, A 6.20).

[176] Newman, *The Idea of a University*, *op. cit.*, p. 77.

[177] *Ibid.*, p. 78.   [178] *Ibid.*, p. 82.

[179] *Ibid.*, pp. 83-84.   [180] *Ibid.*, p. 84.

[181] *Ibid.*, p. 96.   [182] *Ibid.*, p. 106.

[183] *Ibid.*, pp. 148-149.   [184] *Ibid.*, p. 171.

[185] *Ibid.*, p. 135. Newman claimed, on the other hand, in *ibid.*, p. 144, that: "Knowledge is one thing, virtue is another; good sense is not conscience, refinement is not humility, nor is largeness and justness of view faith."

[186] *Ibid.*, p. 146.   [187] *Ibid.*, pp. 195, 224.

[188] *Ibid.*, p. 203.   [189] *Ibid.*, pp. 219, 224.

[190] *Ibid.*, p. 229.   [191] *Ibid.*, pp. 367-369.

[192] *Ibid.*, pp. 400-401, 404.

[193] *Ibid.*, p. 417. Cf. *ibid.*, p. 392, where Newman noted, as he did later in the *Grammar*, that expert judgment of one area of knowledge is in no way a sufficient qualification in another area.

CHAPTER IV

THREE USES OF CHRISTIAN DISCOURSE:
AN INTERPRETATIVE ANALYSIS

The purpose guiding my study to this point has been primarily negative and my method, principally descriptive. In chapter two, I gave an account of four types of criticism that I consider to be inadequate interpretations of Newman because of their reductive tendencies. In chapter three, by amassing testimony from Newman regarding different uses of Christian discourse, I sought to oppose the desire for a simple unity in Newman. The burden of this study has been to argue that the unity of Christian thinking does not rest in a meta-functional analysis of the uses of Christian discourse which, in some way, involves their reducibility to some one description (a simple unity), but lies rather in a complex manifold of uses related to one another in non-reductive ways and, therefore, subject to various descriptions (a complex unity).

Heretofore, I have offered examples of efforts to force a simple unity upon Newman's work and have offered evidence that points to the superficiality of such attempts. In this chapter, both my purpose and my method alter. I turn to a more detailed discussion and interpretation of the descriptions which Newman offered of the three uses of Christian discourse which I have isolated. This metatheological description is not intended, in any sense, to be foundational, i.e., logically necessary as a preparation for reflecting on Christianity, either for Newman or for any one who so reflects. The purpose of the analysis is to display Newman's own manner of reflection and to bring it to that allowable, though not necessary, level of explicit awareness of which Newman himself wrote.

I am interested, by making this explicit metatheological analysis, in presenting a more definite case for Newman's avoidance of reductionism and for his adherence to a complex unity of reflection. In this way, I argue not only that reductive interpretations of Newman are superficial but that they are positively erroneous and, therefore, illegitimate. In the

first section of the chapter, I argue that Newman's description
of religious inquiry in terms of certain characteristics of the
moral life and of the central phenomenon of the conscience
should not be understood to account for the content or truth
of the Christian faith. This account is, rather, an attempt
to display that religious inquiry is a rational human enterprise.
In the second section, I seek to describe how the imaginative
adoption and employment of the Christian picture of the world
and of one's place in it is not either the same as, or substi-
tutable for, religious inquiry or theological reflection.
In the third section, I describe the way in which Newman
explicated the objective reality and authority of the Christian
faith. In the fifth chapter of my study, I shall consider
more fully the nature of the "complex unity" that accounts for
Newman's not reducing any of these functions of Christian
discourse to another of the three or to some other description.

I. COMING TO FAITH: THE CONTEXT OF RELIGIOUS INQUIRY

Several matters must be considered in describing the
nature of coming to faith and the function of Christian discourse in relation to that pilgrimage. I shall have to consider the roles of the conscience and of moral dispositions as
well as the elements of evidence, argument and the illative
sense. These factors constitute what David Pailin calls the
"antecedents of faith."[1] After a summary of the consideration
which I gave to these factors in chapter three, I shall turn
to an ordered presentation of their relationships and meaning
within the context of religious inquiry, specifically, inquiry
into the Christian faith.

In the course of the earlier parts of this essay, I
noted that Newman gave frequent attention to the nature of
religious inquiry. I pointed, even in his earliest essays, to
an effort to distinguish between several senses of the word
"reason," only some of which he felt were applicable to the
domain of religion. His most insistent point was the denial
that any neutral rational criteria beyond the most formal in
character, such as the law of non-contradiction, were applicable
across boundaries of subject matter. In other words, he argued
for the preponderantly material quality of reason. Newman's

insistence on this point is especially significant for the nature of religious inquiry and for the explication of the Creed, but also necessarily has an impact on his understanding of the exercise of faith.

In relation to the nature of religious inquiry, the claim involved Newman's describing what he felt were the identifiable characteristics of the process of coming to believe. There are two significant elements in this description: one, an emphasis on the variety of approaches to faith; two, an isolation of certain characteristics that have more than an accidental relation to religious inquiry. Of course, it is the second factor that makes a description of religious inquiry possible. If Newman's remarks had been limited to his claim that no universally binding course of conversion could be described, I could then suggest only that one consult the biographies of individuals for further particulars regarding that process. For example, in Newman's case, one would consult the Apologia but not the Grammar since under these conditions the latter could not even have been undertaken. Newman felt, however, that more was possible. Some generalizations regarding the process of religious inquiry could be made; thus, he could write the Grammar of Assent.

Newman's earliest attempts to understand the nature of religious inquiry emphasized that religious faith is peculiar in two respects: one, in the role of a person's state of mind and of heart in preparing him for proper inquiry; two, in the peculiar nature of the evidence which one will accept as counting in favor of one's beliefs. More than any other source in the Anglican period, Newman's sermons reveal his reflections on the appropriate "disposition of the mind" in religious inquiry. In particular, this disposition seems to involve an openness to the dictates of conscience, or, more completely stated, to the witness of natural religion. This openness implies, in turn, an openness, even an eagerness, for revelation in the light of the incomplete witness of natural religion.

Newman felt that this kind of active inquiry altered the nature of the evidence necessary to convince one that deciding to believe a certain thing is warranted. In the first place, one accepts the testimony of others, not demanding firsthand experience for himself. Active inquiry and eager

anticipation make one open to learning from others. In the
second place, since this openness is a function of a desire for
the mending of their lives in the case of most men, it results
in the willing acceptance of a message able to meet that need.
The <u>Oxford</u> <u>University</u> <u>Sermons</u> gave an early indication of the
kind of rational process which he felt this inquiry to involve.
These sermons, often thought by critics to be his most thoroughly
subjective statement of the issues, allowed, however, that this
need may evidence itself in many diverse ways, including a need
for assurance regarding evidence for the truth of the Christian
faith. In no sense, then, did he seem to suggest the common
sin-salvation dialectic as the inevitable pattern of conversion
for all men. On the contrary, against excessive evangelicalism,
he deprecated such a prescription.

In describing the nature of religious inquiry, Newman
indicated a personal involvement varying in its specific nature
but constant in its opening men to the possibility of revelation. Thus, rather than use the misleading word "need" (candidly realizing that Newman himself often used the word), perhaps I could more helpfully employ the word "mystery" as Newman
sometimes used it, that is, to indicate the designation of a
problem that causes inquiry to arise. "Mystery" is the preferable term because it does not limit the possibilities as to
what that problem may be. Thus, for Newman, inquiry presupposed
the presence of certain kinds of questions. One duty of a
person describing the nature of religious inquiry is clarifying
the nature of those questions. Newman wanted to avoid a
simplistic identification of the questions with any one description. His insights in this regard have important implications
for apologetics and other issues involved in the study of the
relation of culture and Christianity.

Newman concluded that religious inquiry involves questions that evidence a pursuit of personal involvement rather
than one of detachment or curiosity. One's personal involvement
causes him to be on the "look out" for evidence rather than
waiting for it to "strike him in the face." In religious
matters, evidence arises in this way both because of the general character of experience and because of the peculiar nature
of revelation. On the one hand, one's general experience
indicates that life is such that conclusive proof is not

possible practically, considering one's manifold duties and
activities and the limits of one's training. On the other hand,
such proof is not even required for the man seeking religious
truths since God has so ordained matters that one can believe
on the basis of a cumulation of arguments functioning implicitly
and requiring no explication in order to be good reasons for
believing. Such reasons involve the dispositions and needs of
the inquirer as well as evidence. For this reason Newman constantly emphasized the necessity of attention to individual
life histories and peculiarities of personality in presenting
the faith.

The evidence afforded by inquiry makes credible the belief
he is bidden to embrace. The cumulation of these credibilia
or separate pieces of evidence leads one to consider the belief
worthy of believing. But religious faith, while involving
these personal dispositions and credibilia, is not reducible to
them. An act of the will by which one actually believes what
he comes to feel he ought to believe on the basis of its credibility is needed to overcome objections suggested by the
imagination and to embrace elements of revelation which actually
go beyond man's natural capacities of reasoning. With these
concerns, one encounters Newman's distinction between fides
acquisita, under consideration in this section, and fides
divina, considered in the third section of this chapter.
Actually the distinction separates his discussion of religious
inquiry from the matter of conversion, the latter being the
result of divine grace.

Likewise the description of the nature of religious
inquiry does not account for the content of one's religious
faith. In having described both the accidental or personal
and formal elements in a religious pilgrimage, one has not
thereby described the faith to which the pilgrimage led. To
understand how one came to believe something is not in itself
to understand what one believes. To fail in making this distinction is to reduce the objectivity of Christianity to a
pattern of appropriation. My concern is to show that Newman
did not commit that kind of reduction.

Natural Religion and the Testimony of Conscience

I want to consider, therefore, Newman's reflections on

the nature of religious inquiry or <u>fides acquisita</u> in the <u>Grammar of Assent</u> and in some other philosophical papers from the period of the <u>Grammar</u>'s writing in order to account for his having held to these important distinctions. The first and basic element in these writings, as one should expect, is the phenomenon of natural religion, understood by Newman in terms of the testimony of conscience. Newman set forth the essential framework for this description in his <u>Grammar of Assent</u>, but his most detailed and carefully considered work on the subject is a manuscript entitled "Proof of Theism."

In the <u>Grammar</u>, he noted that ". . . we have by nature a conscience."[2] Newman understood the conscience to be a kind of "mental act" like those of memory, reasoning, and imagination. In this mental act, there are two elements: a moral sense or critical office by which one makes moral decisions and a sense of obligation or a judicial office by which one is aware that right conduct is sanctioned. This element of sanction is what Newman usually means by conscience although he realizes that the two elements are not strictly separable. He considered the element of sanction basic and logically prior. The dictates of sanction in the conscience arouse one's affections and passions of hope and fear, reverence and awe. As such, conscience implies an object, an intelligent being since, said Newman, inanimate things cannot stir our emotions; thus, the experience of shame, fear, and responsibility imply that ". . . there is One to whom we are responsible, before whom we are responsible, before whom we are ashamed, whose claims upon us we fear."[3] Newman concluded:

> . . . the phenomena of Conscience, as a dictate, avail to impress the imagination with the picture of a Supreme Governor, a Judge, holy, just, powerful, all-seeing, retributive, and is [sic] the creative principle of religion, as the Moral Sense is the principle of ethics.[4]

For Newman, this belief comes to him ". . . like an impulse of nature to entertain it."[5]

In the important section on "natural religion" in the <u>Grammar</u>, Newman described conscience as the "great internal teacher of religion. . . . "[6] In his manuscript on the "Proof of Theism" of 1859, Newman stated outright that "there is a God, because there is a moral obligation."[7] Newman argued that, like consciousness and reasoning, conscience is the very nature of human existence. One should not speak of accepting these elements as if one could discard them, for they simply constitute what it is to exist as a human being. Newman claimed that ". . . it is as absurd to speak of being sceptical of consciousness, reasoning, memory, sensation, as to say that I am sceptical that I am."[8]

When one analyzes this basic sense of obligation, said Newman, one finds that it involves the idea of a Judge. Newman described this move as his "own chosen proof" for the being of God.[9] On the other hand, in the *Grammar*, he expressed doubt as to whether the picture of God as Moral Governor would ever arise apart from some external stimulation and suggests that a special divine aid which is above nature is the cause for its arising in the mind.[10] Even if this testimony is produced by divine assistance, the essential attributes of God according to conscience are those of retributive justice and almighty power. In short, God appears as one angry with us and as one who threatens to punish us. The doctrines and devotions of natural religion are also shaped by the centrality of justice. The sense of sin and of guilt make a doctrine of atonement and a means of appropriating forgiveness central. In addition to these gloomier aspects, however, there are elements of hope in natural religion. The general existence of religious beliefs and institutions argue for man's essential hope for benefits to alleviate the gloom and misery. Such beliefs can lead one to interpret the course of things from such a point of view that every event seems guided by a providential hand. Prayer also offers relief and solace from trouble. Finally, and most inclusively,

> . . . it is another alleviation of the darkness and distress which weigh upon the religions of the world, that in one way or other such religions are founded on some idea of express revelation, coming from the unseen agents whose anger they deprecate. . . .[11]

Newman argued, therefore, that the notion of revelation is quite congenial to the human mind. More specifically, he pointed out, natural religions almost universally contain a rite of sacrifice for the removal of guilt and the principle of meritorious intercession as a basis of that sacrifice.

Interestingly enough, however, Newman did not conclude that the truths of revelation derive from or even depend on the truths of natural religion as he described them. In other words, he did not argue that there is a kind of reasoning that takes one from the dictates of conscience and the resulting religious framework to the revealed truths. Revelation is separate, distinct and complete within itself. What the dictates of conscience and the elements of natural religion do bring to fruition is a "special preparation of mind."

> Accordingly, instead of saying that the truths of Revelation depend on those of Natural Religion, it is more pertinent to say that belief in revealed truths depends on belief in natural. Belief is a state of mind; belief generates belief; states of mind correspond to each other; the habits of thought and the reasonings which lead us on to a higher state of belief than our present, are the very same which we already possess in connexion with the lower state.[12]

Those persons who are prepared to receive revealed truth, then, are those ". . . imbued with the religious opinions and sentiments which I have identified with natural religion."[13] Such a preparation is opposed to what Newman characteristically called the "religion of civilization."[14]

The religion of civilization almost solely emphasizes the intellect, recognizing the moral sense but not the sanction of the conscience and, thus, according to Newman, giving no attention to the hopes and fears of man's soul. It was advocates of this religion whom Newman had in view when he wrote:

> I do not address myself to those, who in moral evil and physical see nothing more than imperfections of a parallel nature; who consider that the difference in gravity between the two is one of degree only, not of kind; that moral evil is merely the offspring of physical, and that as we remove the latter so we inevitably remove the former; that there is a progress of the human race which tends to the annihilation of moral evil; that knowledge is virtue, and vice is ignorance; that sin is a bugbear, not a reality; that the Creator does not punish except in the sense of correcting; that vengeance in Him would of necessity be vindictiveness; that all we know of Him, be it much or little, is through the laws of nature; that miracles are impossible; that prayer to Him is a superstition; that the fear of Him is unmanly; that sorrow for sin is slavish and abject; that the only intelligible worship of Him is to act well our part in the world, and the only sensible repentance to do better in future; that if we do our duties in this life, we may take our chance for the next; and that it is of no use perplexing our minds about the future state, for it is all a matter of guess. These opinions characterize a civilized age; and if I say that I will not argue about Christianity with men who hold them, I do so, not as claiming any right to be impatient or peremptory with any one, but because it is plainly absurd to attempt to prove a second proposition to those who do not admit the first.[15]

Clearly the first proposition which Newman had in mind is one that dissolves prejudice against the possibility of revelation by opening one to anticipation of it. This state of mind he described in this way:

> . . . a belief and perception of the Divine Presence, a recognition of His attributes and an admiration of His Person viewed under them, a conviction of the worth of the soul and of the reality and momentousness of the unseen world, an understanding that, in proportion as we partake in our own persons of the attributes which we admire in Him, we are dear to Him, a consciousness on the contrary that we are far from exemplifying them, a consequent insight into our guilt and misery, an eager hope of reconciliation to Him, a desire to know and to love Him, and a sensitive looking-out in all that happens, whether in the course of nature or of human life, for tokens, if such there be, of his bestowing on us what we so greatly need. These are specimens of the state of mind for which I stipulate in those who would inquire into the truth of Christianity. . . . [16]

In many contexts, therefore, Newman employed the so-called argument from conscience as a kind of description of the religious sphere of life in opposition to an interpretation that, in his eyes, failed to do justice to the character and dynamics of that sphere. He was by no means offering a description of the nature of Christianity; he was seeking to identify an element of religious faith which the religion of civilization failed to recognize.

There is no doubt, however, that Newman placed more than casual emphasis on the testimony of the conscience. Indeed he even felt that it was possible to establish a kind of argument for the existence of God on the basis of a proper understanding of the phenomenon of conscience as sanction. In his paper on the "Proof of Theism," he distinguished between intuition or the recognition of that which is a constitutive element of our existence as such and belief in external objects. According to Newman, one cannot properly be said to have faith in his constitution as a human being for that is simply what one is; on the other hand, it is appropriate to speak of belief in external objects. For example, he pointed out, sensations as internal acts or mental operations are known in our consciousness by intuition, but the objects which are their cause are "objects of faith" since the truth of their existence is not bound up with that act of consciousness.[17] The general principle behind this observation was: "My point is not to deny that our knowledge comes from experience, not to advocate innate forms, but to say that our experience is not so much of external things, but of our own minds."[18] At the same time, he argued that the external fact of God's existence is different from all other such facts in that its intuition necessarily involves an external reference.[19] Faith is the nature of one's relation to God but intuition provides the usual means of conviction of His existence. Thus Newman can state: ". . . to recognize our nature is really to recognize God."[20]

Adrian J. Boekraad bases his interpretation of Newman's views on this understanding of conscience as a reflexive act bearing witness to the existence of God.[21] While some of Newman's own words legitimize Boekraad's view, there is contrary evidence that mitigates the centrality of conscience in an overall interpretation of Newman's work. The basic point in this regard has been the thesis of this entire study: The tendency to reduce Newman's reflections to a simply unity overlooks the varying contexts in which he writes and his guiding metatheological principles. I shall have more to say about this important point below. Let it suffice to say that the temptation to reduction is nowhere greater than at this point.

A second consideration against the centrality of conscience is that the "proof" was never so rigidly made in any of Newman's published works. In those writings, the testimony of conscience seems to serve another purpose. A third matter to consider is the fact that the value of the testimony of conscience is a matter of some contradiction in his work. There are at least two reasons for this observation. One, Newman understood the failings of conscience, the power of man's imagination to deface its testimony.[22] Two, he must or at least should have remembered some of his own warnings regarding fitting one's apologetic to the capacities of the hearer and being aware of the accidents of life histories which attend religious inquiry. The emphasis on the accidents of life, the peculiarities of capacity and circumstance, suggests that a rigid demand that one come to faith through a dependence on the testimony of conscience is out of place and self-defeating. The evidence indicates that Newman himself depended too heavily on this avenue to faith. Nevertheless he did openly admit that this kind of evidence was the kind that was convincing to him and that he offered it in that manner of personal testimony.[23] He wrote of that personal quality of the argument:

> In religious inquiry each of us can speak only for himself, and for himself he has a right to speak. His own experiences are enough for himself, but he cannot speak for others: He cannot lay down the law; he can only bring his own experiences to the common stock of psychological facts. He knows what has satisfied and satisfies himself; if it satisfies him, it is likely to satisfy others. . . . [24]

This contrast between the persuasiveness of personal testimony and the setting of rules could have served Newman better than it did at times in relation to his fascination with the testimony of conscience. Such a distinction surely would have shaken the confidence that sometimes appears in Newman regarding the universal validity of his description of the witness of conscience. On the occasions of this confidence, Newman suggested that his conclusions regarding the testimony of conscience constitute a proposal of something one might describe as a universally present "religious attitude" underlying all experience or what Boekraad understands as a religious aspect at the very root of our human being.[25] In a letter written April 13, 1870, Newman observed:

> I believe in design because I believe in God, not in God because I see design. You will say that the nineteenth century does not believe in conscience either--true--but then it does not believe in a God at all. Something I must assume, and in assuming conscience I assume what is least to assume, and what most will admit.[26]

He counseled a young man in doubt to interrogate his heart or his conscience for, he says, ". . . the God who dwells there."[27]

My suggestion is that Newman might have been more cautious about this kind of proposal in the light of his understanding of the variability of approaches to faith according to the accidents of individual life histories. His own words in this connection are very persuasive; he argued that faith is produced

> . . . in different minds by various experiences and disposing causes, variously combined; such as a warm or strong imagination, great sensibility, compunction and horror at sin, frequenting the Mass and other rites of the Church, meditating on the contents of the Gospels, familiarity with hymns and religious poems, dwelling on the Evidences, parental example and instruction, religious friends, strange providences, powerful preaching.[28]

Conscience and the Nature of Religious Inquiry

Having given attention to considerations that suggest the lack of harmony between the centrality which Newman sometimes gave to the conscience and the negative remarks which he made about the testimony which the conscience affords and about the standardization of a pattern of conversion, I want to consider another function which the concept of the conscience has in Newman's writings. In this case, descriptions of the testimony of conscience serve as analogous descriptions of the nature of religious inquiry. I noted above that Newman held that in "religious inquiry each of us can speak only for himself. . . ."[29] In this sense, a person who did come to the Christian faith on the basis of certain moral experiences could not demand that others come to faith in that same way. Yet, an analysis of Newman suggests that he might have used the nature of moral experience as a means for claiming, by analogy, something about the nature of religious inquiry that is more universally true.

Newman himself drew at least three parallels between moral and religious inquiry: the importance of personal dispositions and of the will, the peculiar nature of evidence and of argument, and the kind of judgment required.[30] In drawing these parallels, he opposed a certain understanding of reason characteristic of what he called the "religion of civilization" and sought to reveal the nature of ". . . the grounds on which the mass of men believe in Christianity, or in other words, the relation of faith viewed in the concrete as a habit and act of the mind."[31]

Religious inquiry and personal involvement. In the first place, reasoned Newman, the indispensability of personal involvement and decision is a characteristic of religious inquiry as it is of moral inquiry. Religious inquiry undertaken only for the sake of an increase in knowledge can be perfectly in harmony with historical or other purposes but not with strictly religious ones. In large measure, making this distinction is the goal of Newman's further distinction between inference and assent. By inference, Newman indicated a process by which one holds to a proposition on the basis of arguments for the truth of other propositions in addition to those for the main proposition. Thus, an inference is a conclusion conditioned upon the truth of other propositions. An assertion is categorical, implying the absence of any conditions, in a matter of assent. An assent to an assertion also involves the apprehension of that which one asserts.[32] By apprehension, Newman meant the ability to impose meaning on a proposition.[33] "Apprehension then is simply an intelligent acceptance of the idea or of the fact which a proposition enunciates."[34]

Newman's differentiation between "idea" and "fact" is not accidental; rather it is related to his differentiation of two modes of apprehension, notional and real. ". . . according as language expresses things external to us, or our own thoughts, so is apprehension real or notional."[35] Newman argued in turn that the human mind is more moved by the apprehension of the concrete thing than by the apprehension of an abstract idea. Since notional apprehensions are most congenial to inference and real apprehension to assent, in Newman's view, real apprehension implies that the object of the assent is not a notion but a fact. Both types of apprehension are exercised on propositions, but one on propositions apprehended as images standing for things and the other on propositions as notions or as representing notions.[36]

Newman described the nature of real apprehension or assent as dependent on "moral experiences;" that is, on personal formation or life history. One cannot arrive at real apprehension secondhand by means of general ideas or notions; one can only do so by means of lived experience that suggests images of things.[37] In the religious life, for example, there is

> . . . an imaginative or real assent to the doctrine that there is One God, that is, an assent made with an apprehension, not only of what the words of the proposition mean, but of the object denoted by them.[38]

These images arise, for Newman, in the conjunction of the development of "moral experiences" and of the facts of revelation and doctrine.[39] Religious inquiry, therefore, consists not only in matters of information but also in the way in which those matters come to have personal significance for the individual.

<u>Religious inquiry and informal inference.</u> The whole point of Newman's distinctions, in relation to the second

parallel he finds between moral and religious experience, is
the difference between the types of reasoning operative in the
religious context and those operative in other contexts.
His most important point is that notional or detached and
conditional inference does not characterize religious inquiry.
Religious inquiry involves concrete, particular realities
rather than ideas alone. For Newman, particulars involve a
person's imagination, which in turn relates to his passions and,
subsequently and consequently, his actions. Notional apprehension, on the other hand, can largely leave a man unmoved,
uncommitted, inactive. Newman clarified this distinction more
fully by describing the nature of evidence and of argument in
relation to the two types of apprehension.

Notional apprehension, as we have observed, is characterized by inference, i.e., by the founding of the truth of a
proposition on the truth of other premises and propositions.
As such, then, inferential exercises and notional apprehension
are always conditional in their hold on propositions. These
propositions can be analyzed, however, so that a method can be
established to describe and make standard the process of inference. Newman wrote of this method:

> Ratiocination, thus restricted and put into grooves, is
> what I have called Inference, and the science, which is
> its regulating principle, is Logic.[40]

This method fails, said Newman, insofar as what enters into
human reasoning cannot be adequately expressed in propositions
and in syllogisms. Newman seemed to suggest in this regard
that words are somehow inadequate bearers of human thought.
Perhaps he could more helpfully have suggested that the contexts in which propositions have real meaning sometimes involve
non-linguistic factors, e.g., symbolic or other kinds of gestures, actions.[41] In that way, he might have made clear, what
seems more likely the case, that language is adequate for its
task though it is not the only factor to be considered in every
situation. Certainly the importance which Newman placed on
dogmas should suggest that any attempt to devalue the importance
of language in Newman is ill conceived.

What Newman did conclude is that logic conceived according to the Aristotelian model does not adequately account for
concrete things, their historical life, and other associations
and connotations. In particular, said Newman, inference falls

short of proof in concrete matters because it merely assumes its premises and because its conclusions are abstract and not concrete. The former deficiency results from the fact that some assumptions are necessary if one is not to be involved in an infinite regress. The latter results from dealing with notional propositions which are unable to reach the concrete thing. General notions and definitions can never give the reality of the concrete object; such notions are only aspects of what is the whole real thing. The conclusion of such a process of reasoning is always probable since one can never be sure that the conclusion will fit a concrete case.

Newman amplified his conclusions in this way:

> As to logic, its chain of conclusions hangs loose at both ends; both the point from which the proof should start, and the point at which it should arrive, are beyond its reach; it comes short both of first principles and of concrete issues. Even its most elaborate exhibitions fail to represent adequately the sum total of considerations by which an individual mind is determined in its judgment of things. . . .[42]

In the *Grammar*, Newman made this distinction between notional and real apprehension quoting long passages from "The Tamworth Reading Room." But he went beyond the appeal to personal involvement in reasoning to a description of the form that evidence and argument take. Newman described what he calls "informal inference" in this way:

> It is the cumulation of probabilities, independent of each other, arising out of the nature and circumstances of the particular case which is under review; probabilities too fine to avail separately, too subtle and circuitous to be convertible into syllogisms, too numerous and various for such conversion, even were they convertible.[43]

This type of inference is characterized by a cumulation of probabilities arising in the course of human living and not simply abstractions. This process, arising as it does, is more or less implicit and incapable of complete analysis by the mind of the reasoner. Yet the fact is that it remains a process of inference, and consequently, one dependent on premises and conditional in character. The case developed by this cumulation becomes non-conditional only as the individual appropriates the evidence as legitimizing certitude. Each person must judge for himself, by his own principles and on the basis of his own character or development in his personal life history. Thus, one's assents are the result of the personal exercise of a living individual and not merely of argumentative skill.[44]

Religious inquiry and the illative sense. The personal element in reasoning indicates the need for the development of an <u>organum investigandi</u> by which one can judge a mass of evidence to warrant certitude regarding the matter to which the evidence relates. Newman argued that this <u>organum investigandi</u> is characterized by prudence, an endowment not natural to man but one gained by personal development.[45] Thus, one notes the third parallel which Newman drew between moral and religious inquiry. In addition to suggesting the importance of personal dispositions and of the will and to indicating the peculiar nature of evidence and argument, he pointed to the similarity between the kind of judgment required in moral and religious inquiry. Newman described the faculty of judgment in religious inquiry or the "illative sense" in terms of Aristotle's notion of <u>phronesis</u> or judgment in ethical matters.

<u>Phronesis</u>, according to Newman's understanding of Aristotle, ". . . is seated in the mind of the individual, who is thus his own law, his own teacher, and his own judge in those special cases of duty which are personal to him."[46] <u>Phronesis</u> is an acquired habit, something formed and nurtured by experience and practice, sufficient for decision in a given situation though not characterized by a systematic point of view or method. Of course, Newman realized that there are differences between <u>phronesis</u> as a moral phenomenon and as an epistemological one. Most apparently, though duties change, truth never does. Nevertheless, said Newman, the parallel holds that ". . . the reasonings which carry us to truth and certitude are many and distinct, and vary with the inquirer. . . ."[47] Thus, in matters of personal decision in ethics or religion, a living, present authority, either oneself or another, is the immediate guide. The illative sense does what formal inference could never do: "It determines . . . the limit of converging probabilities and the reasons sufficient for a proof."[48] Certainty is a function of authoritative decision.

The character of authority was clarified by Newman in his pointing out that such authority is gained only by long standing experience in a given subject matter. In particular he denied that the illative sense is a general instrument which once gained admits of free and ready exercise in any and every field of knowledge. Newman understood the illative sense to have its authority only within provinces or departments of knowledge. Newman pointed out that:

> It is not so much one faculty, as a collection of similar or analogous faculties under one name, there being really as many faculties as there are distinct subject-matters, though in the same person some of them may, if it so happens, be united. . . .[49]

Thus, concluded Newman, one should trust persons rather than logical science; the long acquaintance of individuals with a given body of subject matter gives them the capacity and the right to judge. Newman wrote of the means of acquiring an "illative sense":

> And if we wish ourselves to share in their convictions and the grounds of them, we must follow their history, and learn as they have learned. We must take up their particular subject as they took it up, beginning at the beginning, give ourselves to it, depend on practice and experience more than on reasoning, and thus gain that mental insight into truth, whatever its subject-matter may be, which our masters have gained before us.[50]

This passage reveals one source of possible confusion for readers and a possible confusion in Newman's own mind. Newman seemed to suggest that reasoning is invalid or is insufficient and that practice and experience are what is required for sound judgment. Yet his analysis of the illative sense was expressly intended as a description of the natural reasoning process, particularly as it evidences itself in religious inquiry. What is the reason for this seeming contradiction? Perhaps the most adequate explanation would suggest that the seeming contradiction is actually an expression of the distinction made by Newman between reasoning in an appropriate and in an inappropriate way, between a field dependent or material reason and a formal and supposed generally valid reason, between a positive sense of notional apprehension and a negative sense. Reasoning that exempts experience and practice is, therefore, inappropriate, illicitly formal, and negatively notional. The illative sense is the <u>organum investigandi</u> of a reasoning process in which practice, acquired habit and experience in a given subject matter are important to reasoning well and being certain.

Conclusions

In drawing these three parallels between religious inquiry and moral inquiry, Newman described the nature of the process of reasoning, making judgments, and reaching certainty regarding religious matters. He took personal involvement or what he calls "moral experiences" to be inextricably involved in reasoning in religious contexts. Detached, notional, and conditional inference is not sufficient in the context of religious inquiry. One's passions, affections, and volitions are involved in religious as well as moral inquiry. The kind of evidence which brings religious conclusions and images to the mind cannot be forced into syllogisms; such evidence is too varied and subtle for that. Thus, evidence has the nature of a cumulation of probabilities rather than a single, formally rigid proof. Newman did not mean that the collection of probabilities itself only had probable argumentative force. He meant that, since no one piece of argument was conclusive in itself, only a cumulation of such pieces of evidence could be sufficient.[51] This cumulation remains probable only in the sense that the evidence is not coercive, forcing the mind to accept a certain conclusion. The individual must, by an exercise of the acquired habit of judgment, decide the issue. By an acquired familiarity with the subject matter and, consequently, with the kinds of evidence for its truth, the judgment can be made.

What must be kept in mind is that the formation of the illative sense comes about in different persons in different ways. Indeed, evidence of different kinds convinces different persons. In Wilfrid Ward's rendering of his words, Newman bemoaned the fact that the "typical Italian professor often failed to realize the actual state of mind of the man who was to be convinced. . . ."[52] Thus, each individual case is a "personal result . . . idiosyncratic in its circumstances."[53] Ward pointed out that:

> Newman was specially careful to suit his words to the mind or mood of a correspondent in his letters to those whose belief in Christianity or even Thomism was in danger or actually dying. . . . he feared lest staking too much on an argument which might not prove convincing might make things worse instead of better.[54]

Thus, one must not make the experience of one man to fit the experience of another since accidents of individual life histories are so very important in understanding the process by which notional apprehension or knowledge of certain religious ideas and doctrines become real apprehension or assent to certain realities. Newman described this change as "religious conversion," the point of passing from religious inquiry to faith. Newman noted in this connection:

> The most awful truths are to him but sublime or beautiful conceptions, and are advanced and used by him, in season and out of season, for his own purposes, for embellishing his style or rounding his period. But let his heart at length be ploughed by some keen grief or deep anxiety, and Scripture is a new book to him.[55]

Two questions remain to be answered regarding this transition from religious inquiry to faith. First, did Newman judge biographical incidents to constitute reasons? Another way of asking the same question is: Did Newman suppose, as Baudin believed, that faith is the result of the contagion of a certain sensibility? Are causes, needs, and motives good _reasons_ for believing a given thing? Second, is the transition from inquiry to faith described when one has offered an analysis of _fides acquisita_? As a conclusion to this section, I shall direct myself to each of these two questions in turn.

First, did Newman believe that causes for one's adopting a given belief could be good reasons for doing so as well? Brother F. James Kaiser suggests that the answer to this question is affirmative when he describes the act of conscience, in Newman, as

> . . . merely a specification of the act of human belief; the same mental operation, the same kind of certitude, and the same procedure and difficulties in reaching certitude are found in both.[56]

In short, Newman did believe that personal needs and dispositions could be reasons for believing something which met or complemented those personal "accidents." A letter to Wilfrid Ward in 1884 reveals clearly that this was Newman's position:

> . . . it seems to me you mean to say that the same considerations which make you wish to believe are among the reasons which, when you actually do inquire, lead you prudently to believe, thus serving a double purpose. Do you bring this out anywhere? On the contrary, are you not shy of calling those considerations reasons? Why?[57]

Clearly Newman was not so shy about making that kind of conclusion: Personal need could be a reason not only for inquiry but also for believing. Two important qualifications should be made at this point. First, this kind of reason constitutes only one kind of reason that could be given for coming to faith. Second, and more importantly, although these kinds of reasons may be the only kind offered by a given individual, the Church could not rely solely on them. These matters will be clarified in the remainder of this chapter.

Our second question is: Has the transition from religious inquiry to faith been described when one has made an analysis of *fides acquisita*? I noted above that Newman's account of the nature of religious inquiry includes a reference to conversion as the transition from notional to real assent. He had referred to the transition in "The Tamworth Reading Room" which he quoted in the *Grammar* as a movement consisting in turn of ". . . knowledge, then a view, then reasoning, and then belief."[58] This process of *fides acquisita*, however, was always distinguished in the most definite fashion from *fides divina*. In fact, the transition from *fides acquisita* to *fides divina* does not permit description. For instance, he noted that the imagination suggests objections to the individual which rational religious inquiry cannot overcome. In these cases, only an act of the will can move a person to assent. But, Newman noted, that act of the will is not a human possibility but a gift of grace. At this point, Newman suggested, the inquirer can only pray and wait upon God's grace. Newman offered the following as an example of an appropriate prayer:

> O my God, I confess that Thou canst enliven my darkness. I confess that Thou only canst. I wish my darkness to be enlightened. I do not know whether Thou wilt; but that Thou canst, and that I wish, are reasons for me to ask, what Thou at least has not forbidden my asking. I hereby promise Thee that, by Thy grace which I am seeking, I will embrace whatever I at length feel certain is the truth, if ever I come to be certain. And by Thy grace I will guard against self deceit which may lead me take what nature would have, rather than what reason approves.[59]

In explanation, Newman went on to say:

> If a man tells me he has thus heroically cast himself upon God, and persisted in such a prayer, and yet is in the dark, of course my argument with him is at an end. I retire from the discussion and leave the matter to God. . . .[60]

He even suggested more broadly that grace and prayer were the divine and human elements that were necessary for an openness to arguments in the subject matter of religion.[61] What is certain, however, is that the transition from inquiry to faith is a matter dependent on the activity of God through the Holy Spirit and not describable or prescribable in any way by man. In the words of the priest who counsels the main character of Newman's novel <u>Loss and Gain</u>: "You approach the Church in the way of reason, you enter into it in the light of the Spirit."[62]

Newman pointed to the distinction between <u>fides acquisita</u> and <u>fides divina</u> in this way in the <u>Grammar</u>:

> Nor . . . does this doctrine of the intrinsic integrity and indivisibility of assent (if I may so speak) interfere with the teaching of Catholic theology as to the pre-eminence of strength in divine faith, which has a supernatural origin, when compared with all belief which is merely human and natural. For first, that pre-eminence consists, not in its differing from human faith, merely in degree of assent, but in its being superior in nature and kind, so that the one does not admit of a comparison with the other; and next, its intrinsic superiority is not a matter of experience, but is above experience. Assent is ever assent; but in the assent which follows on a divine announcement, and is vivified by a divine grace, there is, from the nature of the case, a transcendent adhesion of mind, intellectual and moral, and a special self-protection, beyond the operation of these ordinary laws of thought, which alone have a place in my discussion.[63]

In <u>fides divina</u>, noted Newman, religious inquiry no longer has a place. The inquirer is still in doubt regarding what is the truth. Thus, Newman clearly wanted to distinguish between the inquirer and the believer.[64] The believer has not only exercised the judgment implied by the illative sense; he has also made, by means of God's grace, a decision to believe and no longer to inquire. He has the security of faith available, not through the exercise of the illative sense despite its effectiveness in religious inquiry, but only through God's grace. The kind of rational inquiry made prior to faith involves the exercise of the illative sense; and Newman's description of the organ of judgment was a part of his effort to display the nature of religious inquiry as a rational enterprise. But the decision to believe and no longer to inquire involves the purging of all objections raised by the imagination for the illative sense and is not itself a judgment understandable in terms of the illative sense alone. For this reason, to have described the <u>fides acquisita</u> is not to have understood the nature or cause of <u>fides divina</u>.

Newman did allow what he called "investigation" by the believer to be legitimate. In this case, the believer investigates the grounds and meaning of propositions or doctrines without doubting the truth of the proposition. The next section of this chapter explores the shape of the life of the believer or the man of _fides divina_. The third and last section considers the nature of "investigation" or theology. Newman did not propose that his description of the nature of religious inquiry and of the role of moral dispositions and implicit reasoning sufficed as an account either of the life of faith or of reflection on one's faith. To have argued for that sufficiency would indeed have made him guilty of that reductionism, which I contend he sought to avoid.

II. EXERCISING FAITH: THE CONTEXT OF THE CHRISTIAN LIFE

I have given lengthy attention to the nature of religious inquiry or, in Newman's phrase, the grammar of assent. One could gain the false impression that Newman's concern with the uses of Christian discourse was limited to his description of the illative sense. In fact, I have shown in an earlier chapter that concentration on Newman's understanding of religious inquiry has been all too common in books proposing to describe Newman's understanding of Christian faith. Against this reductive tendency, I have distinguished several perspectives in order to explore them as elements in Newman's complete understanding of the issues. As Newman himself did, I have concentrated on three of these perspectives. Having given attention to coming to faith or religious inquiry, I now turn to consider the Christian life or the exercising of faith.

In chapter three, I noted Newman's understanding of the poetic quality of faith or the role of the imagination in the life of faith. The peculiar vision of the world and of one's own and others' places in it is the factor in terms of which Newman sought to account for the affections and actions of the Christian, that is to say, for the Christian character.

As we should expect, Newman made a clear distinction between religious inquiry and the Christian life. The latter was never understood as the result to which a process of inquiry, no matter how complex and intertwined with moral dispositions and prudent judgment, leads one. Viewed from the perspective of man's inquiry, the life of faith appears as the culmination of a personal history ending in an act of will by which one achieves certitude. But, viewed from the perspective of divine activity, the life of faith is constituted by an act of grace that gives power to the will and molds the imagination. In describing the life of faith, Newman analyzed the character of the imagination and of the will following upon this act of divine grace.

Imagination

The concept "image" was a very important one for Newman. An "image" is related more directly to the object of sensation than a notion and, consequently, is central to real apprehension in a way that it is not for notional apprehension.[65] According to Newman, things act upon the imagination so as to leave impressions or images of themselves.[66] Imagination or, more concretely, these images stimulate the affections or motive powers to action in accordance with the image.[67] Newman indicated that such images can be formed by what he calls the "faculty of composition." This inventive faculty follows

> . . . the description of things which have never come before us, and . . . [forms] . . . out of such passive impressions as experience has heretofore left on our minds, new images, which, though mental creations, are not notional. They are concrete units in the mind . . . .[68]

By means of this faculty of composition, one is able to appropriate past or distant realities. The faculty provides a capacity for interpreting the statements of others. A characteristic image formed in these ways, according to Newman, is the picture of a Moral Governor.[69] Although he seemed to suggest that this image is a natural result of the inner development of an individual person, he explicitly stated his doubt that the image ". . . would ever be elicited without extrinsic help . . . ."[70] He did not seem interested in pursuing this question, however, giving his attention to the way in which the image functions rather than to the history of its origin.

The picture of God as Moral Governor comes to inform one's view of the world of nature and of man. The religious imagination

> . . . interprets what it sees around it by this previous inward teaching, as the true key of that maze of vast complicated disorder; and thus it gains a more and more consistent and luminous vision of God from the most uncompromising materials.[71]

Beginning with this image, men soon find that ". . . everything that happens tends to confirm them in the truths about Him which live in the imagination, varied and unearthly as those truths may be."[72] While Newman seemed to feel that this image is possible apart from revelation, he did argue that one main purpose of revelation is to give man a clear, full, exact, and sufficient object for his faith.[73] In fact, Newman explained the power and influence of Christianity in the history of the world as a function of the imprinting of the image of Christ by Christ Himself in the minds of His followers individually. Newman concluded:

> . . . that Image, apprehended and worshipped in individual minds, becomes a principle of association, and a real bond of those subjects one with another, who are thus united to the body by being united to that Image; and moreover that Image, which is their moral life, when they have been already converted, is also the original instrument of their conversion.[74]

Such a conclusion only illustrates what Newman held as a fundamental principle: "The heart is commonly reached, not through the reason, but through the imagination, by means of direct impressions, by the testimony of facts and events, by history, by description."[75]

For all of his emphasis on the imagination, Newman was careful to distinguish it from the power of conceiving. Newman urged that "we can imagine things which we cannot conceive."[76] As an example, he argued that one can imagine, or gain knowledge by means of an image of, a mystery which is in itself inconceivable. Yet images by themselves are not sufficient for judgment or assent since one cannot give assent without grounds for assenting.[77] Newman warned, therefore, against the danger of confusing the distinctness and power of an image functioning in a real assent and the actual existence of the objects which those images represent.[78] Newman reasoned in this way:

> A proposition, be it ever so keenly apprehended, may be true or false. If we simply put aside all inferential information, such as is derived from testimony, from general belief, from the concurrence of the senses, from common sense, or otherwise, we have no right to consider that we have apprehended a truth, merely because of the strength of our mental impression of it.[79]

In this way, Newman argued that the imagination must not be allowed to usurp the functions of reason. I have already considered how reason functions in religious inquiry; in the next section, I shall consider the way in which reason functions for the man of faith. What role, however, is left to the imagination? What function did it have in Newman's analysis?

I would suggest that the concept "imagination" most often served as a tool for describing the way in which the Christian faith molds the life of its followers. He did speak of the way in which the facts of the Christian revelation strike the imagination of the religious inquirer and gain a foothold in his consciousness. But the consequences of this foothold are Newman's primary interest in the use of this concept. In that regard, he noted, imagination stirs the motive powers of the man who adopts a given image and by stirring "hope and fear, likes and dislikes, appetites, passion, affection, . . . selfishness and self-love" leads to action. ". . . the imagination may be said in some sense to be of a practical nature, inasmuch as it leads to practice indirectly by the action of its object upon the affections."[80] Thus, as a man begins to see the world, things and events with the image of a Moral Governor or of Christ in his mind, his affections become moved in a certain way and his actions follow in a certain course. In this way, faith,

> . . . being concerned with things concrete, not abstract, which variously excite the mind from their moral and imaginative properties, has for its objects, not only directly what is true, but inclusively what is beautiful, useful, admirable, heroic; objects which kindle devotion, rouse the passions, and attach the affections; and thus it leads the way to actions of every kind, to the establishment of principles, and the formation of character, and is thus again intimately connected with what is individual and personal.[81]

The Visible and the Invisible

Newman returned to the description of elements in the Christian imagination again and again in his writings, particularly in his sermons. The basic image, for Newman, involved a distinction between a visible and invisible world. The recommendation implied by the image is that one look at the world in a different way. Instead of cataloging the disclosure of the five senses and nothing more, another kind of perception is recommended for those who want to comprehend what is real. "There are two worlds, 'the visible and the invisible,' as the Creed speaks,--the world we see, and the world we do not see; and the world we do not see as really exists as the world we do see."[82]

In the <u>Apologia</u>, Newman referred to aspects of his own personality that were congenial to this dual view of the world. He noted his superstition and imagination which operated in

> . . . isolating me from the objects which surrounded me, in confirming me in my mistrust of the reality of material phenomena, and making me rest in the thought of two and two only supreme and luminously self-evident beings, myself and my Creator . . . .[83]

It was Bishop Butler's <u>Analogy</u> <u>of</u> <u>Religion</u> which first suggested to him that:

> . . . the very idea of an analogy between the separate works of God leads to the conclusion that the system which is of less importance is economically or sacramentally connected with the more momentous system, and of this conclusion the theory, to which I was inclined as a boy, viz. the unreality of material phenomena, is an ultimate resolution.[84]

Newman also noted the influence of John Keble in his developing awareness of the sacramental system or "the doctrine that material phenomena are both the types and the instruments of real things unseen. . . ."[85] This sacramental system Newman took to include not only the sacraments proper but also the communion of the saints and the mysteries of the faith. In this connection, he noted that the study of the philosophy of Clement and Origen made in connection with his study of Arianism confirmed him in his view of the mystical and sacramental principle.

> I understand them to mean that the exterior world, physical and historical, was but the outward manifestation of realities greater than itself. Nature was a parable: Scripture was an allegory: pagan literature, philosophy, and mythology, properly understood, were but a preparation for the Gospel. There had been a divine dispensation granted to the Jews; there had been in some sense a dispensation carried on in favour of the Gentiles. He who had taken the seed of Jacob for His elect people, had not therefore cast the rest of mankind out of His sight. In the fulness of time both Judaism and Paganism had come to nought; the outward framework, which concealed yet suggested the Living Truth, had never been intended to last, and it was dissolving under the beams of the Sun of Justice behind it and through it. The process of change had been slow; it had been done not rashly, but by rule and measure, 'at sundry times and in divers manners,' first one disclosure and then another, till the whole was brought into full manifestation. And thus room was made for the anticipation of further and deeper disclosures, of truth still under the veil of the letter, and in their season to be revealed. The visible world still remains without its divine interpretation; Holy Church in her sacraments and her hierarchical appointments, will remain even to the end of the world, only a symbol of those heavenly facts which fill eternity. Her mysteries are but the

expressions in human language of truths to which the human mind is unequal. It is evident how much there was in all this in correspondence with the thoughts which had attracted me when I was young, and with the doctrine which I have already connected with the <u>Analogy</u> and the <u>Christian Year</u>.[86]

Included in this remarkably consistent image was a belief that angels were not only the ministers of the Jewish and Christian dispensations but also the agents responsible for the elementary principles of the universe, the laws of nature, or what Newman called the "Economy of the Visible World."[87]

And that there is such an invisible world, ". . . Scripture tells us."[88] Newman argued that the appropriate image of this world, as contained in Scripture, represents the world not on its natural but on its supernatural side. While Newman's views regarding the sufficiency of Scripture in itself underwent change, he maintained a belief that revelation, whatever the relative importance of its various media, offered the authoritative picture of the world. The peculiar nature of revelation is that it views providence in its complete fulfillment or total design rather than simply in the measure of fulfillment which it has at a given time in history. "All accidents are excluded, when He speaks; the present and the to come, delays and failures, vanish before the thought of His perfect work."[89]

Many of Newman's sermons concentrated on this distinction of the invisible and the visible worlds. He explained:

. . . how different are the character and effect of the Scripture notices of the structure of the physical world, from those which philosophers deliver. I am not deciding whether or not the one and the other are reconcilable; I merely say their respective <u>effect</u> is different. And when we have deduced what we deduce by our reason from the study of visible nature, and then read what we read in His inspired word, and find the two apparently discordant, <u>this</u> is the feeling I think we ought to have on our minds;-- not an impatience to do what is beyond our powers, to weigh evidence, balance, decide, and reconcile, to arbitrate between the two voices of God,--but a sense of the utter nothingness of worms such as we are; of our plain and absolute incapacity to contemplate things <u>as they really are</u>; a perception of our emptiness, before the great Vision of God. . . .[90]

In short, Newman declared: "We are then in a world of spirits, as well as in a world of sense, and we hold communion with it, and take part in it, though we are not conscious of doing so."[91]

What I need to make clear at this point, however, is

that Newman's imagery should not be taken to imply that he held
a philosophical position akin to that one usually attributed to
Bishop Berkeley. Newman himself wrote:

> As to Berkeley, I do not know enough to talk, but it seems
> to me, while a man holds the moral governance of God as
> <u>existing in and through</u> his <u>conscience</u>, it matters not
> whether he believes his senses or not. For at least he
> will hold the external world as a <u>divine</u> intimation, a scene
> of trial whether a reality or not. . . . I conceive Hume
> denied conscience, Berkeley confessed it. To what extent
> Berkeley denied the existence of the external world, I
> am not aware; nor do I mean to go so far myself (far from
> it) as to deny the existence of matter. . . .[92]

The importance of the distinction then seems to be to establish
a priority, not that the material world does not exist but
that its existence is dependent on another world and power than
itself.

The Christian then must keep this picture of the world,
as it really is in God, before himself at all times. To do so
is to realize the secrecy of divine action in the world and the
danger that the visible world poses to our spiritual interests.[93]
To do so is to enter into a kind of warfare with the world
because of one's concern for the welfare of his soul now and
in the future when the invisible world is fully revealed.
Newman argued that:

> To understand that we have souls, is to feel our separation
> from things visible, our independence of them, our distinct
> existence in ourselves, our individuality, our power of
> acting for ourselves this way or that way, our accountable-
> ness for what we do.[94]

In the light of this picture, one becomes aware of his place in
God's great system of providence which, though secret now, will
reach its fulfillment. In that complete revelation, God's
action will be manifest and man's actions will receive their
just rewards as the illusory stabilities and false securities
of this world fade away.[95]

<u>Tokens of the invisible in the visible.</u> Even presently,
however, said Newman, there is evidence of the invisible world
in the visible one. Newman urged that ". . . tokens of Omnipotence are all around us, in the world of matter, and in the
world of man; in the dispensation of nature, and in the dispensation of grace."[96] He noted that we ". . . have been granted
Apostles, Prophets, Evangelists, pastors, and teachers. We
celebrate those true Festivals which the Jews possessed only in

shadow. For us Christ has died; on us the Spirit has descended."[97] Thus, the sacramental principle, the economy of God's dispensation, the incursion of the invisible world into the visible is evident in the testimony of conscience prior to revelation, uniquely in Christ and His Church, consequently in the sacraments and services of the Church and in the lives of the saints. Conscience provides some of the basic elements of a picture of the world that goes beyond immediate experience by suggesting the element of judgment and the existence of One who judges. To be aware of the testimony of conscience and of the image of the unseen world which it suggests is to desire knowledge of that unseen world and its Lord.[98]

God has not left man without trustworthy evidence of this unseen world. "Wonderful things had taken place, while the world seemed to go on as usual . . . . Herod went on in his career of sin, and having seen and put to death one prophet, hoped to see miracles from a second. They all viewed things as of this world . . . ."[99] In the meantime, the Son of God had humbled Himself in condescending to come into the world in the form of a servant and in the weakness and likeness of fallen man. The Son of the Lord of the invisible world became an offspring in the visible world. Newman returned to this theme or model for the incarnation in various ways but the essential elements relate to the basic image of the visible-invisible worlds: The Son of glory and of power in the invisible world became, out of His love for man, weak, hidden, and despised in the visible world in order to restore man to his original image and to bring him to life eternal.[100] Newman dwelt on Christ's sympathy for man's plight, His suffering, His crucifixion as evidence of the true nature of the world and its values.[101] Yet even in the midst of that revelation, the epiphany, the transfiguration, and the resurrection are manifestations of the glory of Christ as King over the visible world rather than as one defeated by it.[102]

There are two ways in which Christ's condescension and final exaltation aid men presently. First, the remembrance of that life gives man a pattern by which to live his own life and, thus, to prepare himself for meeting God. We have His "words and deeds, in order that we may have that on which to fix our eyes."[103] Christians ". . . are tried, and then they triumph;

they are humbled, and then are exalted. . . ."[104] Christians are ". . . bound to rise in spirit after His pattern."[105] Second, Christ is present, though not visibly so, through the power of the Holy Spirit.[106]

The Church is Christ's special dwelling place and the sacraments are His visible presence.[107] The world does not recognize the church for her true nature.

> It knows nothing . . . of that hidden life, of that faith, that love, that spirit of adoration, which is our incorporating principle. It knows nothing of His Divine Presence, who, when He left the earth visibly, told us that we should still possess Him, though the world would not. It has no experience of the operations of grace, of the efficacy of the Sacraments, of the power of prayer, of the virtue of holy relics, of the communion of Saints, of the glorious intercession of the Mother of God, and of the care and tenderness of the Guardian Angel.[108]

The world does not realize that the Church is "a visible image of Heaven . . . " on earth.[109] It does not recognize that "He has appeared to His Holy Church first of all, and in the Church he dispenses blessings, such as the world knows not of."[110] One aspect of that bestowal is the sacramental system of the Church by which ". . . a high invisible grace . . . [is] . . . lodged in an outward form. . . ."[111] Thus, the sacraments and sacred services of the Church are the means by which men may appropriate God's grace and by which they may grow in their spiritual lives as a preparation for life in the unseen world.[112]

Some of those justified in Christ are judged by the Church to have grown in grace to such an extent that they are called "saints." Though these individuals were born in sin and once lived in sin, grace has made them different. Men of the world, not recognizing that any power is able to overcome nature in this way, do not recognize the special importance of the saints.[113] But, members of the communion of the Church ". . . have a standard for their principles of conduct, and it is the image, the pattern of the Saints which forms it for them."[114] The saints serve as a special witness to the light of the unseen world of which they are servants. "They enlarge the mind with ideas it had not before, and they show to the multitude what God can do, and what man can be."[115]

The Christian and the man of the world. The dialectic of invisible and visible, church and world, sinner and saint continues on the level of the contrast between the man of the world and the Christian.[116] The religion of the man of the world is both a false security for him and a temptation to the man of faith. The religion of the man of the world is an attachment to the praise of other men and, thus, to self-importance; Christians are to act for the glory of God and to evidence self-denial.[117] The man of the world thinks it enough to know the precepts of religion without seriously applying them to his own life, choosing rather to continue to act according to custom, according to generally accepted standards of decent and refined behavior.[118] The Christian understands, on the other hand, that he must genuinely attempt to do what is commanded in such a way that he acts not in imitation of custom but from an awareness of his own sin and inadequacy and from the habit of obedience to Christ. In short, the man of the world lives essentially for and according to the standards of the visible world;[119] the Christian lives according to the image of an unseen world.[120]

The Christian realizes that this world is but the type of another, more basic and real world and that his life should be lived in separation from the standards and goals of this world and in accordance with the image of that invisible, yet ultimately real, world.[121] As Newman put it, ". . . nothing but a clear apprehension of things unseen, a simple trust in God's promises, and the greatness of mind thence arising, can make us act above the world . . . ."[122] To be a Christian is to live in reverence, that is, under the conviction of God's presence even though we do not see Him.[123] To be a Christian is to desire the end of this world and to be watching for the coming of Christ.[124]

> This then is to watch; to be detached from what is present, and to live in what is unseen; to live in the thought of Christ as He came once and as He will come again; to desire His second coming, from our affectionate and grateful remembrance of His first.[125]

Thus, Christians ". . . are but on pilgrimage . . ."[126] in this world to which they are "foreigners,"[127] "strangers and pilgrims"[128] and from which Christ is calling them to their home.[129]

Newman noted at least three general ways in which the Christian differs from the man of the world. In the first place, as I have been describing, the Christian has a picture

of the world which differs from that of the man of the world.
As such they account for the world, for events in it, and for
the lives and acts of men in very different ways. The picture
of the world generally held by men depends on some temporal
end, not necessarily selfish, but always temporal and of this
world. Consequently, in accounting for Christians, the man of
the world fails to understand them because he cannot, within
his picture of the world, allow for a motive that has its end
beyond this world. The religious picture of the world is hidden to his understanding, unseen by him.

> They do not know the ideas and motives which religion
> sets before that mind which it has made its own. They
> do not enter into them, or realize them, even when they
> are told them; and they do not believe that a man can be
> influenced by them, even when he professes them.[130]

Yet, said Newman, "only admit us [Christians] to believe what
we profess, and you [the world] will understand without difficulty what we are doing."[131] And it is this connection between
believing and doing and feeling that introduces the other two
areas of difference between the man of the world and the Christian.

First, as to the affections of the Christian, Newman
made some important distinctions regarding the nature of "religious emotion." Newman was fearful of "excited feelings" lest
one substitute them for the Christian life. In the case of
such a substitution, one assumes that to be ". . . agitated is
to be religious . . . " so that one indulges himself in feelings
for their own sake. He is found to be ". . . resting in them
as if they were engaged in a religious exercise, and boasting
of them as if they were an evidence of their own exalted
spiritual state; not using them (the one only thing they ought
to do), using them as an incitement to _deeds_ of love, mercy,
truth, meekness, holiness."[132] For Newman, ". . . there is an
immeasurable distance between feeling right and doing right."[133]
Thus, one must not mistake transient emotion for the Christian
life. Nevertheless, noted Newman, the aim of all religious
instruction is to involve the affections in one's religion.
Such a training of the affections, however, based on that perfect or sound state of mind

> . . . which the Holy Spirit imparts, is a deliberate preference of God's service to every thing else, a determined
> resolution to give up all for Him; and a love for Him, not
> tumultuous and passionate, but such love as a child bears

toward his parents, calm, full, reverent, contemplative, obedient.[134]

Excited emotions may or may not accompany such a state of mind, for they are accidents natural only to some men and not to be cultivated or prized in and for themselves as an essential part of faith. In fact, such feelings can be dangerous as they may supplant true faith and lead to self-deception. These judgments represent Newman's criticisms of Evangelicalism.

On the other hand, Newman did point to the need for affections which do not come and go but become habits fixed in one's life by the power of faith.[135] Such habits result not from direct concentration on one's inner state, but through one's concentration on the "view of God in Christ" and the aim to obey Him.[136] The ideal state of mind is one free from tumult, anxiety, and excitement and one under the rule of faith. In this regard, the life of Jesus Christ is the supreme example of such tranquility.[137] The basic characteristic of this state of mind or of this set of affective habits is self-denial. The centrality of this quality is significant evidence of the connection which Newman made between the affections and action. This attitude is basic both to the affective life and to the active or moral life of the Christian.

The basic affections of faith involve a sense of one's dependence upon the Unseen God.[138] Such dependence arouses feelings both of fear and of love.

> We cannot understand Christ's mercies till we understand His power, His glory, His unspeakable holiness, and our demerits, that is, until we first fear Him. Not that fear comes first, and then love; for the most part they will proceed together. Fear is allayed by the love of Him, and our love sobered by our fear of Him.[139]

That sense of dependence on God is brought to mind by self-denial or the recognition that, without God's assistance, one is unable to do what he ought. According to Newman, self-denial is the test of religious earnestness.[140]

> This then is one of the first elements of Christian knowledge and a Christian spirit, to refer all that is good in us, all that we have of spiritual life and righteousness to Christ our Saviour; to believe that He works in us, or, to put the same thing more pointedly, to believe that saving truth, life, light, and holiness are not _of_ us, though they must be _in_ us.[141]

To change one's heart from self-satisfaction and self-gratification to self-denial is to "unlearn the love of the world" by a "thwarting of our natural wishes and tastes."[142]

Thus, the basic imagery of the dual reference operates on this level also. Newman suggested that self-denial is a denial of the self which the world offers and seeks to impose on man. The denial itself offers the possible realization of that self which the pattern of the life of the man from heaven suggests and which the grace of the unseen God seeks to impress on our lives. Self-denial is also the basis for love of one's fellow man.[143] To know one's own nature as a sinner but as redeemed is to recognize one's essential brotherhood with all man.[144] Whereas the man of the world weighs differences and advantages in relation to other men, the Christian sees basic similarities.

The duality of fear and love is the explanation of the peculiar quality of those other basic Christian affections, joy and peace. The belief on which their peculiar quality rests is that one's good lies with God even if one be guilty of sin. This conviction results in

> . . . the combined feeling that God loves us yet punishes us, that we are in His favour, yet are under, or may be brought under His rod; the feeling of mingled hope and fear, of suspense, of not seeing our way, yet having a general conviction that God will bring us on it, if we trust to Him.[145]

The world cannot understand how such sorrow and pain can be endured without gloom. Such an ignorance rests on a failure to recognize the two worlds basic to the Christian picture of reality. Because self-confident men do not know their hearts and do not recognize an unseen world, they cannot see reasons for being dissatisfied with themselves; they do not fear God. Others who lack such confidence may fear Him and yet not recognize the mercies of that unseen world that allow love.[146] The Christian both rejoices in the grace of God and the sense of peace which it brings, and also remembers and repents of his sins lest God should remember them. Self-denial forbids confidence in absolute forgiveness or holiness; confidence in God forbids despair and gloom. Holding to some view of purgatory, Newman argued that the Christian can rejoice in punishment which comes to him in this life as being better than that which would come in the next.[147]

Thus, the Christian concentrates on that next, unseen world; he is a stranger in this world in which he sees no need

to establish himself nor of which he deems it necessary to
demand unmixed blessing. The Christian manifests a certain
indifference to the course of human affairs and to his place
in them.[148] That is not to say that the Christian has no joy
in the present blessings of this life, for the

> . . . true Christian rejoices in these earthly things which give joy, but in such a way as not to care for them when they go.[149]

A Christian is to be grateful for the enjoyment of life's
pleasures as they come to him, but he is not to seek them
earnestly. To seek them is childish for one who has a higher
view of things. Religious joy is a function of humility and
not of what the world esteems. In this sense, one can be
joyful even in obscure circumstances which the world scorns.[150]
One can be at peace in the most troubled and tumultuous times.[151]
"There is an inward world into which they enter who come near
to Christ, though to men in general they seem the same as
before."[152] This joy and peace stem from the awareness that
one's life is open to God in whose dealings with us we can
have confidence.[153]

As I have already suggested, however, self-denial should
never be construed to involve a state of mind only. For, no
matter how important certain affections, they are never to be
cultivated or even contemplated apart from obedient action.
Such obedient action is both ritual and moral. As to ritual
obedience, Newman urged that

> . . . we may as well expect that the spirits of men might be seen by us without the intervention of their bodies, as suppose that the object of faith can be realized in a world of sense and excitement, without the instrumentality of an outward form to arrest and fix attention, to stimulate the careless, and to encourage the desponding.[154]

In this sense, ". . . the forms of devotion are parts of devotion."[155] By these observances, one acts over again and
celebrates the history of Christ.[156] Such regular acts of
devotion allow one to see continually ". . . the skirts of
powers and providences beyond this world . . . " and exposes
one to invisible influences.[157] Daily prayer, the public
services of the Church, and the Eucharist are the means of
hidden grace which sustain one's spiritual life in the midst
of this world.[158] Also these ritual devotions are a means of
the preparation of affection and thought for one's future
sight of God. These ordinances are ". . . anticipations and

first-fruits of that sight of Him which one day must be."[159]

Yet, Newman realized that such ritual devotion can become a substitute for other duties since it is its completeness and tangible form which is likely to satisfy one.[160] Newman advised that a certain care be exercised, but he also warned that excessive fear regarding such a possibility is not characteristic of faith in the God who commanded these observances. Attempting to do one's whole duty--ritual and moral--is the remedy for religious perplexity. "When we set about to obey God, in the ordinary business of daily life, we are at once interested by realities which withdraw our minds from vague fears and uncertain indefinite surmises about the future."[161] Nevertheless, said Newman, there is a clear distinction between conscientious obedience and Christian obedience. In the first case, a man uses religion as a corrective or restraint on his attachment to the world, judging it sufficient to have a sort of moderate love of the world and, consequently, moderate avarice, ambition, selfishness.[162] The Christian character, however, is not merely a superior kind of worldly character but a new character by which the sufficiency and the curse of the law are overcome in Christ.[163] Christ is a Master to whom the Christian is strictly subjected; yet, at the same time, Christ makes us righteous or obedient through the presence of the Holy Spirit in us.[164]

This lengthy description of the various ways in which the image of an invisible world imposes itself on the thought and the life of the Christian illustrates the manner in which Newman understood the mind to be drawn in a particular direction and to be formed in a particular way in those who embraced it in belief.[165] For those who did not share that belief or that picture

> . . . one season is the same as another, and they take no account of any. Feast-day and fast-day, holy tide and other tide, are one and the same to them. Hence they do not realize the next world at all. To them the Gospels are but like another history; a course of events which took place eighteen hundred years since. They do not make our Saviour's life and death present to them; they do not transport themselves back to the time of His sojourn on earth. They do not act over again, and celebrate His history, in their own observance; and the consequence is, that they feel no interest in it. They have neither faith nor love towards it; it has no hold on them. They do not form their estimate of things upon it; they do not hold

it as a sort of practical principle in their heart.[166]

Thus, the wellspring for motivation and coherence in the exercise of the Christian life is the image or picture which forms the basis of his estimate of things and serves as a practical principle molding his affections and guiding his actions. It should be emphasized, however, that Newman concluded that ". . . it is . . . the things believed, not the act of believing them, which is peculiar to religion."[167] Newman warned that one must not make the test of being religious to consist in a spiritual state of the heart to ". . . the comparative neglect of the Object from which it must arise. . . ."[168] Of course, his understanding of the role of a picture itself indicates the emphasis which he placed on an external factor or control in religious belief. Nevertheless, the use of the categories of the imagination and of "picture" still does not account adequately for what he wanted to claim about the content of the Christian faith.[169]

III. EXPLICATING THE FAITH: THE CONTEXT OF GOD'S REVELATION AND CHRISTIAN THEOLOGY

Newman was explicit in his awareness of the limitations of an analysis of Christian faith in terms of the imagination. He warned that the vividness of the apprehension of an image was no assurance of the existence of the object represented by the image. To assume that such vividness did give this kind of assurance would mean that the ". . . imagination usurps the functions of reason."[170] He also warned that, in relation to a theological claim, ". . . it is no argument to assert that those who discern it do discern it, though those who do not discern it do not."[171] No matter how serious the devotion of the believer, he must always recall: "As well can there be filial love without the fact of a father, as devotion without the fact of a Supreme Being."[172] His statements in his *Apologia* summarize his understanding of this matter:

> From the age of fifteen, dogma has been the fundamental principle of my religion: I know no other religion; I cannot enter into the idea of any sort of religion; religion, as a mere sentiment, is to me a dream and a mockery.[173]

Despite several changes in his understanding of the locus of authority, or more correctly, in his understanding of the relationships between the loci of authority in Christianity, Newman remained convinced that objective authority, reality and cognitivity were the necessary basis of faith. A second way in which this conviction manifested itself, beyond that of the limitations imposed on the influence of the imagination, was Newman's equally decided limitations on the role of the implicit reasoning which, in his view, characterized religious inquiry. In this case, he pointed out that *fides acquisita* did not account for the character of Christian faith as *fides divina*.

Newman referred to the dogmatic character of the Christian faith in the introduction to the last chapter of the *Grammar*. There he concluded that Christian faith involves the recognition that

> . . . the Gospel Revelation is divine, and that it carries with it the evidence of its divinity . . . it is a definite message from God to man directly conveyed by his chosen instruments, and to be received as such a message; and therefore to be positively acknowledged, embraced and maintained as true, on the ground of its being divine, not as true on intrinsic grounds, not as probably true, or partially true, but as absolutely certain knowledge, certain in a sense in which nothing else can be certain, because it comes from Him who can neither deceive nor be deceived.[174]

By "dogma," Newman meant to indicate ". . . supernatural truths irrevocably committed to human language, imperfect because it is human, but definitive and necessary because given from above."[175] My purpose in this section is to analyze what elements he took that Gospel to involve as a definite message and in what ways he took it to be true in so categorical a way.

My survey of the Newman literature has already given us the necessary clues for isolating these matters and some of the means for understanding Newman's view of them. I noted Newman's emphasis on the distinctive character of the Christian Gospel. He warned against the use of formal reason or the use of a material reason from another discipline, in particular science, in analyzing and evaluating Christianity. He called for a material reason attentive to the peculiarities of content, of rules, and of evidence in the Christian dispensation. This call involved two important corollaries: one, the analysis of the peculiar content of revelation and the method of its transmission; two, the analysis of the nature of theological reason or investigation.

Regarding the first corollary, Newman emphasized the

fact that the transmission of the Christian revelation had its birth in the testimony of the Apostles. That testimony reveals that the fabric of Christian truth is interwoven with miracles and other evidential elements, with established rules of interpretation and usage, and with central concepts. As a second corollary, the responsibility of the theologian is to attend to this testimony in order to grasp the meaning of given aspects of the revelation and in order to understand the way in which the truth of that revelation is made known. As testimony, the Christian revelation is a system given with its own criteria of meaning and of truth; as such, it is a matter open to unlimited inquiry. The Creeds were formulated to prevent vain speculations, to make clear pronouncements regarding issues of meaning and truth. As keeper and interpreter of the Scriptures and the Creeds, the Church is an authority in matters of faith.

Newman understood the characteristic attitude of the Christian in relation to the revelation to be obedience, evidenced most directly in a reception of the testimony of the Apostles in faith. The ultimate reason for this obedience is that the author of the revelation and the architect of its structure is God whom no one should question. Such unquestioning obedience to the authority of God and of His message, though the characteristic response of the Christian, does not preclude another equally appropriate response, namely, the natural tendency of the mind that results in the explication of the meaning of and the grounds for the truth of the revelation both in its separate parts and in its totality. Theology involves understanding what has been made known, how it has been made known, and why one is warranted in claiming it to have been made known.

The discipline of theology, unlike religious inquiry, does not question that the revelation has indeed been made known. The possibility of the enterprise depends on the attentiveness of the theologian to the testimony which he has received as a member of the Church and not on his personal ingenuity. Newman was particularly concerned that theologians avoid a false systematization or reduction of the testimony that would obscure the full and complete character of the revelation. Attention to revelation did not mean, for Newman, that all mysteries can be dispelled and that all elements of the revelation can be made immediately powerful as a practical force in one's life. Theology is a science which has truth as its object, truth not in itself reducible or even always apprehensible in terms of its moral or affective impact on the life of the individual believer. Thus, what is the case about God and His revelation, what makes real assent a possibility is not itself dependent on real assent. In fact, some elements of the Creed such as the doctrine of the Trinity are not even a possibility for real assent. One gives a notional assent to them on the basis of the authority of the testimony which demands them.

What I propose to undertake in this section is a closer examination of the two matters introduced above: the mode of the transmission of authoritative revelation and the character of proper reflection upon that revelation. In relation to these matters, Newman was no longer talking about coming to faith, the illative sense, or a cumulation of probabilities; he is not describing the role of a certain picture dominating the imagination in the Christian life as an interpretative, behavioral, and passional guide. For him, explicating the faith involves dogmas which have been subjected to the test of agreement with scripture and to the protection of the church's authority in religious matters.

In the _Development of Christian Doctrine_, he expressed his understanding of this matter by claiming that "a revelation is not given, if there be no authority to decide what it is that is given."[176] Since he felt that an invidious private judgment was associated with any principle of the sole authority of the Bible, Newman argued that the content of the faith could be secured against error only by the teaching authority of the Holy See. Creed, tradition, and ecclesiastical authority guard and develop the truths of dogma which are themselves grounded in Scripture. It was this authority that Newman had in mind when he claimed that ". . . religion cannot maintain its ground at all without theology" and that ". . . devotion falls back upon dogma."[177]

The function of the discourse of dogma or authority has a primacy in relation to the other two functions under discussion without, however, reducing the other two to itself.

In fact, Newman showed how an undue concern with the explication of the faith can lead one from appropriating and exercising faith. Nevertheless, the question of the meaning and truth of the faith is not to be left to the discussion of <u>fides</u> <u>acquisita</u>, that is, to the individual's personal acceptance of the Creed as true and binding for him. Newman wanted to describe in what sense the Creed is, for the lack of a better description, "objectively" true. Pailin makes a helpful distinction in this regard:

> It [the word "certainty"] is used 'subjectively' when it refers to our unreserved commitment to a proposition while it is used 'objectively' when it expresses the fact that something is true, whatever people may think about it.[178]

Newman himself made this kind of distinction:

> We must distinguish between a revelation and a reception of it, not between its earlier and later stages. A revelation in itself divine, and guaranteed as such, may from first to last be received, doubted, argued against, perverted, rejected, by individuals according to the state of mind of each. . . . It is no objection then to the idea of a peremptory authority, such as I am supposing, that it lessens the task of personal inquiry unless it be an objection to the authority of Revelation altogether.[179]

What I need to explore is how Newman understood that objectivity and authority of revelation.

The Loci of Authority

Newman obviously assumed that an explicit and describable revelation had been given. From an early emphasis on the sufficiency of Scripture in isolating that revelation, through an emphasis on the role of tradition, he finally moved to an emphasis on the authority of the Church and of the Pope as the earthly representatives of the authority of God. The isolation of the loci of authority for Newman is no easy matter. The loci which I have isolated are not to be considered an exhaustive list, though they certainly seem to be some of the most important. One could include the locus of religious experience discussed as a factor in religious inquiry and in the life of faith if the proper provisos are made clear regarding its limitations and possible exaggerations. Since these matters are discussed at length in the first two sections of this chapter, I shall not repeat them here.

<u>Scripture.</u> Although he did not hold to the sufficiency

of Scripture in itself to reveal Christian dogma for any great
part of his life, Newman was concerned throughout his life
with the nature of the inspiration of Scripture as the initial,
though not the sole, element in an understanding of the authority of Christian truth. Inspiration of Scripture implied, for
Newman, that God Himself is its main author, making use of
human writers as His organs or instruments. Scripture then
involves that economy of divine wisdom and truth which is most
definitely instanced in the incarnation. Jaak Seynaeve writes
about Newman's view in this regard:

> The Bible is in the strictest sense of the word a reli-
> gious, that is, a divine and supernatural work, for it
> comes from God, tends to God and has Almighty God as its
> subject-matter. However, as the Bible has not been given
> to angels but to men, it is adapted to human capacities
> and human nature.[180]

The unity of Scripture is a function of its every part
being, as it were, from God's point of view, or from the view
of His providence. As an economical revelation, however, the
successive providential disclosures anticipate by type the
full end of that revelation. Newman had full awareness of the
promise-fulfillment motif that characterizes the unity of the
two testaments through typology and prophecy. Newman also
argued for the essential uniformity of New Testament teachings
despite the obvious peculiarities of separate books. The
unifying element in both respects, for Newman, is Christ as
anticipated in the Old Testament and as the constant object
of reflection in the New Testament.

Seynaeve has argued that Newman's emphasis on the
economical or sacramental character of Scripture tempted him
to emphasize the mystical sense of the text as against the
literal.[181] Whatever the critical judgment on that question,
what is clear is that Newman felt that Scripture had some one
definite sense, sometimes literally put, sometimes not. The
reader of Scripture is dependent on tradition and Church
authority for the authoritative interpretation of that one
sense. In his <u>Lectures on Justification</u>, Newman made his view
clear:

> I say, then, that the words of Scripture, as of every other
> book, have their own meaning, which must be sought in
> order to be found. . . . The words of Scripture were
> appropriated to their respective senses by their <u>writers</u>;
> they had a meaning before we approached them, and <u>they</u>
> will have that same meaning, whether we find it out or not.

> And our business is to find the real meaning, not to impose what will serve for a meaning.[182]

Private judgment is not sufficient.[183] Objective, external rules guide the reception of Divine revelation. Argument from context only shows what Scripture may mean; argument from antiquity and its authority shows what it does mean.[184]

Tradition. Günter Biemer asserts regarding Newman's view of tradition:

> His reflections on revelation as the legacy of the Apostles, as truth transmitted to be preserved and handed on, brought up the problem of faith in the form of tradition with the question of how the historical nature of tradition affected the transmission of the doctrine of Jesus Christ.[185]

Although Newman's early experiences as a Christian were primarily a matter of adherence to <u>sola scriptura</u>, his experiences as a fellow of Oriel College soon brought the issue of tradition to the fore in his personal development as a religious thinker. In the <u>Apologia</u> he tells us what he learned at this point:

> . . . the sacred text was never intended to teach doctrine, but only to prove it, and that, if we would learn doctrine, we must have recourse to the formularies of the Church; for instance to the Catechism and to the Creed . . . after learning from them the doctrines of Christianity, the inquirer must verify them by Scripture.[186]

Thus Newman came to take for granted the existence of a tradition given fixed and unaltered expression in the Creeds of the Church. Such a view did not, however, mean that he impugned the Scripture; he simply assigned tradition a role in addition to, but inseparable from, that of Scripture. As Biemer concludes in his monograph studying Newman's view of tradition, Newman's principles in understanding the relationship between the two were: ". . . scripture contains particulars which were not taken over by tradition, and tradition contains truths which do not lie on the surface of scripture."[187] In that sense, Newman never held tradition to be an additional source of revelation. Scripture presents the whole of revelation in the midst of a multitude of detail; tradition, as the life of the universal Church throughout the ages, hands over the whole tradition faithfully to each succeeding generation of Christians.[188]

What Newman did give up was his confidence in the formula of St. Vincent of Lerins, i.e., <u>Quod semper</u>, <u>quod ubique</u>, <u>quod ab omnibus</u>. He could not maintain confidence in what increasingly seemed to him a sterile and mechanical repetition. In "Lectures on the Prophetical Office of the Church" (1837), he came to distinguish episcopal tradition or that unchanging and unadulterated element to which Vincent's formula testified and prophetical tradition or that changing, corruptible element of the Church that displays its searching, lively investigation into faith.[189] In this way, Newman was struggling toward the formulation of a notion of doctrinal development that did justice both to the element of constancy in the object of faith and the historical reality of the system of ideas that have come to be known as Christian doctrine. As the Church has responsibility to preserve the revelation entrusted to it by the Apostles, she also has a duty to meditate upon that revelation. That reflection must, however, be in accordance with Scripture.

Church. At the beginning of the chain of tradition which goes back to Christ Himself are the Apostles, the founders of the Church on its human side. Since their inspired reception of revelation, revelation has not been altered. The transmission of doctrine has been guaranteed by apostolic succession. Undue emphasis on apostolic succession as preserved in the sacrament of ordination must be tempered by Newman's observation that the whole body of the faithful are responsible for the faithfulness of the Church to the depositum fidei. Sometimes the laity are led to exercise this responsibility in the presence of clerical irresponsibility.[190] Nevertheless, Newman did place special emphasis on the role of Bishops in the preservation of doctrinal authority in the Church ". . . apart from that of the infallible magisterium of the pope, in which, however, they have a certain share."[191] They are authorities not as judges of revelation but as the authorized keepers, guardians, and teachers of the divine word. Even more, when the bishops are gathered in council and in union with the pope, under the guidance of the Holy Spirit, they have the depositum fidei before them in such fullness and clarity that they can make appropriate decisions in relation to it. The authority of the Church and her ministers, even that of the Pope, never goes beyond the deposit of faith contained in Scripture and made explicit by explanation and development in tradition.[192]

Newman wrote:

> The Church's infallibility is wholly ministrative to the
> depositum . . . and does not exist except as far as she
> is custos, testis, judex, magistra depositi.[193]

Nevertheless, Newman did hold that the existence of a living, supreme authority with the power of final judgment on such matters was necessary if the transmission is to have absolute, objective validity. Although I cannot develop this topic fully within the limits of this study, one should be aware that Newman was opposed throughout his life to extreme statements or positions regarding the infallibility of the pope. In his Anglican career, he clearly favored a view of the indefectibility of the Church as opposed to the infallibility of the Church or of the pope.[194] Even in the days immediately preceding Vatican I, he held that the doctrine of papal infallibility was only a theological opinion and not a dogma, an opinion that must be "fenced round and limited by conditions."[195]

Newman was particularly concerned that the efforts of some representatives to Vatican I did not give due consideration to proper discussion and reflection and only to devotion. He wrote to Bishop Ullathorne on January 28, 1870, declaring:

> I look with anxiety at the prospect of having to defend
> decisions which may not be difficult to my private judgment,
> but may be most difficult to defend logically in the face
> of historical fact. What have we done to be treated as
> the Faithful never were treated before? When has definition
> of doctrine de fide been a luxury of devotion and not a
> stern painful necessity?[196]

The pain with which he viewed the matter is evident in this sentence from a letter to a staunch opponent of the definition, a Dr. Moriarty, Bishop of Kerry: "If it be God's will that some definition in favour of the Pope's infallibility is passed, I then should at once submit--but up to that very moment I shall pray most heartily and earnestly against it."[197] Or, in another letter, he wrote: "When it is actually done, I will accept it as His act, but, till then, I will believe it impossible."[198] When the definition was passed, Newman was pleased at what he considered its moderation in the light of the intentions of the Ultramontanists, but he added ". . . that is, if the doctrine in question is to be defined at all."[199] Newman was particularly distressed by the increased centralization which he felt the decree would lead to and by the difficulties which it raised for Catholic apologists.[200] Newman's

"Letter to the Duke of Norfolk," written in response to Gladstone's attack on the definition, reveals more clearly than anything else the conditions which Newman finally judged to permit his submission to the definition.

In that letter Newman established the norm that ". . . to determine . . . what is meant by the infallibility of the Pope we must turn first to consider the infallibility of the Church. And again, to determine the character of the Church's infallibility, we must consider what is the characteristic of Christianity, considered as a revelation of God's will."[201] In a summary fashion, Newman set forth the understanding of revelation and tradition which we have reviewed above. God willed both the Gospel as a public and fixed deposit and the Church as its means of transmission, preservation, and protection. And, claimed Newman,

> . . . the proposition defined will be without any claim to be considered binding on the belief of Catholics, unless it is referable to the Apostolic depositum, through the channel either of Scripture or Tradition; and, though the Pope is the judge whether it is so referable or not, yet the necessity of his professing to abide by this reference is in itself a certain limitation of his dogmatic action.[202]

In fact, in consequence of this kind of limitation, Newman felt that the extent of doctrinal matters involved to be quite limited. Beyond these limited matters, open investigation and opinion are freely allowed.[203] And, within these limits, he seemed to have viewed papal authority as a negative authority guarding the original deposit by placing a check on excesses and incautious, overly rapid developments in Catholic theology while not preventing legitimate exercises of reflection.[204]

Considering all that Newman wrote on the question of the authority of the Church and of the Pope, his essential claim seems well summarized by Wilfrid Ward:

> The claim for Christianity is at its strongest as exhibited, not in the reasoning of a single mind, but in the life and thought of the Church as a whole and from the beginning. The individual member of the Church participates in thought and life larger and deeper than his own.[205]

God. The ultimate authority of which Scripture, tradition, and Church are all sacraments and ministers, however, is God. His sacramental presence in His Son initiated the witness of the Apostles and the gift of the Holy Spirit both founded the Church and now guides her in her life in the world.

Specifically the Holy Spirit guarantees the Church's faithfulness to the Divine Word.[206] The Holy Spirit first "inspired the Holy Evangelists to record the life of Christ and directed them" and "next . . . commented upon these, and unfolded their meaning in the Apostolic Epistles."[207] The Holy Spirit likewise guides attempts to understand what has been given in revelation so that, by His help, the truth brought by Christ is handed on, collected, and interpreted in a faithful and helpful way.[208]

In understanding this mode of transmission, one should understand how the revelation witnessed to by the Apostles as an objective, miraculous fact still maintains the uncorrupted objectivity of the witness. On the human side, that objectivity is guaranteed by an uncorrupted transmission of the witness in the Church and by means of the authoritative instrumentality of laity and clergy. On the divine side, one is led to recognize that this human authority has its ultimate authority in the One who reveals. God through His Son is the source of the testimony and through His Holy Spirit is its preserver. That divine authority constitutes the "objective religion" which Newman sought to define over against rationalism and other subjective interpretations.

His concern for defining that authority should not be limited to his years as a Roman Catholic. The direction of his thought throughout his life pointed toward an objective authority as the security of the believer. His own personal flirtations with rationalism and evangelicalism were rejected long before the ardent reflections of the Tractarian period with their intense efforts to illumine the nature of objective religion. The locus of authority was not always placed similarly by Newman, but there is more continuity in that respect than many interpreters have seen. In an accurate sense, his conversion was motivated by his having found what he considered to be the proper locus for the kind of authority that he had always felt was necessary for the viability of the Christian faith.

The Nature of Theological Reflection

Newman's concern for objective religion has one other primary aspect, namely, reflection upon the meaning and truth of the revelation which has been given. After having given a description of the manner in which revelation comes to man, he recognized that the question of its truth and meaning could still be raised. His description of the mode of transmission has important consequences for his conclusions regarding this second question, but that description does not resolve all the kinds of questions which an investigation of the Christian faith involves.

In order to understand the province of this second concern, perhaps I should consider more carefully the nature of investigation in contrast to the character of inquiry which I explored above. I noted that Newman devoted most of his attention in the *Grammar of Assent* to a description of religious inquiry or the nature of implicit reasoning in those who come to have faith. Newman described inquiry in this way:

> . . . an act of the intellect, direct, absolute, complete in itself, unconditional, arbitrary, yet not incompatible with an appeal to argument, and at least in many cases exercised unconsciously. On this last characteristic of assent I have not insisted, as it has not come in my way; nor is it more than an accident of acts of assent, though an ordinary accident . . . those assents which we give with a direct knowledge of what we are doing, are few compared with the multitude of like acts which pass through our minds in long succession without our observing them.[209]

Nevertheless, despite their relative scarcity, "complex" or conscious and deliberate assents are natural to man. These complex assents involve the inferring of a proposition while assenting to it without doubt as to its truth at the same time.

Inference, said Newman, is not only the usual antecedent of assent but also the usual concomitant of assent after assenting.[210] Newman claimed, for this reason, that it is possible to look at a proposition either as an assent or as an inference, i.e., under two different aspects. These two views are not contradictory because they are indeed aspects. Newman continued:

> Therefore to set about concluding a proposition is not *ipso facto* to doubt its truth; we may aim at inferring a proposition, while all the time we assent to it . . . . We may employ ourselves in proving what we already believe to be true, simply in order to ascertain the producible evidence in its favour, and in order to fulfill what is due to ourselves and to the claims of responsibilities of our education and social position.[211]

Newman carefully distinguished this kind of investigation from the kind of inquiry which leads to assent. Inquiry is inconsistent with faith because, as prior to assent, it implies that one is still in doubt as to what the truth of the matter under inquiry is. Newman concluded: "We cannot without absurdity call ourselves at once believers and inquirers also."[212] Though inquiry implies doubt, investigation does not and ". . . those who assent to a doctrine or fact may without inconsistency investigate its credibility, though they cannot literally inquire about its truth."[213] In fact, Newman understood investigation to be both an obligation and a necessity in the case of educated individuals. No doubt, admitted Newman, such investigation can possibly result in a reversal of one's beliefs, but such a possibility does not interfere with the honesty and firmness of one's belief by itself. He pointed out that:

> To incur a risk is not to expect reverse; and if my opinions are true, I have a right to think that they will bear examining. Nor, on the other hand, does belief, viewed in its idea, imply a positive resolution in the party believing never to abandon that belief. What belief, as such, does imply is, not an intention never to change, but the utter absence of all thought, or expectation, or fear of changing. A spontaneous resolution never to change is inconsistent with the idea of belief; for the very force and absoluteness of the act of assent precludes any such resolution. We do not commonly determine not to do what we cannot fancy ourselves ever doing.[214]

To investigate, then, is not to doubt.

On the other hand, to investigate is a second-order activity, not directed by real assent to a reality designated by a proposition and controlling our actions and affections through our imagination and the objects before it. Such reflex activity is notional or intellectual in character. It represents the positive function of theology which I isolated in the previous chapter:

> . . . a simple assent need not be notional; but the reflex or confirmatory assent of certitude always is given to a notional proposition, viz. to the truth, necessity, duty, etc., of our assent to the simple assent and its proposition. Its predicate is a general term, and cannot stand for a fact, whereas the original proposition, included in it, may, and often does, express a fact.[215]

While Newman's understanding of the role of propositional terms may not be entirely adequate, the point of his distinction seems safely certain: Theological reflection constitutes a separate context from that of the normal exercise of Christian faith, though the formal context is more natural to some persons

than others. It is a second-order discipline not directly
operative in the Christian life, but indisputably a part of a
proper understanding of the relation of faith and reason within
the total reality of Christianity. In a word, Newman's claim
was that the reality of Christianity cannot be adequately
accounted for without considering the legitimate and necessary
role of investigation in the life of faith in the Church.

This investigation is important for at least two reasons.
First, investigation can settle disputes regarding the proper
meaning of given words, concepts, and doctrines. Such an issue
is resolved, for Newman, by an appeal to Scripture and tradition,
i.e., by an appeal to authority. Newman's investigative study
of the doctrines of the incarnation and of the Trinity in his
book on the Arians was based on the assumption that a clarity
regarding the teaching of the Fathers and of the ecumenical
councils will reveal the correct understanding of the issue.
Likewise his <u>Lectures on the Doctrine of Justification</u> involved
this same method of investigation. He described his procedure
in that book:

> I have been endeavoring to represent the Lutheran,
> or extreme Protestant idea of justifying faith in its
> <u>internal consistence</u>; to examine how its parts hang together,
> and how it disposes of objections which arise, apart from
> the arguments on which it rests.[216]

This description is a helpful indication of Newman's method of
clarifying the explicative meaning of Christian discourse. He
sought its internal consistency in Scripture and tradition so
as to illumine the proper place and meaning of a given piece
of Christian discourse in revelation. He did all these things
apart from giving arguments for the truth of the claims which
the discourse makes.

Yet Newman's understanding of the authority of testimony
regarding revelation is the foundation of his understanding of
theological method not only in resolving disputes over questions
of meaning but also in settling questions of truth. We have
already seen that, for Newman, religious inquiry need not
necessarily but may legitimately involve questions regarding
evidence for the truth of what one is considering for belief.
Likewise we have seen that the character of faith as a principle
of interpretation, action, and affection does not in that
respect involve any truth questions. Assent rests on the
adequacy of a picture to direct one's life. Truth, in its

theological relevance, is the object of complex assent or notional reflection on the object of faith. Above all, Newman wanted to maintain that some reflection can legitimately claim to be an instance of knowledge. That claim was one of the principal theses guiding his lectures on the nature of the university. In fact, those lectures contain the clue to Newman's understanding of the conditions of the truth of revelation: ". . . God Himself is the author as well as the subject of theology."[217]

Perhaps I can clarify the nature of Newman's understanding by utilizing a helpful distinction which Roderick Chisholm makes between "criteria of evidence" and "conditions of truth."[218] An appeal to "conditions of truth" in Christian discourse designates an appeal to those things which a Christian believes to be the case about God and man. This appeal is an appeal to Scripture, tradition, and Church pronouncement. Only the faith itself announces that God is Creator, that Christ was raised from the dead, and that God will be "all in all." The claim is that Christians hold these assertions of belief to be true, and, that if they can be shown to be false, Christians can no longer retain their faith.

But to appeal to conditions of truth in this way is to do nothing more than to refer to what has been written or to what has been said.[219] This kind of reasoning is clearly closely related to questions of meaning and, as such, is a very important element of reasoning about the Christian faith. In this mode of reasoning, one's arguments are made on the basis of principles of coherence and consistency. In relation to these principles, Christian discourse fulfills certain criteria of intelligibility based on its character as authoritative testimony. Appeal to authoritative sources seeks to settle disputes involving rival interpretations of elements of the faith. Reflection on testimony regarding the incarnation reveals the necessity for a Trinitarian faith. In many ways, rules of consistency, coherence, and implication as well as genuine development (the rules of which were explored in Newman's essay on development) reveal the conditions of truth for Christianity.

Once conditions of truth have been described and analyzed in this way, however, it is still in order to ask whether things

are as Christians take them to be. Explication of the internal
structure of the Christian faith does not sufficiently account
for the matters that concern one in an investigation of the
faith. As I pointed out above, to appeal to conditions of
truth in this way is to do nothing more than to refer to what
has been written or to what has been said. Criteria of evidence refer, however, not only to what Christians say but also
to how things are. Criteria of evidence in Christian discourse
designate those rules governing the relation of the content of
the faith to the scope of human experience. They are context
bound in that only the faith enunciates these criteria; they
are not derived from some external source; they are not neutral.
For Newman, to ascertain the criteria of evidence for the truth
of Christianity as well as the conditions of truth, Christians
appeal to authority. Newman concluded that: ". . . the Gospel
Revelation is divine, and that it carries with it the evidence
of its divinity . . . ."[220] Or, he said, in another place:
". . . the exhibition of credentials, that is, of evidence,
that it is what it professes to be, is essential to Christianity,
as it comes to us. . . . "[221]

The kinds of individual pieces of evidence which we
found to have force in religious inquiry also play a role in
theological investigation. I must emphasize again that Newman
would not allow that these *motiva credibilia* whether implicitly
present in inquiry or explicitly considered in theological
argument are the only element in faith as a matter of knowledge.
Newman suggested ". . . faith, in its theological sense,
includes a belief, not only in the thing believed, but also in
the ground of believing; that is, not only belief in certain
doctrines, but belief in them expressly because God has
revealed them. . . ."[222] That authority of God comes concretely
in the form of the authority of the Church witnessed to by her
notes of being a voice of God in the world.[223] In the final
analysis, however, the truth of Christianity is dependent on
the truthfulness of God in what He has done in the past, in
what He evidences of Himself through the Holy Spirit in the
present, and in what He will do in the end. This formal
aspect of theological faith is a function of the externality
and objectivity of God and of man's dependence on Him.

The nature of the faith and of theology is non-circular

or non-fideistic in that the criteria of evidence impel one to appeal to states of affairs, facts, and other "public" matters as implicit in its own conditions of truth. Newman wrote: "Let the doctrine of the Incarnation be true: is it not at once of the nature of a historical fact, and of a metaphysical?"[224] Owen Chadwick points out that Newman's understanding of Christian doctrine allows that historical inquiry could theoretically disprove Christian teaching.[225] The development of Christian doctrine through history can be studied according to the kinds of principles which Newman enunciated in the essay on development. Breaks or deliberate falsifications in that development bring the entire edifice of dogma and the authoritative transmission of dogma into question.

Nevertheless the nature of faith finally makes the certainty of the truth of the faith as *fides divina* dependent on the One who speaks of Himself. It is His presence in and through the loci of authority that constitutes their authority and in which "objective religion" finally and essentially consists. The certainty of the Christian depends not on the level of his feelings, the perspicacity and cogency of his arguments, but on the effective action and being of God. The frame of Christian discourse is not a function of certain human goals or needs but of the authority of God.

Newman did not believe that the transition from religious inquiry to religious faith, i.e., conversion, could be described; one can only wait on the grace of God to bridge that gap. The use of the Christian picture of the world is not, by itself, a satisfactory justification for the Church despite its possible sufficiency for a given individual to whose life that use brings sustenance and order; the Church must also give attention to *justificatio cognitionis*. Appeals to scripture and tradition make no sense as mechanical adherence to accepted forms and dogmas; one must hear the voice of God speaking to him through these sources. Newman's words are definite:

> . . . the absolute and perfect certitude of Divine faith does not appeal to ratiocination or to human *motiva*, but simply to this one fact, that God, the eternal Truth, has spoken, who can neither deceive nor be deceived.[226]

Newman understood Christian discourse to have these separate contexts of use, i.e., these separate functions. My analyses of these functions are not different descriptions of the same context of use or of the same use; they are descriptions of various contexts in which Christian discourse functions. Because I have dealt with different contexts and different uses, no one of the descriptions will do by itself to set forth Newman's understanding of Christian discourse. What is clear, therefore, is that at least each of these three descriptions must be given if the reduction of Christianity is to be avoided. Their unity does not lie in their reducibility to any one of the three uses or to some other description which accounts in itself for the three uses.

There is no systematic theology found in Newman's corpus; there is the reflection of a highly consistent thinker who was too consistent and too subtle and clear in his insight into the nature of the Christian faith to reduce it to a system. My analysis simply seeks to display how his work can be understood to hold together metatheologically without being systematic in principle. The unity of Newman's work is simply the conjunction, without reduction, of these three diverse uses exercised adeptly according to their appropriate contexts and described in their individuality in metatheological reflection. No other description can or need be given. My concentration on this metatheological analysis is simply one possible, though not necessary, exercise of explicit reflection. I have attempted to clarify and to explicate that analysis as it occurs, for the most part, implicitly in Newman's work.

NOTES TO CHAPTER IV

[1]Cf. David A. Pailin, *The Way to Faith: An Examination of Newman's Grammar of Assent as a Response to the Search for Certainty in Faith* (London: Epworth Press, 1969), pp. 125-260.

[2]John Henry Newman, *An Essay in Aid of a Grammar of Assent*, Charles Frederick Harrold, editor (new edition; London: Longmans, Green, and Co., 1947), p. 80. This work will hereafter be cited as *Grammar*. Only Newman's last name will appear in future citations within this chapter even in cases where the book cited has not been included in the chapter before that citation.

[3]Ibid., p. 83.   [4]Ibid., p. 84.

[5]Ibid., p. 85.   [6]Ibid., p. 296.

[7]Newman, "Proof of Theism," *The Text*, Edward J. Sillem and A. J. Boekraad, editors (Vol. II of *The Philosophical Notebook of John Henry Newman*. 2 vols.; New York: Humanities Press, 1969), p. 31. Hereafter this work is cited as *Text: PN*.

[8]Ibid., p. 37.   [9]Ibid., p. 67.

[10]Newman, *Grammar*, op. cit., pp. 87-88.

[11]Ibid., p. 307.   [12]Ibid., p. 314.

[13]Ibid., p. 316.   [14]Ibid., p. 301.

[15]Ibid., p. 316.   [16]Ibid., p. 317.

[17]Newman, "Proof of Theism," op. cit., pp. 37, 75-77.

[18]Newman, "Elements of Thought," *Text: PN*, op. cit., p. 22.

[19]Newman, "Proof of Theism," op. cit., pp. 39, 41, 43.

[20]From a letter from Newman to Dr. Charles Meynell dated July 25, 1869. Cf. Zeno, "Appendix: The Newman-Meynell Correspondence," *John Henry Newman: Our Way to Certitude; an Introduction to Newman's Psychological Discovery: The Illative Sense, and His Grammar of Assent* (Leiden: E. J. Brill, 1957), p. 232.

[21]Adrian J. Boekraad and Henry Tristram, *The Argument from Conscience to the Existence of God according to John Henry Newman* (Louvain: Editions Nauwelaerts, 1961), pp. 53-87. Boekraad had responsibility for the interpretative as opposed to the historical portion of the book. Boekraad claims: "The argument for God's existence par excellence is thus nothing else than: 'a realisation of what we are.'" Cf. ibid., p. 57.

[22]Cf. F. James Kaiser, *The Concept of Conscience according to John Henry Newman* (The Catholic University of America Studies in Sacred Theology, No. 106; Washington, D. C.: Catholic University of America Press, 1958), pp. 145-152, 240-265, for collected references to these negative factors.

[23]In this regard Newman claimed, in the *Grammar*, op. cit.,

p. 292, that in the area of religious inquiry ". . . egotism is true modesty . . . each of us can speak only for himself. . . ." Newman did have some confidence in the arguments which occupy the last one hundred pages of the Grammar, not viewing them simply as psychological idiosyncrasies. He wrote to Miss Holmes on March 26, 1870, concerning his purpose in this section: "I wanted to show that, keeping to broad facts of history, which everyone knows and no one can doubt, there is evidence and reason enough for an honest inquirer to believe in revelation." For this letter, see Wilfrid Ward, The Life of John Henry Cardinal Newman (two volumes; London: Longmans, Green, and Co., 1912), II, 275. Ward's biography will be cited hereafter as Life.

[24] Newman, Grammar, op. cit., p. 292.

[25] Boekraad and Tristram, op. cit., p. 62.

[26] Ward, Life, II, 269.

[27] Ibid., 331.

[28] Newman, Grammar, op. cit., p. 66.

[29] Ibid., p. 292.

[30] In making these comparisons, I am generally in agreement with the analysis of the concept of conscience made by Brother F. James Kaiser, op. cit., rather than with Boekraad's conclusions regarding an "argument" from conscience. In the second chapter of his book, Kaiser makes some of the same parallels that I do between Newman's understanding of conscience and the nature of religious inquiry as the broad concern of the Grammar of Assent.

[31] From a manuscript paper entitled "The Evidence of Religion" dated January 12, 1860. Found in Boekraad and Tristram, op. cit., pp. 171-172.

[32] Newman, Grammar, op. cit., pp. 3, 11.

[33] Ibid., p. 7.   [34] Ibid., pp. 16-17.

[35] Ibid., p. 17.   [36] Ibid., p. 32.

[37] Ibid., pp. 66-67. Cf. Ward, Life, I, 122, for a letter of February, 1846, in which Newman refused to give an account of his conversion to the truth of Roman Catholicism:

No, you have not got them, you cannot get them, except at the cost of some portion of the trouble I have been at myself. You cannot buy them for a crown prince--you cannot take them in your hand at your will, and toss them about. You must consent to think--and you must exercise such resignation to the Divine Hand which leads you, as to follow it any whither. I am not assuming that my reasons are sufficient or unanswerable, when I say this--but describing the way in which our intellect can be successfully exercised on the great subject in question, if the intellect is to be the instrument of conversion. Moral proofs are grown into, not learnt by heart.

[38] Newman, Grammar, op. cit., p. 90.

[39] Ibid., p. 75.   [40] Ibid., p. 200.

[41] Cf. James Munro Cameron, "Faith and the Mind: I. The

Night Battle," The Listener, LVII (January 3, 1957), 15-16.

⁴²Newman, Grammar, op. cit., p. 216.

⁴³Ibid., p. 219.

⁴⁴Ibid., p. 230. Newman should not be interpreted as implying that the unbeliever is consciously insincere in his appraisal of faith, uncommitted, uninvolved. A passage in a letter to Father Coleridge written on February 5, 1871, concerning the Grammar suggests a moral judgment is being made on the non-believer: "My book is to show that a right moral state of mind germinates or even generates good intellectual principles." Cf. Ward, Life, II, 270. The reference to a "right moral state of mind" indicates a mode of inquiry that goes along with full and accurate knowledge of the evidences and is not a moral judgment. In Wilfrid Ward's words, Life, II, 247-248:

. . . he did away with the old contrast, to which Protestants as well as Catholics had long been accustomed, between believer and unbeliever as two men looking at and apprehending precisely the same evidence, which was so obviously cogent that only a man whose will was here and now perverse could disbelieve. He substituted a far subtler analysis in which circumstances and education played their part in the power of mental vision on the particular subject; in which the appreciation of reasons was personal, and gradual; religious earnestness and true principles being necessary not only to the acceptance of the reasoning for Christianity, but to its adequate apprehension.

⁴⁵Newman, Grammar, op. cit., pp. 241, 382.

⁴⁶Ibid., p. 269. ⁴⁷Ibid., p. 270.

⁴⁸Ibid., p. 273. ⁴⁹Ibid., p. 257.

⁵⁰Ibid., p. 259.

⁵¹Cf. Ward, Life, II, 43, for a letter from Newman to Canon Walker on July 6, 1864, voicing his view in an apt metaphor:

. . . The best illustration of what I hold is that of a cable, which is made up of a number of separate threads, each feeble, yet together as sufficient as an iron rod.

An iron rod represents mathematical or strict demonstration; a cable represents moral demonstration, which is an assemblage of probabilities, separately insufficient for certainty, but, when put together, irrefragable. A man who said 'I cannot trust a cable, I must have an iron bar,' would in certain given cases, be irrational and unreasonable:--so too is a man who says I must have a rigid demonstration, not moral demonstration, of religious truth.

For other illuminating passages, see Ward, Life, I, 442-443, and Newman, An Essay on the Development of Christian Doctrine (New York: Longmans, Green, and Co., 1949), pp. 93-94.

⁵²Ward, Life, I, 244.

⁵³Newman, Grammar, op. cit., p. 66.

⁵⁴Ward, Life, II, 329. Note Newman's attention to these nuances of personal history in his correspondence. Cf., for example, letters to Henry Wilberforce and Mrs. William Froude in Ward, Life, I, 235-242. Ward points out, in Life, II, 317, that

there ". . . are very subtle differences in style and in subject between his letters to different persons. Even when the subject is the same, the way of treating it will differ. It was a saying of his that the same thought in different persons is probably as different as their faces."

⁵⁵Newman, *Grammar*, *op. cit.*, p. 61.

⁵⁶Kaiser, *op. cit.*, p. 87.

⁵⁷Ward, *Life*, *op. cit.*, II, 489.

⁵⁸Newman, *Grammar*, *op. cit.*, p. 70.

⁵⁹Gordon Huntington Harper, *Cardinal Newman and William Froude, F.R.S.: A Correspondence* (Baltimore: The Johns Hopkins Press, 1933), pp. 88-89.

⁶⁰*Ibid.*, p. 89.

⁶¹Ward, *Life*, *op. cit.*, I, 624.

⁶²Newman, *Loss and Gain: The Story of a Convert* (London: Burns and Oates, Ltd., 1904), p. 297.

⁶³Newman, *Grammar*, *op. cit.*, pp. 140-141.

⁶⁴Cf. *ibid.*, pp. 6, 143ff.

⁶⁵*Ibid.*, p. 27.   ⁶⁶*Ibid.*, p. 57.

⁶⁷*Ibid.*, p. 63.   ⁶⁸*Ibid.*, p. 22.

⁶⁹*Ibid.*, p. 84.   ⁷⁰*Ibid.*, p. 88.

⁷¹*Ibid.*, p. 89.   ⁷²*Ibid.*, pp. 89, 239.

⁷³*Ibid.*, p. 90.   ⁷⁴*Ibid.*, p. 354.

⁷⁵*Ibid.*, pp. 70-71.

⁷⁶Newman, "Sundries Continued," *Text: PN*, *op. cit.*, p. 153.

⁷⁷*Ibid.*, p. 152.

⁷⁸Newman, *Grammar*, *op. cit.*, p. 61.

⁷⁹*Ibid.*   ⁸⁰*Ibid.*, p. 63.

⁸¹*Ibid.*, p. 69.

⁸²Newman, *Parochial and Plain Sermons* (8 vols., new edition; London: Rivingtons, 1873), IV, 200. Title of these collected volumes hereafter cited as *PPS*.

⁸³Newman, *Apologia pro vita sua* (New York: The Modern Library, 1950), p. 36. Hereafter cited as *Apologia*.

⁸⁴*Ibid.*, p. 41.   ⁸⁵*Ibid.*, p. 48.

⁸⁶*Ibid.*, pp. 55-56.   ⁸⁷*Ibid.*, p. 56.

⁸⁸Newman, *PPS*, IV, 202; cf. *PPS*, VI, 237, 252.

⁸⁹Newman, *PPS*, II, 90.

⁹⁰*Ibid.*, 208-209.

⁹¹Newman, *PPS*, IV, 205.

⁹²Anne Mozeley (ed.), *Letters and Correspondence of J. H. Newman* (London: Longmans, Green, and Co., 1890), II, 36.

⁹³Cf. Newman, *PPS*, II, 107-116; IV, 265; VII, 27-73; and

Discourses addressed to Mixed Congregations (fifth edition; London: Burns, Oates, and Co., 1876), pp. 1-21. Discourses addressed to Mixed Congregations will hereafter be cited as DMC.

[94]Newman, PPS, I, 19. Cf. PPS, I, 15-26; IV, 80-93; VIII, 141-153, 154-171; DMC, 146-169, 239-260.

[95]Newman, PPS, III, 102-113; IV, 214-225; and Faith and Prejudice and Other Unpublished Sermons of Cardinal Newman, Birmingham Oratory, editors (New York: Sheed and Ward, 1956), pp. 74-84. Faith and Prejudice will hereafter be cited as FP.

[96]Newman, Sermons Preached on Various Occasions (sixth edition; London: Burns and Oates, Limited, 1887), pp. 121-122. Sermons Preached on Various Occasions will hereafter be cited as SVO.

[97]Newman, PPS, VII, 256.

[98]Newman, PPS, I, 42-43; IV, 133; VIII, 110-123, 201-216; SVO, pp. 60-74; DMC, pp. 104-123; FP, pp. 31-40.

[99]Newman, PPS, VI, 216.

[100]Cf. Newman, PPS, II, 26-40, 41-50, 139-150; III, 156-172; IV, 239-252; V, 86-98; VI, 53-68; DMC, pp. 285-305, 306-323; SVO, pp. 75-90, 221-233.

[101]Cf. Newman, PPS, III, 114-127, 128-138, 139-155; VI, 39-52, 69-82, 83-93; VII, 133-145; DMC, pp. 324-342.

[102]Cf. Newman, PPS, I, 295-308; VI, 105-119; VII, 74-85.

[103]Newman, PPS, III, 130-131.

[104]Newman, PPS, VI, 228.

[105]Newman, PPS, VI, 208; cf. ibid., IV, 252-266; V, 93, 96; VI, 208-220, 221-233.

[106]Cf. Newman, PPS, III, 254-270; VI, 120-135.

[107]Cf. Newman, PPS, III, 270; VI, 132.

[108]Newman, SVO, pp. 195-196. Cf. ibid., p. 141.

[109]Ibid., p. 197. Cf. PPS, VII, 230-242. The Church is worthy of care then, ibid., VI, 270-312; but still not perfect, divided in itself and, thus, only an image, ibid., III, 180-235.

[110]Newman, PPS, II, 148. Cf. PPS, III, 236-253; IV, 150-167, 248-252; SVO, pp. 47-59.

[111]Newman, PPS, II, 211. Cf. ibid., VI, 174-189.

[112]Cf. Newman, PPS, VII, 301-317, 318-335, 336-349.

[113]Cf. Newman, DMC, pp. 43-61.

[114]Ibid., pp. 94-95.   [115]Ibid., pp. 99-100.

[116]Cf. Newman, PPS, VII, 13-16.

[117]Cf. Newman, PPS, I, 24-25, 57-71, 124-138; VIII, 172-184; SVO, pp. 263-280 and Fifteen Sermons preached before the University of Oxford, between A.D. 1826 and 1843 (new edition; London: Rivingtons, 1887), pp. 37-53. The last work is hereafter cited as OUS.

[118]Cf. Newman, PPS, I, 27-40, 72-82, 215-227, 309-324; II, 368-378; IV, 1-17; VII, 1-12; VIII, 256-268; SVO, 15-30.

119 Cf. Newman, *PPS*, II, 343-357.

120 Cf. Newman, *PPS*, IV, 295-306.

121 Cf. Newman, *PPS*, I, 1-14; V, 27-40.

122 Newman, *PPS*, III, 1.

123 Cf. Newman, *PPS*, II, 61-68, 151; V, 13-28, 313-326; VIII, 1-16.

124 Cf. Newman, *PPS*, IV, 319-333; V, 46-57; VI, 234-254; *SVO*, pp. 31-46.

125 Newman, *PPS*, IV, 325.

126 Newman, *PPS*, VI, 233.

127 *Ibid.*, IV, 236.

128 *Ibid.*, VI, 326. Cf. *DMC*, pp. 1-25.

129 Newman, *PPS*, VI, 233.

130 Newman, *DMC*, p. 4.   131 *Ibid.*, p. 18.

132 Newman, *PPS*, I, 118.

133 *Ibid.*, 171.   134 *Ibid.*, 180.

135 *Ibid.*, 185.

136 Newman, *PPS*, II, 153. Cf. *ibid.*, 163.

137 Cf. Newman, *PPS*, I, 185-189; VI, 39-52.

138 Newman, *PPS*, I, 173.

139 *Ibid.*, 304.   140 Cf. *ibid.*, 57-71.

141 Newman, *PPS*, V, 132. Cf. *ibid.*, VI, 319, 324-325.

142 Newman, *PPS*, VII, 86.

143 *Ibid.*, VI, 29.

144 Cf. *ibid.*, V, 116-127.

145 Newman, *PPS*, IV, 21.

146 *Ibid.*, I, 303-304.   147 *Ibid.*, IV, 132.

148 *Ibid.*, V, 61-64.

149 *Ibid.*, I, 133. Cf. *ibid.*, I, 336-349; II, 51-60; V, 270-283.

150 *Ibid.*, VIII, 246.   151 *Ibid.*, V, 69.

152 *Ibid.*, V, 295.

153 *Ibid.*, V, 319; cf. *ibid.*, VI, 362-371.

154 *Ibid.*, II, 75.   155 *Ibid.*

156 *Ibid.*, IV, 338.   157 *Ibid.*, IV, 335-336.

158 *Ibid.*, I, 93-94. Cf. *ibid.*, VII, 179-191, 192-203.

159 *Ibid.*, V, 9.   160 *Ibid.*, IV, 70.

161 *Ibid.*, I, 241.

162 *Ibid.*, IV, 29. Cf. *ibid.*, 124-138; IV, 307-318; V, 222-236; 327-340, 341-356.

163 *Ibid.*, VII, 113. Cf. *PPS*, I, 139-151; *OUS*, 136-155.

[164] Newman, PPS, V, 143-163. This claim reminds me of Newman's thesis in his Lectures on the Doctrine of Justification (fourth edition; London: Rivingtons, 1885) where he argues that faith and obedience are but one thing--the indwelling of the Holy Spirit in the life of the Christian--viewed in two different, but not contradictory, ways. Lectures on the Doctrine of Justification shall hereafter be cited as LJ. Cf. PPS, I, 165-176; III, 80-81; V, 164-177, 178-194, 195-208, 209-221, 237-253. Charles Stephen Dessain comments on the centrality of the doctrine of the indwelling of the Holy Spirit to the whole of Newman's Parochial and Plain Sermons, even more to the whole of his theological perspective, in "The Biblical Basis of Newman's Ecumenical Theology," The Rediscovery of Newman: An Oxford Symposium, John Coulson and Arthur Macdonald Allchin (London: Sheed and Ward, 1967), pp. 100-122.

[165] Newman, PPS, IV, 292-293.

[166] Ibid., 337-338.   [167] Ibid., I, 191.

[168] Ibid., II, 154.

[169] The concept "picture" has been given reasonably careful analysis as a mode for understanding the nature of religious belief in Peter Munz, Problems of Religious Knowledge (The Library of Philosophy and Theology, John McIntyre and Alasdair MacIntyre, editors; London: SCM Press, Ltd., 1959) and Ludwig Wittgenstein, Lectures and Conversations on Aesthetics, Psychology and Religious Belief, Cyril Barrett, editor (Berkeley: University of California Press, 1967). A parallel instance of a similar analysis without specific concern with religious belief is found in Stuart Hampshire's Thought and Action (New York: The Viking Press, Compass Books, 1967) and Freedom of the Individual (New York: Harper and Row, Publishers, 1965). Each of these analyses posits that one's picture of his situation and, more broadly, of his world forms the framework within which he makes judgments of value and of truth; the framework itself, each concludes, cannot be justified, only decided for or against. In that conclusion, they are in agreement with the analysis of justification offered by Herbert Feigl in "De Principiis Non Disputandum . . .? On the Meaning and Limits of Justification," Philosophical Analysis, Max Black, editor (Ithaca, New York: Cornell University Press, 1950), pp. 119-155 and "Validation and Vindication: An Analysis of the Nature and Limits of Ethical Arguments," Readings in Ethical Theory, Wilfrid Sellars and John Hospers, editors (New York: Appleton-Century-Crofts, Inc., 1952), pp. 667-680. They agree with Feigl that the justification of one's picture or framework of judgment can only be a justificatio actionis, a decision to pursue certain ends, and never a justificatio cognitionis or a proof that these ends should be pursued because they are somehow rooted in "fact" or "truth." I have been helped by these analyses to separate and to distinguish the sense in which Newman felt justificatio cognitionis was not only possible but necessary for the Church. Justificatio actionis is a satisfactory analysis, according to Newman, of coming to faith and of exercising faith but not satisfactory as an analysis of what an explication of the faith involves.

[170] Newman, Grammar, op. cit., p. 62.

[171] Newman, "Lectures on the Prophetical Office of the

Church viewed relatively to Romanism and Popular Protestantism," The Via Media of the Anglican Church (2 vols.; new impression; New York: Longmans, Green, and Co., 1901), I, p. 123.

[172]Newman, Apologia, op. cit., p. 75.

[173]Ibid.

[174]Newman, Grammar, op. cit., p. 294.

[175]Newman, An Essay on the Development of Christian Doctrine, op. cit., p. 303.

[176]Ibid., p. 82.

[177]Newman, Grammar, op. cit., p. 92.

[178]Pailin, op. cit., p. 177.

[179]Newman, An Essay on the Development of Christian Doctrine, op. cit., p. 76.

[180]Jaak Seynaeve, Cardinal Newman's Doctrine on Holy Scripture according to His Published Works and Previously Unedited Manuscripts (Louvain: Publications Universitaires de Louvain, 1953), p. 220. Cf. Newman, "Newman Manuscripts on Holy Scripture," Cardinal Newman's Doctrine on Holy Scripture according to His Published Works and Previously Unedited Manuscripts, appendices, Jaak Seynaeve, editor (Oxford: Basil Blackwell, 1953), pp. 1-150; Newman, On the Inspiration of Scripture, J. Derek Holmes and Robert Murray, S. J., editors (London: Geoffrey Chapman, 1967); Newman, "What is of Obligation for a Catholic to Believe concerning the Inspiration of Scripture? Being a Postscript to an Article in the February No. of the 'Nineteenth Century Review,' in answer to Professor Healy" (London: Burns and Oates, 1884).

[181]Seynaeve, op. cit., p. 348.

[182]Newman, LJ, op. cit., pp. 118-119.

[183]Cf. Newman, PPS, IV, 275-276; SSD, 276-277; Apologia, pp. 294-295; "Lectures on the Prophetical Office of the Church . . .," op. cit., pp. 128-188.

[184]Newman, LJ, op. cit., p. 122.

[185]Günter Biemer, Newman on Tradition, Kevin Smyth, translator and editor (London: Burns and Oates, 1967), p. 2. This is a revised version of the original German edition, Uberlieferung und Offerbarung, Die Lehre von der Tradition nach John Henry Newman (Freiburg: Herder, 1961). Cf. also Jean Stern, Bible et Tradition, aux Origenes de la Théorie du Developpement (Theologie: Etudes Publiées Sous la Direction de la Facultie de Théologie S. J. de Lyon-Fourviére; Aubier, 1967).

[186]Newman, Apologia, op. cit., p. 40.

[187]Biemer, op. cit., p. 164.

[188]Ibid., p. 165.

[189]Cf. Newman, "Lectures on the Prophetical Office of the Church . . .," op. cit., p. 56.

[190]Newman, On Consulting the Faithful in Matters of Doctrine, John Coulson, editor (New York: Sheed and Ward, 1961). The article was originally published in the Rambler for July,

1859. Cf. Samuel D. Femiano, *Infallibility of the Laity: The Legacy of Newman* (New York: Herder and Herder, 1967) for a history of the issues involved in a controversy which the article was meant to address. Webster T. Patterson's *Newman: Pioneer for the Layman* (Washington, D. C.: Corpus Books, 1968), while concerned with the historical situation to which the article was addressed, is more concerned to understand the theological significance of the article and the relation of its principal claims to Newman's theological commitments as found in his other writings.

[191] Biemer, op. cit., p. 103.

[192] Ibid., p. 109.

[193] Newman, "Notes on Church and Pope" (unpublished manuscript, Birmingham Oratory, England; microfilmed copy, Yale University Beinecke Library, New Haven, reel 14, batch 75, A 18.20).

[194] Newman, "On the Prophetical Office of the Church . . .," op. cit., pp. 84, 192. Cf. J. Richard Quinn, *The Recognition of the True Church According to John Henry Newman* (The Catholic University of America Studies in Sacred Theology, second series, No. 81; Washington, D. C.: The Catholic University of America Press, 1954), pp. 86-91.

[195] Ward, *Life*, op. cit., II, 236. Letter to Mr. Peter le Page Renouf, June 21, 1868.

[196] Ibid., 238.   [197] Ibid., 289.

[198] Ibid., 293.   [199] Ibid., 307.

[200] Ibid., 309-312.

[201] Newman, "A Letter addressed to His Grace the Duke of Norfolk on occasion of Mr. Gladstone's Expostulation in 1874," *Certain Difficulties felt by Anglicans in Catholic Teaching* (2 vols.; London: Longmans, Green, and Co., 1910), II, 322.

[202] Ibid., pp. 329-330.

[203] Ibid., pp. 341, 346.

[204] Newman, *Apologia*, op. cit., pp. 243-263. A very negative judgment of Newman's views, essentially agreeing with my interpretation but finding Newman's position "dangerously" misleading, is Joseph Clifford Fenton, "Newman and Papal Infallibility," *American Essays for the Newman Centenial*, John K. Ryan and Edmond Darvil Benard, editors (Washington, D. C.: The Catholic University of America Press, 1947), pp. 163-185. Romuald A. Dibble, *John Henry Newman: The Concept of Infallible Doctrinal Authority* (The Catholic University of America Studies in Sacred Theology, second series, no. 91; Washington, D. C.: The Catholic University of America Press, 1955) sees Newman's views in essential harmony with a fully and traditionally orthodox position.

[205] Wilfrid Ward, "Preface," *Men and Matters* (London: Longmans, Green, and Co., 1914), p. v. Cf. John Coulson's excellent article on the matter of the full, multifaceted reality of the Church: "Newman on the Church--His Final View; its Origin and Influence," *The Rediscovery of Newman: An Oxford Symposium*, op. cit., pp. 123-143.

206Newman, "The Prophetical Office of the Church . . .," op. cit., pp. 4, 6.

207Newman, PPS, II, 227.

208Newman, "Report of JHN's Sermons 1873-74-75" (unpublished manuscript, Birmingham Oratory, England; microfilmed copy, Yale University Beinecke Library, New Haven, reel 52, batch 173, C5.1).

209Newman, Grammar, op. cit., p. 142.

210Ibid., p. 143.   211Ibid., p. 144.

212Ibid.   213Ibid., p. 145.

214Ibid., p. 146.   215Ibid., p. 162.

216Newman, LJ, op. cit., pp. 15-16.

217Newman, The Idea of a University (Garden City, New York: Doubleday and Company, Inc., Image Books, 1959), p. 229.

218For this distinction, I am indebted to Roderick Chisholm, Theory of Knowledge (Foundations of Philosophy Series, Elizabeth and Monroe Beardsley, editors; Englewood Cliffs, New Jersey: Prentice-Hall, Inc., 1966), p. 111. Cf. his Perceiving: A Philosophical Study (Contemporary Philosophy, Max Black, editor; Ithaca, New York: Cornell University Press, 1957).

219Chisholm, Theory of Knowledge, op. cit., p. 111, says that ". . . to give the truth conditions for any belief, it is sufficient merely to express or formulate that belief."

220Newman, Grammar, op. cit., p. 294.

221Ibid.   222Ibid., p. 76.

223Cf. Quinn, op. cit.

224Newman, The Idea of a University, op. cit., p. 67.

225Owen Chadwick, From Bossuet to Newman: The Idea of Doctrinal Development (Cambridge: Cambridge University Press, 1957), p. 148. Newman's own exercises in historical inquiry, in particular his Two Essays on Biblical and Ecclesiastical Miracles (fourth edition; London: Basil Montagu Pickering, 1875), have not always been valued as critically sound. Cf. Thomas S. Bokenkotter, Cardinal Newman as an Historian (Louvain: Publications Universitaires de Louvain, 1959) for a balanced judgment.

226Newman, "Theses De Fide," The Expositor, fourth series, II (1890), 350. These Theses were translated by Arthur W. Hutton.

CHAPTER V

THE COMPLEX UNITY OF THE CHRISTIAN FAITH:
NEWMAN'S METATHEOLOGICAL PRINCIPLES

In the preceding chapters of this study, I have sought to clarify by description and interpretation the kind of complex unity which characterizes the reflections of John Henry Newman on Christianity. My purpose in doing so has been twofold. First, I have sought to provide an interpretation of Newman's diverse uses of Christian discourse that calls into question the reductive tendency long present in criticism of Newman's thought. Second, in explicating the complex unity which Newman felt to characterize an adequate understanding of Christian discourse, I have isolated and clarified certain metatheological principles which seem to guide Newman's work.

Hopefully my analysis has already enabled me to achieve my first goal. In this last chapter, as a way of reaching the second goal, I shall review the conclusions of my descriptive and interpretative analyses, add some observations regarding Newman's metatheological principles, and note the impact of both matters on the history of Newman criticism.

Three Uses of Christian Discourse: A Summary Review

Perhaps Newman's own words best summarize my conclusions regarding his metatheological principles: "Whatever is great refuses to be reduced to human rule, and to be made consistent in its many aspects with itself."[1] Newman's guiding principle in analyzing and in using Christian discourse involves an adherence to the nonreducible, multi-faceted reality of revealed truth in its complex unity and a resistance to all temptations to find one "leading idea" that characterizes Christianity. That principle allowed, for Newman, the employment of Christian discourse within a given context for a given purpose if one was clear that the context and the purpose were conditioning factors.[2]

Newman recognized certain rather broadly but well defined dimensions of Christian faith evidenced in the way that

Christian discourse functions in three diverse contexts. He was particularly interested in delineating three ways in which the relation of faith and reason could be understood.

First, he gave attention to the nature of religious inquiry and its relation to specifically Christian confessions of faith. He noted that religious inquiry involves a definite preparation of mind, a peculiar mode of reasoning, and special kinds of evidence. I was concerned in giving attention to these matters to oppose the notion that Newman's view of conscience and of the role of moral dispositions in religious inquiry must be understood as an argument for the existence of God. While I admitted that Newman viewed the testimony of conscience as the most generally plausible and persuasive argument, I also pointed out that he himself did not employ it in any rigidly argumentative fashion in his published writings. He did not judge an argument from conscience or any other single piece of argument or evidence to be more than a <u>motivum</u> <u>credibilium</u>. Insofar as he seemed to place some exclusive value on the effectiveness of the argument from conscience or to make moral considerations the basis of a universal description of the process of conversion, he transgressed his own soundest principles and most astute warnings.

What I have argued is that he did not characteristically view the testimony of conscience as material for probative argument. He seems rather to have used moral activity and reflection as a model for understanding and for making understood the nature of religious inquiry without reference to its role as an argument for God's existence or as the one and only pattern of conversion. Insofar as the testimony of conscience does lead man to inquire after God, Newman was positing a minimal natural theology that allows for the question concerning God being a possibility for man. But his negative conclusions regarding the testimony of conscience rendered its testimony as ineffective as those natural testimonies referred to by St. Paul in Romans and by John Calvin in the opening sentences of his <u>Institutes</u> <u>of</u> <u>the</u> <u>Christian</u> <u>Religion</u>. It is the attitude of need and anticipation that characterizes this minimal awareness and which provides the basis for an openness to the reception of God's Word. Thus, the import of the testimony of conscience is less a matter of information than of disposition.

One should note that this disposition is given the most formal description possible with the intention of distinguishing the nature of religious inquiry from other kinds of inquiry. In no sense should his description be taken to be a description of the process of conversion on a material level. Religious inquiry and its outcome assume widely different material characters even though a very few formal characteristics hold true across these differences. One's need and anticipation may as easily be expressions of an eagerness for understanding as a search for relief of guilt.

Second, Newman gave attention to the matter of Christian living or to the exercise of Christian faith in the life of the individual. Whatever his journey in coming to faith, a person of faith understands himself, others, history, and the world in a different way from one who has not come to faith. Whatever his port of entry, he now inhabits a world made up of different realities, controlled by different principles, and inviting as well as demanding a different set of actions and passions. He now has a different "picture" of the world; his imagination is imbued with a view of the unseen, yet present, reality and power of God and of His activity. While Newman felt that Scripture and Christian tradition gave no authority for giving a material description of the process of conversion, he obviously did conclude, as his sermons reveal, that these sources make very detailed observations regarding the character and quality of Christian life.

Third, since Newman did not allow a consideration of religious inquiry or of the Christian life to explain fully the nature of the Christian faith, I turned to consider what Newman often spoke of as the "objective" character of Christianity. In fact, in a real sense, this "objective" quality of Christianity provided the framework within which the other uses of Christian discourse--those related to contexts of coming to faith and of exercising faith--were discussed. While this conclusion may seem to constitute Newman's own brand of reductionism or my own reductive analysis of his complex unity, I want to show, in this chapter, that it does not. Reductionism would be the result only if religious inquiry and Christian living could be accounted for by reference solely to questions of meaning and truth. That kind of claim is never made by

Newman. When one has completed a description of the meaning
and truth of Christian claims, one still has not accounted for
<u>fides acquisita</u> or for the peculiar way in which one must
employ the Christian picture in his life. The peculiar function
and context of the third use of Christian discourse does not
displace the equally special functions and contexts associated
with the other two uses. Nevertheless, Newman was quite concerned with that third use. He understood that the <u>fact</u> of a
person's coming to faith and exercising faith and the accompany-
ing employment of Christian discourse in these contexts does
not provide a <u>norm</u> guarding against illegitimate judgments in
the third context.

Thus, while Louis Cognet is right that Newman is deducing
rules of discourse <u>a posteriori</u> and that he justifiably uses
the word "grammar" for his principal work on these questions,
one should not conclude with J.D. Bastable that Newman provides
a social rather than an epistemological criterion of knowledge.[3]
To have concerned oneself with the appropriation of faith and
the exercise of faith is not yet, Newman realized, to have
accounted in any normative fashion for the meaning and truth of
one's faith. The explication of faith is itself guarded from
the charge of appealing only to the fact of usage by Newman's
appeal to evidence and to the operation of the Holy Spirit.
Newman concluded that ". . . one aspect of Revelation must not
be allowed to obscure another; . . . Christianity is dogmatical,
devotional, practical all at once. . . ."[4]

What I need to demonstrate, however, is that this sense
of complex unity is characteristic of Newman's more general
reflections on the various uses of Christian discourse. I need
to prove that Newman's suggestions in this regard are compatible
with those actual uses of Christian discourse which I have
investigated in chapters three and four. Newman's reflections
on this matter are not rigorously thorough; he explored the
same question in various, equally incomplete, ways. Newman
was not himself concerned to develop what I have called a metatheological position. Nevertheless, his suggestions in that
direction are remarkably consistent with his actual practice.
What I seek to do, in this chapter, is to draw those reflections together, to show their developing yet consistent point
of view, and to clarify their importance for understanding

Newman.

Newman's Metatheological Principles

Newman always contended that the Christian faith, though definite in content, does not have an ". . . identity of the narrow, absolute, formal kind . . . [which] would shape everything into one mould."[5] The Christian faith is such, argued Newman, that it can afford to be free and spontaneous, to present itself in varying aspects and to accommodate itself to different contexts without loss of principle.[6] He suggested that ". . . the whole system of revelation may be viewed in various, nay antagonistic aspects. . . ."[7] What was important for Newman was that one not deal with one or several aspects in such a way as to suggest that they constitute the sum total of the reality of Christianity. Newman concluded that ". . . as far as Revelation has joined truths together, and has made one depend and throw light on another, it is not for us to put asunder. . . ."[8]

One example of the manner in which Newman held seemingly diverse, even contradictory, interpretations of the Christian faith together so that they become aspects of the same complex unity can be found in his <u>Lectures on the Doctrine of Justification</u>. In that series of lectures, he argued that the Lutheran and the Roman Catholic understandings of justification are both unsatisfactory since each deals with only one aspect of man's justification. What are two modes of the same truth, said Newman, have become separate religions.[9] Each individual description of justification becomes problematic ". . . apart from other truths which serve to repress those tendencies to error, which it, in common with every other separate portion of the Scripture creed, contains, not in itself, but when exclusively cherished by the human mind."[10] One should find the real meaning of "justification" by an investigation of its use in the authoritative sources of the Christian faith and must not impose a meaning. When one does make such an investigation, he finds that the word has many shades of meaning each related to one another although they are not identical; they are of "one family."[11] These different meanings result from modifications of points of view toward the same reality.[12] One only has a full understanding of the reality, concluded

Newman, when he has an awareness of the totality of these descriptions.

Newman refined the expression and discussion of this view of complex unity throughout his career. Three works have peculiar significance: the <u>Oxford University Sermons</u>, the <u>Essay on the Development of Christian Doctrine</u>, and the <u>Essay in Aid of a Grammar of Assent</u>. Each work deserves separate attention.

<u>Metatheological suggestions in the Oxford University Sermons: the role of reasoned reflection in faith and the safeguard of wisdom</u>. In his <u>Oxford University Sermons</u>, Newman attended for the first time to metatheological issues, particularly in relation to the role of reflection in the life of faith. Because of the division, false pride, and cold formality that often accompany theology or explicit reason, many persons seek to divorce that form of reasoning from faith as inconsistent with the character of the affections and habits suggested in Scripture. But, urged Newman, such an opposition, though understandable to some degree, is an extreme and unwarranted resolution of the difficulty.[13] The danger that theological reflection will substitute a kind of religious philosophy for worship and practice is an argument for its careful use, contended Newman, rather than for its dismissal.[14]

Newman understood theological science to include evidence for the divine origin of religion, both natural and supernatural; the interpretation of Scripture; and dogmatic theology or the determination of questions of faith and morals. The implicit reasoning of men of faith by which they believe certain things to be true for certain reasons through certain informants is the subject matter that provides the material for theological analysis. Theology is concerned with the why, the how, and the what of faith.[15] The inherent danger of theology is that it will promise more than it can bring about. Newman explained:

> No analysis is subtle and delicate enough to represent adequately the state of mind under which we believe, or the subjects of belief, as they are presented to our thoughts.[16]

Newman noted the difficulty of depicting the variety of circumstances attending the reception of a doctrine as true from one time and from one individual to another. The kinds of reasons that a theologian adduces are, therefore, only specimens of the more complicated network of reasons existing in the mind.[17] Because of the economical character of coming to faith, no one analysis will fit all individual cases.

Newman mentioned several safeguards against the possible abuse of reasoned reflection. On the one hand, he argued that a right state of heart or love is the safeguard of faith. He rejected reason as the safeguard of faith, for faith requires no intellectual act beside itself to make it authentic and warranted.[18] The holiness of the Christian's new life, his love for Christ guards him from superstition and fanaticism. In large measure, Newman implied that this safeguard is operative for implicit reasoning. In fact, he related his description of the safeguard to a description of natural religion. The grounds of faith animated by love stem from man's need for a revelation and his inclination to believe that God would provide one. These anticipations under the guidance of love lead the honest mind to truth without formal evidence.[19] In this case, love is a sufficient safeguard.

Newman did suggest another safeguard in relation to what he understood as explicit reasoning. This safeguard Newman called "wisdom" or the orderly and mature development of thought usually called science and philosophy.[20] Philosophy is not knowledge of things alone but also knowledge of their mutual relations. Wisdom is an analytical process, a kind of systematizing, by which one ascertains the existing relationships between things and understands the various aspects of each individual thing. Wisdom

> . . . never views any part of the extended subject-matter of knowledge without recollecting that it is but a part, or without the associations which spring from this recollection. It makes every thing lead to every thing else; it communicates the image of the whole body to every separate member, till the whole becomes in imagination like a spirit, every where pervading and penetrating its component parts, and giving them their one definite meaning . . . . [They] are all viewed, not in themselves, but as relative terms, suggesting a multitude of correlatives, and gradually, by successive combinations, converging one and all to their true centre.[21]

Bigotry, said Newman, results from the application of principles too narrow for such a rich understanding and leads one to profess an understanding of that which he, in fact, does not comprehend.[22] Bigoted men ". . . think that any one truth excludes another which is distinct from it . . . ."[23] They tend to settle on some leading idea or simple view as the sum and substance of the Gospel, insisting on this isolated tenet in a way that finally disparages the rest of the revealed system.[24] Men of faith, on the other hand, make no profession of having the ability to describe all the contents of the faith and its doctrines in their mutual relationships. On the other hand, even though faith does not profess to be able to trace out these relationships, explicit faith does seek to trace them out in the spirit of humility and without the presumption of bigotry. Implicit faith simply views each separate aspect of the faith in itself and not as part of a whole.[25] The obedience to and love of revelation that characterizes faith guards it against falsifications of the object of faith. The humility of wisdom allows it to consider reflectively the content of revelation in its various aspects without falling victim to the reductionism of bigotry.

The metatheological proposal in An Essay on the Development of Christian Doctrine: the relationship of an idea and its aspects. In his Essay on the Development of Christian Doctrine, Newman delineated the principles guiding reflection on the complex unity of the Christian faith. The only previous reflection on these metatheological principles had been spelled out in the Oxford University Sermons in terms of the concept of "wisdom" and its conjunction of mutual relations. In the famous essay on development, Newman set forth his understanding of the relationship between an idea and its aspects. For Newman, an "aspect" results from a judgment which one makes on some thing with which he comes into contact; these separate judgments become "aspects" of this thing in one's mind.[26] Newman designated the representation of the thing of which one forms the judgment an "idea." This representation or "idea" is commensurate with the sum total of the possible judgments or aspects.[27] One aspect is, therefore, never sufficient to exhaust the contents of a real idea.

Newman offered man's understanding of God as an example of the relationship between an idea and its aspects in his 1843 sermon on "The Theory of Developments in Religious Doctrine." As God is one, faith has one individual being as its

object rather than a system, ". . . not a philosophy, but an
individual idea in its separate aspects."[28] Though one in Himself, said Newman, the impressions which the idea of God makes
on one's mind are complex and manifold in their relationships
to one another and to their object. Particular propositions
corresponding to these impressions and separate relations
express but aspects of the one object.[29] In his 1845 *Essay*,
however, Newman was more careful about making this kind of
identification of the "idea" with God. In fact, he rejected
that kind of identification:

> Sometimes an attempt is made to determine the 'leading
> idea,' as it has been called, of Christianity, an ambitious
> essay as employed on a supernatural work, when, even as
> regards the visible creation and the inventions of men,
> such a task is beyond us. . . . But one aspect of Revelation must not be allowed to exclude or to obscure
> another. . . .[30]

He urged that such a "leading idea" could be selected only
as a matter of convenience in the pursuit of a specific purpose.[31]

The full impact of the idea on the believer through its
various aspects is described by Newman in this way:

> Theological dogmas are propositions expressive of the
> judgments which the mind forms, or the impressions which
> it receives, of Revealed Truth. Revelation sets before
> it certain supernatural facts and actions, beings and
> principles; these make a certain impression or image upon
> it; and this impression spontaneously, or even necessarily,
> becomes the subject of reflection on the part of the mind
> itself, which proceeds to investigate it, and to draw
> it forth in successive and distinct sentences.[32]

The impressions of revealed truth are the result of practices
such as Bible reading, personal conversation with believers,
and the study of dogmatic theology. These impressions constitute material for reasoned reflection and the regulating
principle and warrant for that reasoning. One must always be
wary, warned Newman, of ". . . the ambition of being wiser
than what is written."[33] The ordinary mistake of those who
reflect on the Christian faith is to embrace one proposition of
the creed or aspect of Christian revelation instead of attending
to the complex unity of the propositions or aspects which
conjointly make up the Christian faith. In fact, Newman felt
that this fastening on one statement as if it were the whole
truth to the denial of all others is almost the definition of
heresy.[34] Of course, Newman did assert that it is the nature

of man's mind that he cannot conceive of an object except under
aspects which are not identical with the object itself; no
individual is able to grasp an object in an integral fashion.[35]
What Newman urged is that the individual realize this inability.

Two basic observations are necessary to clarify Newman's
notion of the relation of an idea and its aspects. First, his
suggestion was that an idea is not equivalent to one or even
several, but to the sum total of its aspects. On this level,
it seems, his point was essentially a metatheological one: one
should not concentrate on one aspect to the exclusion of others.
He suggested that the basic datum is the irreducible conjunction
of a "family" of aspects which are related yet not identical.
To understand the idea, one must grasp this conjunction of
aspects. Specifically, to understand the Christian faith, one
must understand the irreducible presence of various uses of
Christian discourse in relationships of complex unity.

Second, however, the suggestion made by this model of
"aspects" and "idea" was that the object to which the idea
refers can never be grasped; one can only take incomplete and,
consequently, misleading perspectives toward that object. In
other words, man's knowledge of aspects is an indication of his
distance from a knowledge of the object. In this case, no one
aspect or even the total conjunction of aspects can suggest
what is meant by the reality of the object of which the idea
is a representation. That object transcends all man's attempts
to understand it. On this second level, it would seem, Newman
was making a religious point, i.e., he emphasized that God is
God and that man's only appropriate attitude toward Him is
humility.

These two levels are not irreconcilable if their respective purposes are kept in mind. That knowledge of God possible
for man must be understood to involve a complex unity of aspects
even though the sum total of those aspects cannot be taken to
be equivalent to a description of the reality of God who
transcends in Himself what man is able to know of Him.[36]
Wisdom and humility are not irreconcilable virtues. Wisdom is
possible because revealed truth as it is given to man has a
complex unity, demanding the conjunction of diverse aspects or
different uses of Christian discourse but capable of being
grasped by the wise believer implicitly or explicitly. The

"idea," in this case, is revealed truth, the object of faith; and the "aspects" are uses of language necessary in order to fully represent that truth. Humility demands, on the other hand, that one realize that awareness of revealed truth is not equivalent to knowledge of God Himself who remains, in a real sense, a mystery.

Therefore, Newman's use of the model of "idea" and "aspects" should not be taken to involve the proposal that the Christian remains essentially ignorant of God, i.e., with no firm knowledge of the reality of God. The model functions most often as a description of the complex unity of the Christian revelation. In this case, the difficulty for man is not impenetrable mystery so much as it is the tendency to reduce that complex unity, and consequently, to misunderstand the full reality of Christian faith. On the other hand, Newman did not disregard the element of mystery that attends even the revelation that God has given to man. He reminded his readers that no creed or theological formula, not even Scripture itself, is able to describe adequately the reality of God. Before His reality humility is always the appropriate response.

A part of that humility, however, is the proper recognition of what God has made known to man. The complex unity of that knowledge in its various aspects is preserved, according to Newman, in the Church. As such, Christianity comes to man as an objective revelation with certain credentials guaranteeing its truth. The facts and events of revelation are singular, unique, and possess an objective rather than simply a subjective authority. Newman explained:

> Revelation consists in the manifestation of the Invisible Divine Power, or in the substitution of the voice of a Lawgiver for the voice of conscience. The supremacy of conscience is the essence of natural religion; the supremacy of Apostle, or Pope, or Church, or Bishop, is the essence of Revealed . . . . Thus, what conscience is in the system of nature, such is the voice of Scripture, or of the Church, or of the Holy See, as we may determine it, in the system of Revelation.[37]

Revelation is governed by what Newman called the "principle of dogma" or the view that supernatural truths are "irrevocably committed to human language, imperfect because it is human, but definitive and necessary because given from above."[38] One must conclude, therefore, that dogmatic ". . . truth is not the gratification of curiosity; that its attainment has nothing of the excitement of discovery; that the mind is below truth, not above it, and is bound, not to descant upon it, but to venerate it . . . ."[39] For Newman, "Dogmatism is a religion's profession of its own reality as contrasted with other systems. . . ."[40] As a definite body of given revealed truth, the Christian faith is capable of a scientific analysis, by which one is

> . . . handling, examining, explaining, recording, cataloging, defending, the truths which faith, not reason, has gained us . . . providing an intellectual expression of supernatural facts, eliciting what is implicit, comparing, measuring, connecting each with each, and forming one and all into a theological system.[41]

The gift of the theologian is his ability to fix his mind on what is received by tradition with a preciseness and thoroughness of analysis. This gift is clearly distinct from an originality of mind that generates new doctrines; such originality is not appropriate in a revealed religion.[42]

In an essay which was written in his Catholic period and which serves as the "Preface" to the third edition of The Via Media, Newman warned that the fact of this revealed truth being found in the Church should not lead one to think that the reality of the Church or of Christianity can be reduced to the question of the truth of its doctrines. Newman argued that, just as Jesus Christ was prophet, priest, and king at once, so the Church has three offices as teacher, ruler, and sacred minister. "Christianity, then, is at once a philosophy, a political power, and a religious rite . . . ."[43] Newman continued:

> Truth is the guiding principle of theology and theological inquiries; devotion and edification, of worship; and of government, expedience. The instrument of theology is reasoning; of worship, our emotional nature; of rule, command and coercion.[44]

Each of these aspects is influenced and modified by the others. Each has its own distortion: ". . . reasoning tends to rationalism; devotion to superstition and enthusiasm; and power to ambition and tyranny."[45] According to Newman, it is the proper function of each of the individual aspects in its own sphere that eliminates the distortion of excesses in the other spheres. Reasoning can correct fanaticism; proper religious sentiment dispels rationalism. In this interaction of aspects, the Church and the revelation which it preserves are the prime examples of the truth that ". . . whatever is great refuses to be reduced to human rule, and to be made consistent in its many aspects with itself."[46] He warned: "It is not well to exhibit some sides of Christianity and not others . . . . It does not pay to be eclectic in so serious a matter of fact."[47] That warning succinctly summarizes the central concern which animated his distinction between an "idea" and its "aspects."

Metatheology in An Essay in Aid of a Grammar of Assent: "real" and "notional" assent. Many interpreters of the Grammar of Assent have understood that book to involve a reduction of the manifold aspects of the Christian faith. What they have overlooked is that the Grammar, in harmony with Newman's other books, actually distinguishes three diverse uses of Christian discourse, even though the Grammar is by no means a complete exploration of all three.

Newman stated his intentions quite clearly:

> I am not proposing to set forth the arguments in the belief of these doctrines, but to investigate what it is to believe them, what the mind does, what it contemplates, when it makes an act of faith.[48]

The modern interpreters of Newman whom I classed as concerned with his understanding of religious inquiry recognize this avowed purpose and its self-imposed limitations. But they do not sufficiently explain the distinctions which Newman made between the three diverse functions of Christian discourse which I have isolated. While they note in passing that Newman had positive words about the "notional," about reason, and about theology, they do not analyze those concerns in any significant way. They concentrate on Newman's genuinely unique contributions to an analysis of the way in which persons come to knowledge in implicit and personal ways.

What I want to demonstrate in this section is that, while Newman's basic purpose in the Grammar was to describe the act of faith as a phenomenon of human experience, he recognized even in that regard that such a description is a complex matter demanding careful distinctions if one is to avoid confusion. Since so many critics have found the distinction between "real" and "notional" assent to provide a priority of personal, subjective elements in faith, some clarification of the nature and relations of the two types of assent is necessary if I am

to support my claims concerning the complex unity of Newman's
reflections. He summarized his awareness of this complexity
in this way:

> We may of course assent to a number of propositions all
> together, that is, we may take a number of assents all
> at once; but in doing so we run the risk of putting upon
> one level, and treating as if of the same value, acts of
> the mind which are very different from each other in character
> and circumstance . . . . Now a religion is not a
> proposition but a system; it is a rite, a creed, a philosophy,
> a rule of duty, all at once; and to accept a religion
> is neither a simple assent to it nor a complex, neither
> a conviction nor a prejudice, neither a notional assent
> nor a real, not a mere act of profession, nor of credence,
> nor of opinion, nor of speculation, but it is a collection
> of all these various kinds of assent at once and together,
> some of one description, some of another . . . .[49]

In this way, Newman criticized any simplistic reduction of
Christianity and, thus, of his work.

Those who have accused him of some form of subjectivism
have urged that he unfailingly gave real assent precedence over
notional assent and faith over reason, displaying a disdain for
the role of theology. More sophisticated critics have often
agreed to this absolute priority of real assent or faith and
have, consequently, failed to give adequate attention to the
function of theology in Newman's view.

What is clearly necessary is some clarification of
Newman's use of the terms "real" and "notional." My purpose
is to show that, for Newman, real assent did not have uniformly
constant priority over notional assent and that faith and reason
had a legitimate, though different, role in each kind of assent.
I shall keep two questions in mind in my analysis: Was Newman
himself clear as to what the terms meant for him? Did he
obliterate the distinctiveness of the terms by their repeated
and diverse use?

The terms have certain general characteristics. The
term "real assent" appears in conjunction with concepts like
"thing," "external," "image," "imagination," "concrete,"
"individual." Real assent is directed toward concrete, individual
things external to the mind and represented by the
impressions (images) left on the imagination. The term
"notional assent," on the other hand, is associated with concepts
like "thought," "internal," "notion," "reason," "abstract,"
"inference." Notional assent is directed internally to the
creations of our own minds (thoughts, notions) rather than to

things and proceeds by aid of the reason through acts of inference to a conclusion.[50] Real but not notional assent is more characteristically spoken of as concerned directly with facts, with the existence of objects and states of affairs.

For Newman, these distinctions have their immediate practical employment in showing the difference between theology and religion. And it is in making this distinction that he becomes subject to grave misunderstanding. That misunderstanding, we shall see, depends on not recognizing the elasticity with which the terms "real" and "notional" function. The distinctions suggested by the characteristics which I cited above are found to be less definite and consistent than what initially appears to be the case. In regard to that distinction, Newman stated:

> To give a real assent to it [dogma] is an act of religion; to give a notional, is a theological act. It is discerned, rested in, and appropriated as a reality, by the religious imagination; it is held as a truth, by the theological intellect.[51]

One should note carefully, however, that a dogma is the object of both real and notional assent. For Newman, there was no contrariety between dogmatic creed and religion, although there was between an intellectualization of Christianity and the many faceted reality of Christian faith. In fact, this distinction helps in sorting out two senses in which the terms "real" and "notional" are used. In one sense, the terms are opposed to each other in relation to the Christian faith. "Notional" here implies the attitude of the philosopher who assumes a given dogma more or less probable as a conclusion of reason made by certain inferences. "Real" describes the attitude of the believer who has an unhesitating faith.

In this sense, the terms refer to two ". . . distinct states or characters of mind."[52] One might be said to have a "theological habit of mind" if he always talked about Christianity as if it were a set of ideas. In that case, a "religious habit of mind" would indicate an apprehension of the reality of God in one's life and thought.[53] Newman was pointing to the fact that a certain habit of mind can come to characterize one's total response to a given matter. He pointed out that

> . . . the previous labour of coming to a conclusion, and that repose of mind which I have above described as

attendant on an assent to its truth, often counteracts
whatever of lively sensation the fact thus concluded is
in itself adapted to excite; so that what is gained in
depth and exactness of belief is lost as regards freshness
and vigour.[54]

Another passage is even more suggestive:

> Questioning, when encouraged on any subject-matter, readily
> becomes a habit, and leads the mind to substitute exer-
> cises of inference for assent, whether simple or complex.
> Reasons for assenting suggest reasons for not assenting,
> and what were realities to our imagination, while our
> assent was simple, may become little more than notions,
> when we have attained a certitude.[55]

While there can be this kind of opposition between
notional assent and theology, on the one hand, and real assent
and religion, on the other, such antagonism is not inevitable.
Newman recognized that: "As Intellect is common to all men as
well as imagination, every religious man is to a certain extent
a theologian, and no theology can start or thrive without the
initiative and abiding presence of religion."[56] One further
lengthy quotation makes this interdependence clear, although
the relationships depicted are rather complicated.

> People urge that salvation consists, not in believing
> the propositions that there is a God, that there is a
> Saviour, that our Lord is God, that there is a Trinity,
> but in believing in God, in a Saviour, in a Sanctifier;
> and they object that such propositions are but a formal
> and human medium destroying all true reception of the
> Gospel, and making religion a matter of words or of logic,
> instead of its having its seat in the heart. They are
> right, so far as this, that men can and sometimes do rest
> in the propositions themselves as expressing intellectual
> notions; they are wrong, when they maintain that men need
> do so or always do so. The propositions may and must be
> used, and can easily be used, as the expressions of facts,
> not notions, and they are necessary to the mind in the
> same way that language is ever necessary for denoting
> facts, both for ourselves as individuals, and for our
> intercourse with others. Again, they are useful in their
> dogmatic aspect as ascertaining and making clear for us
> the truths on which the religious imagination has to
> rest . . . in religion the imagination and affections
> should always be under the control of reason. Theology
> may stand as a substantive science, though it be without
> the life of religion; but religion cannot maintain its
> ground at all without theology. Sentiment, whether imag-
> inative or emotional, falls back upon the intellect for
> its stay, when sense cannot be called into exercise; and
> it is in this way that devotion falls back upon dogma.[57]

This passage bristles with seeming contradictions, particularly
in relation to other passages already cited. How are these
apparent contradictions to be explained?

One is not surprised when Newman makes real assent equivalent to an apprehension of the realities of the faith. In this sense, real assent is an assent to a proposition as representing facts. In this case, the question of the truth of the proposition and of the grounds of its being true do not arise. These questions are second order; they are reflections on the immediate propositions of the faith. The phrase "is true" and the reasons for assigning that phrase to a proposition are the results of theological questions. Both these uses, however, are opposed to a notional habit of mind. Christians always assent in faith to facts (religious habit of mind) and never to notions alone (theological habit of mind), but they sometimes do this for religious purposes and in religious contexts (real assent) and sometimes for theological purposes and in theological contexts (notional assent). For Newman, assenting to a proposition like "God is our Father" does not preclude going through a process of coming to that conclusion at the same time.[58] Faith does not preclude theological argument; real assent does not entirely replace notional assent.

The kinds of enterprises which are truly opposed by Newman are clarified in notes which he made in 1859 on the "faculty of abstraction."[59] In these notes, he distinguished abstraction as "originality" and abstraction as "ingenuity." Newman noted:

> Different people look at the same thing in different ways—
> and in this difference lies Originality. . . . true
> Originality differs from Ingenuity in this that it hits
> upon differences which have their foundation in fact.[60]

In the case of ingenuity, one judges things from an abstract point of view, or what I have been describing after Newman as an illegitimate formal reason, or from within a system of some kind. Originality, on the other hand, is a perception of the relations which actually exist between elements of a given object or subject matter. Thus ingenuity is equivalent to what I have designated as the negative sense of "notional" thinking while "originality" is equivalent to its positive sense. In the first case, one seeks to impose a point of view foreign to a given object or subject matter on to that matter; in the second case, reasoning is formed by a concentration on the object or the subject matter.

This conclusion does not yet explain, however, Newman's remark to the effect that theology has a real primacy in relation to religion. One would have suspected the reverse to be his conclusion. The overextended use of the same terms is the principal factor in the creation of the confusion. A contemporary reviewer of the <u>Grammar</u> understood the nature of this problem quite clearly in judging that ". . . the sense in which the author uses the terms is somewhat wider than that in which he has defined them; and, therefore, that his meaning is rather to be sought in his examples than in his definition."[61]

Paraphrased, and omitting the overextended uses, this conclusion means that the explication of the received faith of the Church has a priority in relation to the matters of coming to faith and of exercising faith on some occasions and in some contexts. For Newman, the issue of authority is the factor that makes sense of this priority. Certainly he was not suggesting that "theology" is, in this instance, a habit of mind. Nor is theology here "notional" in the sense of being the creation of our own minds. Nor does he mean by theology some second order activity, since whatever he means by the concept in this case, it is obviously fundamental to the very possibility of faith. I believe he is appealing to what is Christian revelation no matter whether anyone gives a real assent to it or not, to what is the object of faith ascertainable by "originality" even if not appropriated. What is the case, what makes real assent a possibility is not itself dependent upon real assent. Just as the distinctiveness and effectiveness of images in the religious life are no warrant ". . . for the existence of objects which those images represent," the lack of such vivid images is no proof of their non-existence.[62] Newman recognized that the mode of the apprehension of a proposition was distinct from the question of its truth or falsity.

The Impact of My Analysis of Newman's Notion of Complex Unity on Newman Criticism

A review of those reductive criticisms which I described in the second chapter, now made in light of my analysis of the complex unity in Newman's literature, provides a helpful conclusion for this study. First, my analysis suggests in relation to his thought what certain biographers have made clear already about Newman's life: His understanding of Christianity cannot be explained in terms of psychological need and predisposition and/or biographical accident alone. Attention to the biographical and psychological data alone does not account for the intellectual questions which led Newman in his search for the true Church and for the full body of revealed truth. While one may not agree that his decision was necessary or even wise, he cannot honestly deny that it was a carefully considered decision made not only from an irresistible personal need but also from an intellectual necessity. Concerning his conversion in 1845, Newman wrote in the *Apologia*:

> I determined to be guided, not by my imagination, but by my reason. . . . Had it not been for this resolve, I should have been a Catholic sooner than I was.[63]

Such a personal history is certainly in line with Newman's conclusions regarding the nature of coming to faith. In matters of religious inquiry reasoned reflection and one's personal history are involved. But, for all their importance for personal inquiry, the pieces of one's personal history are not to be considered as formal conditions of one's coming to faith but material accidents to be respected as such yet not dwelt upon. To reduce Newman's own appropriation of faith or his understanding of personal appropriation in the life of any individual to a wholly psychological or biographical question is to misunderstand both Newman's own life and his theological reflections.

Second, Newman's understanding of Christianity is seriously distorted by those who accuse him of scepticism, fideism, subjectivism, or other similar errors. Some critics of this conviction are simply reflecting the influences of those who are convinced of Newman's personal credulity, but many critics have voiced more serious philosophical reservations regarding Newman's position. Certain English critics like Sir Leslie Stephen understood Newman to be guilty of scepticism because of his lack of adherence to what Stephen felt were generally recognizable criteria of reasoned reflection. Newman understood this widely accepted epistemology as a material form of reason based on the scientific model of knowledge which ruled out the possibility of revelation from the outset. In that case, therefore, he and Stephen disagreed on the criteria of rationality appropriate to matters of religious faith. They did not disagree on the importance of having some criteria.

The modernists emphasized the role of personal experience, imagination, and moral dispositions in Newman and depreciated the role of the _depositum fidei_. As such, they fostered the suspicion in many that he was a fideist or one who believed on the basis of personal need and disposition alone. Ernest Baudin gave voice to these various criticisms and suggested Newman's essential subjectivism. Baudin's criticism to the effect that Newman exalted his own life history and passional dispositions as the norm for Christian experience is simply not supportable as I have already suggested. Newman never took sensibility to be transferable from one person's personal inquiry to that of another person. In fact, he had a suspicion of the role of excited feelings in faith. In addition, Newman cannot be considered to have exempted rational argument from a role in religious inquiry. Even if he did not feel that it would be as important for some individuals as for others, he felt it to be a necessary aspect of the Church's understanding of the reality of her faith.

Perhaps Baudin was right insofar as Newman placed too much emphasis on the testimony of the conscience. But he was wrong in suggesting that Newman did not understand the diversity of beliefs which might satisfy certain human needs of a religious kind. The roles of the _depositum fidei_ and of theology, to which Baudin gave no attention, have a very definite relation to the way in which personal need and imagination can transgress appropriate rules of Christian discourse. Implicit in the recognition of these rules is the awareness that other beliefs than those allowed by the Christian faith might well meet certain needs. In the final analysis, of course, Newman would probably claim with St. Augustine and other great theologians of the Church that man's deepest needs can only be met by God. But that does not mean that he did not recognize the propensity for human fulfillment in other ways. Newman did suggest that Christian faith meets human needs; he warned however, against making descriptions of those needs formally a part of the theological enterprise and certainly against making the fulfillment of those needs the only aspect of the Christian faith.

Third, for many of the same reasons, I must reject the claim that Newman's work can adequately be explained as an apologetic effort. Certainly he did oppose religious liberalism, rationalism, and the centrality of the gentleman in English values. In some sense, the "picture" of the world which Newman proposed and developed so effectively in his sermons is an imaginative proposal meant to displace the "picture" of the world which grasped the minds of his contemporaries. Likewise his entire discussion of the nature of religious inquiry serves the purpose of displaying its peculiar rationality to others in face of charges that Christian faith is irrational at heart. I cannot agree, however, that this involves some depreciation of other strata of discourse or forms of rationality. Newman did attack criteria of rationality, other than a few formal criteria such as non-contradiction, that claimed a generalizability across ranges of subject matter and across disciplines. He did note that criteria of a rigorous, Lockean kind would not fit many aspects of our experience. But he did not deny that different accounts of rationality might be appropriate for different realms of discourse and disciplines.

In some sense, the <u>Grammar of Assent</u> constitutes Newman's attempt to loosen the grip of formal criteria of rationality and to replace them, for the most part, with criteria richly variable and material in character. The "illative sense" is a term designating the element of familiarity with a subject matter, the rules for meaningfulness and truth in that subject matter, and the consequent ability to make appropriate judgments in questions involving that subject matter. In particular, of course, Newman was interested in describing the nature of religious assents. For that reason, illustrations are more numerous from this realm of discourse than from any other. Rather than seeking to show the incompleteness or insufficiency of other realms of discourse, as Davis urges, however, he was suggesting the relative autonomy of modes of rational investigation in various subject matters. This interpretation allows each stratum of discourse its own integrity and rebuts the temptation to depreciate one stratum to the advantage of another. Nevertheless, I should emphasize that this kind of analysis was far from being Newman's only concern; he was equally, if not more, interested in other issues. Likewise, his opposition to certain figures of his time was not the only cause for this concern. Apart from his apologetic interests, he was seeking to provide an analysis that stood on its own as a worthy enterprise in and for itself.

Fourth, the most persuasive and certainly the most troublesome reductive tendency at the present time is that form which emphasizes the role of moral dispositions and of the testimony of the conscience in Newman's understanding of the Christian faith. This analysis is the most persuasive because of the way in which it is aware of other false analyses of Newman and of their limitations. It is the most troublesome because it is not so much obviously reductionistic as it is misleading in its representation of Newman's thought. This analysis is misleading because of its tendency to isolate one aspect of Newman's thought in a way that does not recognize the complex unity of his reflections. A concentration on the nature of Christian discourse as a language of personal commitment (Pailin), or of personal thinking (Boekraad), or of "moral personalism" (Sillem) is a disregard for many important distinctions which Newman made between different functions of Christian discourse and for his concentrated reflection on matters other than the nature of religious inquiry.

Conclusion

Newman's metatheological principles are best described in Newman's own words of description concerning John Chrysostom:

> . . . I am speaking, not of what St. Chrysostom had in common with others, but what he has special to himself; and this speciality, I conceive, is the interest which he takes in all things, not so far as God has made them alike, but as He has made them different from each other. I speak of the discriminating affectionateness with which he accepts every one for what is personal in him and unlike others . . . of the graphic fidelity with which he notes them down upon the tablets of his mind . . . .[64]

The interest which Newman took in all things related to revealed truth was characterized by an attention to the differences between elements within the revelation and between various views which one can take toward revelation. In this regard, he was like the discriminating and graphic saint that he admired. This attentiveness and discrimination protected him from the kind of reductions of which he has so often been accused.

Many discussions of faith and of the nature of Christian

discourse fail to do justice to the kinds of distinctions which Newman employed in his own theological reflections. Undue concentration on one of the contexts which I have isolated in Newman results in a one-sided interpretation of the Christian faith. Newman's analysis could offer the means whereby certain errors or omissions may be corrected and whereby a greater degree of modesty may be exercised in the isolation of an "essence" of Christianity and in the establishment of apologetic programs. In short, Newman calls any one who reflects on the Christian faith to an awareness of the richly variegated contexts in which Christian discourse operates and, correspondingly, to the many forms which intelligent activity and reflection take in matters of faith.

NOTES TO CHAPTER V

[1] John Henry Newman, "Preface to the Third Edition," *The Via Media of the Anglican Church illustrated in Lectures, Letters and Tracts written between 1830 and 1841* (new impression, 2 vols.; London: Longmans, Green, and Co., 1901), I, xciv. Cited hereafter as "Preface," *The Via Media* . . .

[2] Newman, *An Essay on the Development of Christian Doctrine* (seventeenth impression; London: Longmans, Green, and Co., 1927), p. 33.

[3] Cf. Louis Cognet, *Newman ou la Recherche de la Verité* (Paris: Desclée, 1967), p. 216, and James D. Bastable, "Cardinal Newman's Philosophy of Belief," *Philosophical Studies* [Maynooth], V (December, 1955), 65-66.

[4] Newman, *An Essay on the Development of Christian Doctrine*, op. cit., p. 34.

[5] Newman, "Prospects of the Anglican Church," *Essays Critical and Historical* (new edition; London: Longmans, Green, and Co., 1891), I, 285.

[6] Ibid.

[7] Newman, "Milman's View of Christianity," *Essays Critical and Historical*, op. cit., II, 187.

[8] Newman, "Palmer on Faith and Unity," *Essays Critical and Historical*, op. cit., I, 182. One instance of this joining for Newman was the conjunction of what he called "evangelical truth" (the Gospel) and "apostolical order" (the structure responsible for the transmission of the Gospel message). Newman described the conjunction in "The Anglo-American Church," *Essays Critical and Historical*, op. cit., I, 366, in this way:
> Apostolicity is not an addition, or a completion; it is one side, one whole aspect of Christian truth, and Evangelicity is another side. They are different modes of viewing one and the same thing; a man cannot have the Evangelical principle in purity without the Apostolic, nor the Apostolic without the Evangelical; they go together.

[9] Newman, *Lectures on the Doctrine of Justification* (fourth edition; London: Rivingtons, 1885), p. 1.

[10] Ibid., p. 31.   [11] Ibid., p. 120.

[12] Ibid., pp. 132-133, for example, shows how Newman understood "righteousness" viewed in relation to its original source as identical with God's mercy; in relation to its meritorious cause, with the life and death of Christ; in relation to the instrument of it, with Holy Baptism; in relation to the entrance into it, with regeneration; in relation to its ultimate fruit, with everlasting life. Each of these matters Newman took to be an aspect or view of the reality of the inward divine presence of grace.

[13] Newman, "Implicit and Explicit Reason," *Fifteen Sermons*

preached before the University of Oxford between A. D. 1826 and 1843 (new edition; London: Rivingtons, 1887), pp. 262-263. Cited hereafter as OUS. Newman even asserted that his views in the Oxford University Sermons were in his ". . . own mind and reason . . . in parts . . . more sceptical than I now have any temptation to approve." Cf. his letter to Charles Meynell on December 20, 1859, in Charles Stephen Dessain (ed.), Consulting the Laity, January 1859 to June 1861 (Vol. IX of The Letters and Diaries of John Henry Newman. London: Thomas Nelson and Sons, Ltd., 1961).

[14] Newman, "Implicit and Explicit Reason," OUS, pp. 266-267.

[15] Ibid., pp. 263-265.   [16] Ibid., p. 267.

[17] Ibid., p. 275.

[18] Newman, "Love the Safeguard of Faith against Superstition," OUS, p. 234.

[19] Ibid., p. 240.

[20] Newman, "Wisdom, as contrasted with Faith and with Bigotry," OUS, p. 279.

[21] Ibid., p. 291.   [22] Ibid., pp. 297, 300.

[23] Ibid., p. 307.   [24] Ibid., p. 306.

[25] Cf. ibid., pp. 298-307.

[26] Newman, An Essay on the Development of Christian Doctrine, op. cit., p. 33.

[27] Ibid., p. 34.

[28] Newman, "The Theory of Developments in Religious Doctrine," OUS, p. 330.

[29] Ibid., p. 331.

[30] Newman, An Essay on the Development of Christian Doctrine, op. cit., pp. 35-36.

[31] Ibid., p. 36. Newman himself believed the doctrine of the incarnation to be convenient for certain purposes.

[32] Newman, "The Theory of Developments in Religious Doctrine," OUS, p. 320.

[33] Ibid., p. 351.   [34] Ibid., p. 337.

[35] Newman, An Essay on the Development of Christian Doctrine, op. cit., p. 55.

[36] Cf. James Munro Cameron, "Newman and the Empiricist Tradition," The Rediscovery of Newman: An Oxford Symposium, John Coulson and Arthur MacDonald Allchin, editors (London: Sheed and Ward, 1967), p. 83, for a suggestion in this direction.

[37] Newman, An Essay on the Development of Christian Doctrine, op. cit., p. 86.

[38] Ibid., p. 325.   [39] Ibid., p. 357.
[40] Ibid., p. 439.   [41] Ibid., p. 336.
[42] Ibid., p. 367.

[43] Newman, "Preface," The Via Media . . ., op. cit., p. xl.

[44] Ibid., p. xli.   [45] Ibid.

[46] Ibid., p. xciv.

[47] Newman, "An Internal Argument for Christianity," Discussions and Arguments on Various Subjects, (seventh edition; London: Longmans, Green, and Co., 1891), p. 397. Cf. ibid., p. 398, where Newman asserted that "You either accept Christianity, or you do not: if you do, do not garble and patch it . . . ."

[48] Newman, An Essay in Aid of a Grammar of Assent, Charles Frederick Harrold, editor (new edition; London: Longmans, Green, and Co., 1947), p. 76. Hereafter cited as Grammar. Charles Frederick Harrold, John Henry Newman: An Expository and Critical Study of His Mind, Thought and Art (Hamden, Connecticut: Archon Books, 1966), p. ix, quotes Newman as having said of the Grammar that "It is what it is, and is not what it isn't--and what it isn't many people will expect that it is."

[49] Newman, Grammar, op. cit., p. 184.

[50] References distinguishing these two terms can be found in ibid., pp. 8, 18-19, 27-28, 32, 90, et passim.

[51] Ibid., p. 75.   [52] Ibid., p. 5.

[53] Newman used these terms in ibid., p. 75.

[54] Ibid., p. 163.   [55] Ibid., p. 164.

[56] Ibid., p. 5.   [57] Ibid., pp. 91-92.

[58] Ibid., p. 4.

[59] Newman, "Faculty of Abstraction," The Text, Edward J. Sillem and A. J. Boekraad, editors (Vol. II of The Philosophical Notebook of John Henry Newman. 2 vols; New York: Humanities Press, 1969), pp. 8-21.

[60] Ibid., p. 9.

[61] Anonymous, "Dr. Newman's Grammar of Assent," The Catholic World, XII (January, 1871), 605.

[62] Newman, Grammar, op. cit., p. 61.

[63] Newman, Apologia pro vita sua (New York: The Modern Library, 1950), p. 137.

[64] Newman, "John Chrysostom," Historical Sketches (3 vols.; London: Longmans, Green, and Co., 1891), II, 285-286.

BIBLIOGRAPHY

BIBLIOGRAPHY

I. JOHN HENRY NEWMAN: PRIMARY SOURCES

A. Letters

Dessain, Charles Stephen (ed.). *Consulting the Laity, January, 1859 to June, 1863*. Vol. IX of *The Letters and Diaries of John Henry Newman*. London: Thomas Nelson and Sons, Ltd., 1961.

Harper, Gordon Huntington (ed.). *Cardinal Newman and William Froude, F.R.S.: A Correspondence*. Baltimore: The Johns Hopkins Press, 1933.

Mozley, Anne (ed.). *Letters and Correspondence of J. H. Newman during his Life in the English Church*. Vol. II. London: Longmans, Green, and Co., 1890.

Zeno (ed.). "Appendix: The Newman-Meynell Correspondence," *John Henry Newman: Our Way to Certitude; an Introduction to Newman's Psychological Discovery: The Illative Sense, and His Grammar of Assent*. Leiden: E. J. Brill, 1957. Pp. 226-270.

B. Sermons

Newman, John Henry. *Discourses addressed to Mixed Congregations*. Fifth edition. London: Burns, Oates, and Co., 1876.

_____. *Faith and Prejudice and other Unpublished Sermons of Cardinal Newman*. Birmingham Oratory, editors. New York: Sheed and Ward, 1956.

_____. *Fifteen Sermons preached before the University of Oxford between A.D. 1826 and 1834*. New edition. London: Rivingtons, 1887.

_____. *Parochial and Plain Sermons*. 8 vols. New edition. London: Rivingtons, 1870-1873.

_____. "Report of JHN's Sermons 1873-1874-1875." Unpublished manuscript, Birmingham Oratory, England; microfilmed copy, Yale University Beinecke Library, New Haven. Reel 52, batch 173, C 5.1.

_____. *Sermons bearing upon Subjects of the Day*. New edition. London: Rivingtons, 1869.

_____. *Sermon Notes, 1849-1878*. Fathers of the Birmingham Oratory, editors. New York: Longmans, Green, and Co., 1913.

_____. Sermons Preached on Various Occasions. Sixth edition. London: Burns and Oates, Limited, 1887.

_____. Two Sermons preached in the Church of St. Aloysius, Oxford, on Trinity Sunday, 1880. Printed for private circulation. Oxford: James Parker and Co., 1880.

C. Essays and Manuscripts

Newman, John Henry. "Advertissement," Essays Critical and Historical. Vol. I. New edition. London: Longmans, Green, and Co., 1891. Pp. vii-ix.

_____. "The Anglo-American Church," Essays Critical and Historical. Vol. I. New edition. London: Longmans, Green, and Co., 1891. Pp. 309-386.

_____. "Apollonius of Tyana," Historical Sketches. Vol. I. London: Basil Montagu Pickering, 1873. Pp. 301-331.

_____. "The Autobiographical Memoir," John Henry Newman: Autobiographical Writings. Henry Tristram, editor. New York: Sheed and Ward, 1957. Pp. 19-107.

_____. "The Development of Religious Error," The Contemporary Review, XLVIII (October, 1885), 457-469.

_____. Elucidations of Dr. Hampden's Theological Statements. Oxford: J. H. Parker and Messrs. Rivington, 1836.

_____. "Essay (May 4, 1839)." Unpublished manuscript, Birmingham Oratory, England; microfilmed copy, Yale University Beinecke Library, New Haven. Reel 25, batch 127, A 52 B 1.7.

_____. "Essay (December 14, 1838)." Unpublished manuscript, Birmingham Oratory, England; microfilmed copy, Yale University Beinecke Library, New Haven. Reel 25, batch 127, A 52 B 1.7.

_____. "The Evidences of Religion," The Argument from Conscience to the Existence of God according to John Henry Newman. Adrian J. Boekraad and Henry Tristram, editors. Louvain: Editions Nauwelaerts, 1961. Pp. 171-175.

_____. "The Grounds of Our Faith," Tracts for the Times. Vol. I. London: J. G. and F. Rivington, 1834.

_____. "Holy Scripture in its Relation to the Catholic Creed," Discussions and Arguments on Various Subjects. Seventh edition. London: Longmans, Green, and Co., 1891. Pp. 109-253.

_____. "An Internal Argument for Christianity," Discussions and Arguments on Various Subjects. Seventh edition. London: Longmans, Green, and Co., 1891. Pp. 363-398.

_____. "John Chrysostom," Historical Sketches. Vol. II. London: Longmans, Green, and Co., 1891. Pp. 217-302.

_____. "John Keble, Fellow of Oriel," Essays Critical and Historical. Vol. II. Seventh edition. London: Longmans, Green, and Co., 1891. Pp. 421-453.

_____. "Lectures on the Prophetical Office of the Church, viewed relatively to Romanism and Popular Protestantism," *The Via Media of the Anglican Church*. Vol. I. Third edition. London: Longmans, Green, and Co., 1901.

_____. "Lectures on the Theory of Faith." Unpublished manuscript, Birmingham Oratory, England; microfilmed copy, Yale University Beinecke Library, New Haven. Reel 9, batch 55, A 11.

_____. "A Letter addressed to the Duke of Norfolk, on occasion of Mr. Gladstone's Expostulation of 1874," *Certain Difficulties felt by Anglicans in Catholic Teaching*. Vol. II. New impression. London: Longmans, Green, and Co., 1910. Pp. 171-378.

_____. "A Letter addressed to the Rev. E. B. Pusey, D.D., on occasion of his *Eirenicon* of 1864," *Certain Difficulties felt by Anglicans in Catholic Teaching*. Vol. II. New impression. London: Longmans, Green, and Co., 1910. Pp. 1-170.

_____. "A Letter addressed to the Rev. R. W. Jelf, D.D., Canon of Christ Church, in Explanation of No. 90, in the Series called *The Tracts for the Times*." Second edition. Oxford: John Henry Parker, 1841.

_____. "Letter to a Magazine on the Subject of Dr. Pusey's Tract on Baptism," *Tracts for the Times*. Vol. IV. London: J. G. and F. Rivington, 1839.

_____. "Microfilm of Manuscripts," selected from those preserved at the Oratory of St. Philip Neri, Birmingham, England, by A. Dwight Culler. Microfilm files, Yale University Beinecke Library, New Haven.

_____. "Milman's View of Christianity," *Essays Critical and Historical*. Vol. II. New edition. London: Longmans, Green, and Co., 1891. Pp. 186-248.

_____. "Newman Manuscripts on Holy Scripture," *Cardinal Newman's Doctrine on Holy Scripture according to His Published Works and Previously Unedited Manuscripts*, appendices, Jaak Seynaeve, editor; Oxford: Basil Blackwell, 1953. Pp. 1-150.

_____. "Notes on Church and Pope." Unpublished manuscript, Birmingham Oratory, England; microfilmed copy, Yale University Beinecke Library, New Haven. Reel 14, batch 75, A 18.20.

_____. "On Argument, Demonstration." Unpublished manuscript, Birmingham Oratory, England; microfilmed copy, Yale University Beinecke Library, New Haven. Reel 9, batch 33, A 11.

_____. *On Consulting the Faithful in Matters of Doctrine*. John Coulson, editor. New York: Sheed and Ward, 1961.

_____. "On St. Cyril's Formula of the *Mia Phusis Sesarkomene*," *Tracts Theological and Ecclesiastical*. London: Basil Montagu Pickering, 1874. Pp. 285-336.

_____. "On the Controversy with the Romanists," *Tracts for the Times*. Vol. III. London: J. G. and F. Rivington, 1839.

_____. *On the Inspiration of Scripture*. J. Derek Holmes and Robert Murray, editors. London: Geoffrey Chapman, 1967.

_____. "On the Introduction of Rationalistic Principles into Revealed Religion," <u>Essays</u> <u>Critical</u> <u>and</u> <u>Historical</u>. Vol. I. London: Longmans, Green, and Co., 1891.

_____. "On the Study of Modern History." Unpublished manuscript, Birmingham Oratory, England; microfilmed copy, Yale University Beinecke Library, New Haven. Reels 5 and 6, batch 37, A 6.20.

_____. "Palmer on Faith and Unity," <u>Essays</u> <u>Critical</u> <u>and</u> <u>Historical</u>. Vol. I. New edition. London: Longmans, Green, and Co., 1891. Pp. 179-221.

_____. "Paper dated July 20, 1865." Unpublished manuscript, Birmingham Oratory, England; microfilmed copy, Yale University Beinecke Library, New Haven. Reel 14, batch 78, A 23.1.

_____. "Papers on the <u>Grammar</u> <u>of</u> <u>Assent</u>." Unpublished manuscript, Birmingham Oratory, England; microfilmed copy, Yale University Beinecke Library, New Haven. Reel 14, batch 78 A 23.1.

_____. "Papers on Theological Subjects from 1816 to 1834." Unpublished manuscripts, Birmingham Oratory, England; microfilmed copy, Yale University Beinecke Library, New Haven. Reel 7, batch 43, A 9.1.

_____. "The Patristical Idea of Antichrist," <u>Discussions</u> <u>and</u> <u>Arguments</u> <u>on</u> <u>Various</u> <u>Subjects</u>. Seventh edition. London: Longmans, Green, and Co. 1891. Pp. 44-108.

_____. "Poetry, with Reference to Aristotle's <u>Poetics</u>," <u>Essays</u> <u>Critical</u> <u>and</u> <u>Historical</u>. Vol. I. London: Basil Montagu Pickering, 1871. Pp. 1-29.

_____. "Preface," <u>The</u> <u>Via</u> <u>Media</u> <u>of</u> <u>the</u> <u>Anglican</u> <u>Church</u>. Vol. I. Third edition. London: Longmans, Green, and Co., 1901. Pp. xv-xciv.

_____. "Primitive Christianity," <u>Historical</u> <u>Sketches</u>. Vol. I. New impression. London: Longmans, Green, and Co., 1901. Pp. 333-346.

_____. "Private Memoranda, 1816-1826." Unpublished manuscript, Birmingham Oratory, England; microfilmed copy, Yale University Beinecke Library, New Haven. Reel 8, batch 46, A 10.1.

_____. "Private Judgment," <u>Essays</u> <u>Critical</u> <u>and</u> <u>Historical</u>. Vol. II. New edition. London: Longmans, Green, and Co., 1891. Pp. 336-374.

_____. "Proof of Theism," <u>The</u> <u>Text</u>. Edward J. Sillem, editor; revised by A. J. Boekraad. Vol. II of <u>The</u> <u>Philosophical</u> <u>Notebook</u> <u>of</u> <u>John</u> <u>Henry</u> <u>Newman</u>. New York: Humanties Press, 1970. Pp. 31-77.

_____. "Prospects of the Anglican Church," <u>Essays</u> <u>Critical</u> <u>and</u> <u>Historical</u>. Vol. I. New edition. London: Longmans, Green, and Co., 1891. Pp. 262-307.

_____. "Rise and Progress of Universities," <u>Historical</u> <u>Sketches</u>. Vol. III. London: Basil Montagu Pickering, 1873. Pp. 1-251.

_____. "Scientific and Religious Inquiry," *Philosophical Readings in Cardinal Newman*. James Collins, editor. Chicago: Henry Regnery Company, 1961. Pp. 50-54.

_____. "Speech of Cardinal Newman on Receiving the Biglietto in Rome, May 12, 1879," *Catholic University Reports and Other Papers*. Part I of *My Campaign in Ireland*. Printed for private circulation. Aberdeen: A. King and Co., 1896. Pp. 393-400.

_____. "Tamworth Reading Room," *Discussions and Arguments on Various Subjects*. Seventh edition. London: Longmans, Green, and Co., 1891. Pp. 254-305.

_____. *The Text*. Edward J. Sillem, editor; revised by A. J. Boekraad. Vol. II of *The Philosophical Notebook of John Henry Newman*. New York: Humanities Press, 1970.

_____. "Theses de Fide," *The Expositor*, fourth series, II (1890), 349-350.

_____. "Thoughts Respectfully addressed to the Clergy on Alternatives in the Liturgy," *Tracts for the Times*. Vol. I. London: J. G. and F. Rivington, 1834.

_____. "An Unpublished Paper by Cardinal Newman on the Development of Doctrine," Hugo M. de Achaval, editor, *Gregorianum*, XXXIX (1958), 585-596.

_____. "The Visible Church," *Tracts for the Times*. Vol. I. London: J. G. and F. Rivington, 1834.

_____. "What is of Obligation for a Catholic to Believe concerning the Inspiration of the Canonical Scriptures? Being a postscript to an article in the 'Nineteenth Century Review,' in answer to Professor Healy." London: Burns and Oates, 1884.

D. Books

_____. *Apologia pro vita sua*. New York: The Modern Library, 1950.

_____. *The Arians of the Fourth Century, their Doctrine, Temper, and Conduct, chiefly as exhibited in the Councils of the Church between A.D. 325 and A.D. 381*. New edition. London: Longmans, Green, and Co., 1895.

_____. *Certain Difficulties felt by Anglicans in Catholic Teaching considered in Twelve Lectures addressed in 1850 to the Party of the Religious Movement of 1833*. Vol. I. New impression. London: Longmans, Green, and Co., 1908.

_____. *An Essay in Aid of a Grammar of Assent*. Charles Frederick Harrold, editor. New edition. New York: Longmans, Green, and Co., 1947.

_____. *An Essay on the Development of Christian Doctrine*. Seventeenth impression. London: Longmans, Green, and Co., 1927.

_____. *The Idea of a University*. Garden City, New York: Doubleday and Company, Inc., Image Books, 1959.

_____. *Lectures on the Doctrine of Justification*. Fourth edition. London: Rivingtons, 1885.

_____. *Lectures on the Present Position of Catholics in England addressed to the Brothers of the Oratory in the Summer of 1851*. Daniel M. O'Connell, editor. New York: The America Press, 1942.

_____. *Loss and Gain: The Story of a Convert*. London: Burns and Oates, Ltd., 1904.

_____. *Two Essays on Biblical and on Ecclesiastical Miracles*. Fifth edition. London: Longmans, Green, and Co., 1885.

II. JOHN HENRY NEWMAN: SECONDARY SOURCES

A. Bibliography

Culler, A. Dwight. "Catalogue of the Contents of the Cardinal's Cupboards, completed by November 19, 1920. A list of films reproducing the major portion of the Newman manuscripts preserved at the Oratory, as selected by A. Dwight Culler." Typed manuscript, Yale University Beinecke Library, New Haven, 1951.

Fries, Heinrich, and Werner Becker (eds.). *Newman-Studien*. Seven volumes. Nürnberg: Glock und Lutz, 1948-1970.

B. Articles and Essays

Allison, William Henry. "Was Newman a Modernist?" *American Journal of Theology*, XIV (October, 1910), 552-571.

Anonymous. "Cardinal Newman," *The Edinburgh Review*, 215 (April, 1912), 263-290.

_____. "Cardinal Newman's Failure to Blend Rome and Modernism," *Current Literature*, 52 (June, 1912), 678-681.

_____. "The Cause of John Henry Newman," *The Tablet*, 211 (June 21, 1958), 579; 213 (October 24, 1959), 904; 215 (January 21, 1961), 69.

_____. "Editorial: 'The Conversion of Mr. Newman,'" *The Tablet*, CLXXXVI (October 6, 1945), 159-160.

_____. "Dr. Newman's *Grammar of Assent*," *The Edinburgh Review*, 132 (October, 1870), 382-414.

_____. [signed "Theologus"]. "Letter to the Editor: Cardinal Newman and the Mere Probability of Supernatural Revelation," *The Tablet*, LXXIX (January 11, 1908), 59-60.

_____. "*The Month* and John Henry Newman," *The Month*, CI (January, 1903), 1-16; CI (February, 1903), 113-129; CI (March, 1903), 225-240; CI (April, 1903), 337-352.

_____. "Newman's *Grammar of Assent*," *The London Quarterly Review*, 35 (January, 1871), 363-389.

_____. "The Pope and Modernism," *The Manchester Guardian*, November 20, 1907, 4.

Artz, Johannes. "Newman's Contribution to Theory of Knowledge," *Philosophy Today*, IV (Spring, 1960), 12-25.

Aveling, Francis. "Universals and the Illative Sense," *The Dublin Review*, 137 (October, 1905), 236-271.

Bacchus, Francis Joseph, and Henry Tristram. "Newman," *Dictionnaire de Theologie Catholique*, commencé sous la direction de A. Vacant et E. Maugenot et continue sous celle de E. Amann. Tome onzième, premiére partie. Paris: Librarie Letouzey et Ané, 1931. Columns 327-398.

Barmann, Lawrence F. "The Spiritual Teaching of Newman's Early Sermons," *The Downside Review*, 80 (1962), 226-242.

Bastable, James D. "Cardinal Newman's Philosophy of Belief," *Philosophical Studies* [Maynooth], V (December, 1955), 44-70.

Baudin, Ernest. "La Philosophie de la Foi chez Newman," *Revue de Philosophie*, VIII (January-July, 1906), 571-598; IX (July-December, 1906), 20-55, 253-285, 373-390.

Becker, Werner. "Newman's Influence in Germany," *The Rediscovery of Newman: An Oxford Symposium*, John Coulson and Arthur MacDonald Allchin, editors. London: Sheed and Ward, 1967. Pp. 174-189.

_____. "Zum Problem der Einheit von Leben und Werk bei John Henry Newman," *Miscellanea Erfordiana*, herausgegeben von Erich Kleineidam und Heinz Schuermann. Leipzig: St. Benno-Verlag GMBH, 1962. Pp. 291-313.

Beckmann, Joseph F. "Another View of Newman," *The American Ecclesiastical Review*, CXXXVIII (January, 1958), 37-48.

Bellesheim, A. "Newman," *Wetzer und Weltes Kirchenlexikon*, IX 224. Zweite auflage. Freiburg im Breisgau: Herder'sche Verlagshandlung, 1895.

Blakesley, Joseph William. "Dr. Newman's *Grammar of Assent*," *English Catholics and English Ultramontanism: Three Reviews*. Reprinted for private circulation only from the *Times*, April 21, 1870. London: Macmillan and Co., 1874. Pp. 44-70.

Blehl, Vincent Francis. "The Holiness of John Henry Newman," *The Month*, XIX (June, 1958), 325-334.

_____. "Newman and the Missing Miter," *Thought*, XXXV (Spring, 1960), 111-123.

_____. "The Sanctity of Cardinal Newman," *America*, XCIX (June 14, 1958), 328-330.

Boekraad, Adrian J. "Continental Newman Literature," *Philosophical Studies* [Maynooth], VII (December, 1957), 110-116.

_____. "Critical Notice: *Aristotelische Erkenntnislehre bei Whately und Newman*," *Philosophical Studies* [Maynooth], XI (1961/1962), 174-178.

_____. "Critical Notice: Cardinal Newman Studien III," Philosophical Studies [Maynooth], VIII (December, 1958), 140-145.

_____. "Newman in the Low Countries: A Note," The Rediscovery of Newman: An Oxford Symposium, John Coulson and Arthur MacDonald Allchin, editors. London: Sheed and Ward, 1967. Pp. 190-194.

_____. "Newman's Argument to the Existence of God," Philosophical Studies [Maynooth], VI (December, 1956), 50-71.

Bouyer, Louis. "Newman's Influence in France," The Dublin Review, 217 (October, 1945), 182-188.

Bremond, Henri. "Letter to the Editor," The Tablet, LXXIX (January 18, 1908), 100.

_____. "Nouvelle Communication," Revue Pratique d'Apologetique, III (March, 1907), 676-677.

Brickel, Alfred G. "Cardinal Newman's Theory of Knowledge," The American Catholic Quarterly Review, XLIII (July, 1918), 507-518; XLIII (October, 1918), 645-653.

Burgum, Edwin Berry. "Cardinal Newman and the Complexity of Truth," The Sewanee Review, XXXVIII (July, 1930), 310-327.

Cadman, Samuel Parkes. "John Henry Newman and the Oxford Movement of 1833-1845," The Three Religious Leaders of Oxford and their Movements: John Wycliffe, John Wesley, John Henry Newman. New York: The Macmillan Company, 1916. Pp. 385-589.

Cameron, James Munro. "Faith and the Mind: I. The Night Battle," The Listener, LVII (January 3, 1957), 15-16.

_____. "Newman and the Empiricist Tradition," The Rediscovery of Newman: An Oxford Symposium, John Coulson and Arthur MacDonald Allchin, editors. London: Sheed and Ward, 1967. Pp. 76-96.

_____. "The Night Battle: Newman and Empiricism," Victorian Studies [Indiana], IV (1960), 99-117.

Cecil, Algernon. "J. H. Newman," Six Oxford Thinkers. London: John Murray, 1909. Pp. 44-122.

Chesterton, Cecil. "The Art of Controversy: Macaulay, Huxley, and Newman," The Catholic World, CV (July, 1917), 446-456.

Church, R. W. "Cardinal Newman's Course," Occasional Papers. Vol. II. London: Macmillan and Co., Ltd., 1897. Pp. 470-478.

_____. "Cardinal Newman's Naturalness," Occasional Papers. Vol. II. London: Macmillan and Co., Ltd., 1897. Pp. 479-482.

_____. "Newman's 'Apologia,'" Occasional Papers. Vol. II. London: Macmillan and Co., Ltd., 1897. Pp. 379-397.

Coulson, John. "Newman on the Church--His Final View, its Origins and Influences," The Rediscovery of Newman: An Oxford Symposium, John Coulson and Arthur MacDonald Allchin, editors. London: Sheed and Ward, 1967. Pp. 123-143.

Cunliffe-Jones, H. "Note on the Free Church Attitude to Newman," *The Rediscovery of Newman: An Oxford Symposium*, John Coulson and Arthur MacDonald Allchin, editors. London: Sheed and Ward, 1967. Pp. 213-215.

Davis, H. Francis. "The Catholicism of Cardinal Newman," *John Henry Newman: Centenary Essays*. London: Burns, Oates and Washbourne, Ltd., 1945. Pp. 36-54.

_____. "Newman and the Psychology of the Development of Doctrine," *The Dublin Review*, 216 (April, 1945), 97-107.

_____. "Newman and the Theology of the Living Word," *Newman-Studien*, herausgegeben von Heinrich Fries und Werner Becker. Sechste folge. Nürnberg: Glock und Lutz, 1964. Pp. 167-178.

_____. "Newman on Educational Method," *The Dublin Review*, 230 (Winter, 1956), 101-113.

_____. "Newman on Faith and Personal Certitude," *The Journal of Theological Studies*, XII (October, 1961), 248-259.

_____. "Newman's Influence in England," *The Rediscovery of Newman: An Oxford Symposium*, John Coulson and Arthur MacDonald Allchin, editors. London: Sheed and Ward, 1967. Pp. 216-232.

Dessain, Charles Stephen. "The Biblical Basis of Newman's Ecumenical Theology," *The Rediscovery of Newman: An Oxford Symposium*, John Coulson and Arthur MacDonald Allchin, editors. London: Sheed and Ward, 1967. Pp. 100-122.

_____. "Cardinal Newman on the Theory and Practice of Knowledge: The Purpose of the *Grammar of Assent*," *The Downside Review*, LXXV (January, 1957), 1-23.

_____. "Newman's First Conversion," *Studies: An Irish Quarterly Review*, XLVI (Spring, 1957), 44-59.

Dessain, Charles Stephen, and the Fathers of the Birmingham Oratory (eds.). "Introduction," *Faith and Prejudice and Other Unpublished Sermons of Cardinal Newman*. New York: Sheed and Ward, 1956. Pp. 7-16.

Dimnet, Ernest. "Letter to the Editor," *Revue Pratique d'Apologetique*, III (February 15, 1907), 616-618.

_____. "Le Voyant. Quelques Aspects du Cardinal Newman," *La Pensée Catholique dans l'Angleterre Contemporaine*. Paris: Victor Lecoffre, 1906. Pp. 73-129.

Dooley, D. J. "The Newman Question," *Culture*, XX (March, 1959), 41-47.

Fairbairn, Andrew M. "Catholicism and Apologetics," *The Contemporary Review*, XLVII (February, 1885), 164-184.

_____. "Catholicism and Historical Criticism," *The Contemporary Review*, XLVIII (July, 1885), 36-64.

_____. "Catholicism and Modern Thought," *The Contemporary Review*, XLVII (May, 1885), 652-674.

Fawkes, Alfred. "Newman," *Studies in Modernism*. London: Smith, Elder, and Co., 1913. Pp. 24-47.

Fenton, Joseph Clifford. "Newman and Papal Infallibility," *American Essays for the Newman Centennial*, John K. Ryan and Edmond Darvil Benard, editors. Washington, D. C.: The Catholic University of America Press, 1947. Pp. 163-185.

———. "The Newman Legend and Newman's Complaints," *The American Ecclesiastical Review*, CXXXIX (August, 1958), 101-121.

———. "Newman's Complaints examined in the Light of Priestly Spirituality," *The American Ecclesiastical Review*, CXXXVIII (January, 1958), 49-65.

———. "Some Newman Autobiographical Sketches and the Newman Legend," *The American Ecclesiastical Review*, CXXXVI (June, 1957), 394-410.

Froude, James Anthony. "The Oxford Counter-Reformation," *Short Studies on Great Subjects*. Vol. IV. London: Longmans, Green, and Co., 1917. Pp. 231-360.

Gannon, Robert I. "Note on Newman," *America*, XCIX (June 28, 1958), 361.

Gerrard, Thomas J. "Bergson, Newman and Aquinas," *The Catholic World*, XCVI (March, 1913), 748-762.

———. "Dichotomy, A Study in Newman and Aquinas," *The New York Review*, LII (January-April, 1908), 381-390.

———. "The *Grammar of Assent* and the 'Sure Future,'" *The Dublin Review*, 137 (October, 1905), 113-128.

———. "Newman and Conceptualism," *The New York Review*, II (January-February, 1907), 430-441.

Gougaud, L. "Le Prétendu Modernisme Newman," *Revue du Clergé Francais*, LVII (1909), 560-565.

de Grandmaison, Leonce. "John Henry Newman considerée comme Maitre," *Etudes*, CIX (December, 1906), 721-750; CX (January, 1907), 39-69.

Griffith, Gwilyn Oswald. "Newman," *Interpreters of Man*. London: Lutterworth Press, 1943. Pp. 59-74.

Grimshaw, F. J. "The Holiness of Newman," *The Tablet*, 211 (June 21, 1958), 578.

Harper, Thomas Norton. "Dr. Newman's *Essay in Aid of a Grammar of Assent*," *The Month*, XII (May, 1870), 599-611.

———. "Dr. Newman's *Essay in Aid of a Grammar of Assent*. Part II," *The Month*, XII (June, 1870), 667-692.

Hawkins, D. J. B. "Newman the Man: An Approach to Pere Bouyer's Study," *The Dublin Review*, 232 (Spring, 1958), 81-88.

Hedley, J. C. [Bishop]. "Dr. Barry on Newman," *The Ampleforth Journal*, X (July, 1904), 1-12.

Holahan, Mary Benoit [Sister]. "Newman in France." An abstract of a thesis submitted in partial fulfillment of the requirements for the degree of Doctor of Philosophy in English in the graduate school of the University of Illinois, Urbana, 1943.

Hughes, Philip. "Newman and His Age," The Dublin Review, 217 (October, 1945), 111-136.

Hutton, Arthur W. "Personal Reminiscences of Cardinal Newman," The Expositor, fourth series, II (1890), 223-240, 304-320, 336-348.

Hutton, Richard Holt. "Cardinal Newman," Essays on Some of the Modern Guides to English Thought in the Matter of Faith. London: Macmillan and Co., 1888. Pp. 49-101.

Huxley, Thomas H. "Agnosticism and Christianity," The Nineteenth Century, XXV (June, 1889), 937-964.

Klubertanz, George P. "Where is the Evidence for Thomistic Metaphysics?" Revue Philosophique de Louvain, 56 (May, 1958), 294-315.

Lawler, Justus George. "Both-And," Renascence, XV (Fall, 1962), 50-53.

_____. "Newman: Biography or Psychography?" Renascence, XIV (Autumn, 1961), 42-47.

Lebreton, Jules. "Autour de Newman," Revue Pratique d'Apologetique, III (January 15, 1907), 488-504.

_____. "Le Primat de la Conscience d'après Newman," Revue Pratique d'Apologetique, III (March 1, 1907), 667-675.

Leddy, J. F. "Newman and His Critics, a Chapter in the History of Ideas," Report of the Canadian Catholic Historical Association, 1943, 25-38.

_____. "Newman and Modern Educational Thought," American Essays for the Newman Centennial, John K. Ryan and Edmond Darvil Benard, editors. Washington, D. C.: The Catholic University of America Press, 1947. Pp. 115-129.

Lee, George. "Newman's Probabilities," The American Ecclesiastical Review, XXXVIII (May, 1908), 528-541.

Loisy, Alfred (pseud. A. Firmin). "Le Développement Chrétien d'après le Cardinal Newman," Revue du Clergé Francais, XVII (1899), 5-20.

_____. "Les Preuves et l'Economie de la Révélation," Revue du Clergé Francais, XXII (1900), 126-153.

McManus, E. Leo. "Newman and the Newman Legend," The American Ecclesiastical Review, CXXXIX (August, 1958), 93-100.

Maurice, Frederick Denison. "Dr. Newman's Grammar of Assent," The Contemporary Review, 14 (May, 1870), 151-172.

More, Paul Elmer. "Cardinal Newman," The Drift of Romanticism. Shelburne Essays, eighth series. New York: Houghton Mifflin Company, 1913. Pp. 39-79.

Murphy, John L. "The Influence of Bishop Butler on Religious Thought," Theological Studies, 24 (September, 1963), 361-401.

Pius X [Pope]. "Actes du Souverain Pontiff: Newman et la Modernisme, lettre a Mgr. O'Dwyer, Eveque de Limerick," Nouvelle Revue Theologique, XL (1908), 419-420.

Reade, Francis Vincent. "The Sentimental Myth," John Henry Newman: Centenary Essays. Introduction by Henry Tristram. London: Burns, Oates, and Washbourne, Ltd., 1945. Pp. 139-154.

Reilly, Joseph John. "The Tone of the Centre," American Essays for the Newman Centennial, John K. Ryan and Edmond Darvil Benard, editors. Washington, D. C.: The Catholic University of America Press, 1947. Pp. 65-70.

Robinson, Jonathan. "Did Newman 'Fit In'?: Reply to a Critic," The Dublin Review, 232 (Autumn, 1958), 245-259.

──────. "Newman's Use of Butler's Arguments," The Downside Review, LXXVI (Spring, 1958), 161-180.

Rupp, Gordon. "Newman through Nonconformist Eyes," The Rediscovery of Newman: An Oxford Symposium, John Coulson and Arthur MacDonald Allchin, editors. London: Sheed and Ward, 1967. Pp. 195-212.

Russell, H. P. "A Lesson from Newman," The American Ecclesiastical Review, XXXVIII (May, 1908), 514-528.

Ryan, M. J. "The Philosophy of Newman," The American Quarterly Review, 33 (1908), 77-86.

Saunders, Daniel J. "The Psychology of Conversion," American Essays for the Newman Centennial, John K. Ryan and Edmond Darvil Benard, editors. Washington, D. C.: The Catholic University of America Press, 1947. Pp. 39-64.

Simon, Paul. "Newman and German Catholicism," The Dublin Review 219 (July, 1946), 75-84.

Smith, Sydney F. "The 'Edinburgh Review' on Cardinal Newman," The Month, CXIX (June, 1912), 561-578.

──────. "Newman's Relations to Modernism," The Month, CXX (July, 1912), 1-15.

Stephen, Leslie. "Cardinal Newman's Scepticism," The Nineteenth Century, XXIX (February, 1891), 179-201.

──────. "Dr. Newman's Apologia," Frasers Magazine, LXX (September, 1864), 265-303.

──────. "Dr. Newman's Theory of Belief," The Fortnightly Review, XXVIII (November, 1877), 680-697; XXVIII (December, 1877), 792-810.

Toohey, John Joseph. "The Grammar of Assent and the Old Philosophy," The Irish Theological Quarterly, II (October, 1907) 466-484.

──────. "Newman and Modernism," The Tablet, LXXIX (January 4, 1908), 7-9; (January 11, 1908), 47-48; (January 18, 1908), 86-88; (January 25, 1908), 122-125.

──────. "Newman on the Criterion of Certitude," The Irish Theological Quarterly, V (1910), 444-453.

Tucker, John. "Newman as Philosopher and Littérateur," The Catholic World, CXXV (May, 1927), 155-163.

Tyrell, George. "Introduction," The Mystery of Newman, Henri Bremond, author. London: Williams and Norgate, 1907. Pp. ix-xvii.

_____. "The Limits of the Development Theory," The Catholic World, LXXXI (September, 1905), 730-744.

_____. "The Prospects of Modernism," The Hibbert Journal, VI (January, 1908), 241-255.

Versfeld, Martin. "St. Thomas, Newman, and the Existence of God," New Scholasticism, XLI (Winter, 1967), 3-30.

Ward, Wilfrid Philip. "Preface," Men and Matters. London: Longmans, Green, and Co., 1914. Pp. v-ix.

_____. "The True Nature of Newman's Genius: A Criticism of Popular Misconceptions," Last Lectures. London: Longmans, Green, and Co., 1918. Pp. 1-149.

Willam, Franz Michel. "Aristotelische Bausteine der Entwicklungstheorie Newmans," Newman-Studien, herausgegeben von Heinrich Fries und Werner Becker. Sechste folge. Nürnberg: Glock und Lutz, 1964. Pp. 193-226.

_____. "Bezeichnungen und Characterisierungen des Probabilitäten: Beweises bei Newman," Newman-Studien, herausgegeben von Heinrich Fries und Werner Becker. Fünfte folge. Nürnberg: Glock und Lutz, 1962. Pp. 229-250.

_____. "Die Vorgeschichte des Begriffes 'Konvergierende Probabilitäten'," Newman-Studien, herausgegeben von Heinrich Fries und Werner Becker. Vierte folge. Nürnberg: Glock und Lutz, 1960. Pp. 138-143.

C. Books

Abbott, Edwin Abbott. The Anglican Career of Cardinal Newman. Two volumes. London: Macmillan and Co., 1892.

_____. Philomythus: An Antidote to Credulity; A Discussion of Cardinal Newman's Essay on Ecclesiastical Miracles. Second edition. London: Macmillan and Co., 1891.

Atkins, Gaius Glenn. Life of Cardinal Newman. Creative Lives, Harold E. B. Speight, editor. New York: Harper and Brothers Publishers, 1931.

Benard, Edmond Darvil. A Preface to Newman's Theology. London: B. Herder Book Co., 1945.

Biemer, Günther. Newman on Tradition. Kevin Smyth, translator and editor. London: Burns and Oates, 1967.

Boekraad, Adrian J. The Personal Conquest of Truth according to John Henry Newman. Louvain: Editions Nauwelaerts, 1955.

Boekraad, Adrian J., and Henry Tristram. The Argument from Conscience to the Existence of God according to John Henry Newman. Louvain: Editions Nauwelaerts, 1961.

Bokenkotter, Thomas S. Cardinal Newman as Historian. Louvain: Publications Universitaires de Louvain, 1959.

Bouyer, Louis. Newman: His Life and Spirituality. Trans. J. Lewis May. London: Burns and Oates, 1958.

Bremond, Henri. The Mystery of Newman. Trans. H. C. Corrance. London: Williams and Norgate, 1907.

Chadwick, Owen. *From Bossuet to Newman: The Idea of Doctrinal Development*. Cambridge: Cambridge University Press, 1957.

Cognet, Louis. *Newman ou la Recherche de la Verité*. Paris: Declée, 1967.

Cronin, John Francis. *Cardinal Newman: His Theory of Knowledge*. Washington, D. C.: The Catholic University of America Press, 1935.

Culler, A. Dwight. *The Imperial Intellect: A Study of Newman's Educational Ideal*. New Haven: Yale University Press, 1965.

D'Arcy, Martin Cyril. *The Nature of Belief*. London: Sheed and Ward, 1931.

Dessain, Charles Stephen. *John Henry Newman*. London: Thomas Nelson and Sons, Ltd., 1966.

Dibble, Romuald A. *John Henry Newman: The Concept of Infallible Doctrinal Authority*. The Catholic University of America Studies in Sacred Theology, second series, no. 91. Washington, D. C.: The Catholic University of America Press, 1955.

Elbert, John Aloysius. *The Evolution of Newman's Conception of Faith*. Philadelphia: The Dolphin Press, 1932.

Faber, Geoffrey Cuet. *Oxford Apostles: A Character Study of the Oxford Movement*. New York: Charles Scribner's Sons, 1934.

Fairbairn, Andrew M. *Catholicism: Roman and Anglican*. New York: Charles Scribner's Sons, 1899.

Farges, Albert. *La Crise de la Certitude*. Paris: Berche et Tralin, 1907.

Femiano, Samuel D. *Infallibility of the Laity: The Legacy of Newman*. New York: Herder and Herder, 1967.

Firminger, Walter Kelly. *Some Thoughts on the Recent Criticism of the Life and Works of John Henry Cardinal Newman*. Printed for private circulation. Oxford: James Parker and Co., 1892.

Flanagan, Philip. *Newman: Faith and the Believer*. London: Sands and Co., Ltd., 1946.

Garnet, Emmeline. *Tormented Angel: A Life of John Henry Newman*. New York: Ariel Books, Farrar, Straus and Giroux, 1966.

Gout, Raoul. *Du Protestantisme au Catholicisme: John Henry Newman, Notes Psychologiques*. Geneve: Librairie J. H. Jeheber, 1906.

Gundersen, Borghild. *Cardinal Newman and Apologetics*. Oslo: I Kommisjon hos J. Dybwad, 1952.

Harrold, Charles Frederick. *John Henry Newman: An Expository and Critical Study of His Mind, Thought and Art*. Hamden, Connecticut: Archon Books, 1966.

Hollis, Christopher. *Newman and the Modern World*. Garden City, New York: Doubleday and Co., 1968.

Hutton, Richard Holt. *Cardinal Newman*. New York: Houghton Mifflin and Company, 1890.

Kaiser, F. James. The Concept of Conscience according to John Henry Newman. The Catholic University of America Studies in Sacred Theology, no. 106. Washington, D. C.: The Catholic University of America Press, 1958.

Kortenaar, H. ten. A Newman Calendar 1965. Printed on behalf of the American Secretariat for the Cause of Beatification of Cardinal Newman. Pittsburgh.

Juergens, Sylvester P. Newman on the Psychology of Faith in the Individual. New York: The Macmillan Company, 1928.

Morley, John. Critical Miscellanies. Vol. IV. London: The Macmillan Company, 1908.

Nédoncelle, Maurice. La Philosophie Religeuse de John Henry Newman. Strasbourg: Société Strasbourgeosie de Librairie, 1946.

Newman, Francis William. Contributions Chiefly to the Early History of the Late Cardinal Newman. London: Kegan Paul, Trench, Trubner and Co., Ltd., 1891.

O'Dwyer, Edward Thomas. Cardinal Newman and the Encyclical. London: Longmans, Green, and Co., 1908.

Pailin, David. The Way to Faith: An Examination of Newman's Grammar of Assent as a Response to the Search for Certainty in Faith. London: Epworth Press, 1969.

Patterson, Webster T. Newman: Pioneer for the Layman. Washington, D. C.: Corpus Books, 1968.

Paul, Herbert (ed.). Letters of Lord Acton to Mary Gladstone. New York: The Macmillan Company, 1904.

Przywara, Erich. Gottgeheimnis der Welt: Drei Vorträge über die Geistige der Gegenwart. München: Theatiner Verlag, 1923.

Quinn, J. Richard. The Recognition of the True Church according to John Henry Newman. The Catholic University of America Studies in Sacred Theology, second series, no. 81. Washington, D. C.: The Catholic University of America Press, 1954.

Rigg, J. H. Oxford High Anglicanism. London: C. H. Kelly, 1895.

Sarolea, Charles. Cardinal Newman and His Influence on Religious Life and Thought. The World's Epoch-Makers, Oliphant Smeaton, editor. New York: Charles Scribner's Sons, 1908.

Schiffers, Norbert. Die Einheit der Kirche nach John Henry Newman. Dusseldorf: Patmos-Verlag, 1956.

Seynaeve, Jaak. Cardinal Newman's Doctrine on Holy Scripture according to His Published Works and Previously Unedited Manuscripts. Louvain: Publications Universitaires de Louvain, 1953.

Sheridan, Thomas L. Newman on Justification: A Theological Biography. Staten Island, New York: Alba House, Division of the Society of St. Paul, 1967.

Sillem, Edward J. General Introduction to the Study of Newman's Philosophy. Vol. I of The Philosophical Notebook of John Henry Newman. 2 vols. New York: Humanities Press, 1969.

Stern, Jean. *Bible et Tradition chez Newman: Aux Origenes de la Théorie du Developpement*. Theologie: Etudes Publiées sous la Direction de la Facultie de Théologie S. J. De Lyon-Fourviére. Aubier, 1967.

Strachey, Lytton. *Eminent Victorians*. London: Chatto and Windus, 1918.

Trevor, Meriol. *Newman*. 2 vols. Garden City, New York: Doubleday and Company, Inc., 1962.

Tristram, Henry (ed.). *John Henry Newman: Autobiographical Writings*. New York: Sheed and Ward, 1957.

Vidler, Alec R. *The Modernist Movement in the Catholic Church: Its Origins and Outcome*. Cambridge: Cambridge University Press, 1934.

Walgrave, Jan Hendrick. *Newman the Theologian: The Nature of Belief and Doctrine as Exemplified in His Life and Works*. Trans. A. V. Littledale. New York: Sheed and Ward, 1960.

Ward, Wilfrid Philip. *The Life of John Henry Cardinal Newman*. 2 vols. London: Longmans, Green, and Co., 1912.

Willam, Franz Michel. *Aristotelische Erkenntnislehre bei Whately und Newman und Ihre Bezüge zur Gegenwart*. Freiburg: Herder, 1960.

Zeno. *John Henry Newman, Our Way to Certitude: An Introduction to Newman's Psychological Discovery: The Illative Sense, and His Grammar of Assent*. Leiden: E. J. Brill, 1957.

D. Unpublished Materials

Zale, Eric Michael. "The Defenses of John Henry Newman." Microfilmed Ph.D. dissertation, The University of Michigan, 1962.

III. OTHER SOURCES

A. Articles and Essays

Austin, J. L. "Performative Utterances," *Philosophical Papers*, J. O. Urmson and G. J. Warnock, editors. Oxford: The Clarendon Press, 1961. Pp. 220-239.

_____. "A Plea for Excuses," *Philosophical Papers*, J. O. Urmson and G. J. Warnock, editors. Oxford: The Clarendon Press, 1961. Pp. 123-152.

Feigl, Herbert. "De Principiis Non Disputandum . . . ?: On the Meaning and the Limits of Justification," *Philosophical Analysis*, Max Black, editor. Ithaca, New York: Cornell University Press, 1950. Pp. 119-156.

_____. "Validation and Vindication: An Analysis of the Nature and Limits of Ethical Arguments," *Readings in Ethical Theory*, Wilfrid Sellars and John Hospers, editors. New York: Appleton-Century-Crofts, Inc., 1952. Pp. 667-680.

Hampshire, Stuart. "Reply to Walsh on Thought and Action," *The Journal of Philosophy*, LX (July 4, 1963), 410-424.

Harvey, Van A. "Is There an Ethics of Belief?" *The Journal of Religion*, XLIX (January, 1969), 41-58.

MacIntyre, Alasdair. "Is Understanding Religion Compatible with Believing?" *Faith and the Philosophers*, John Hick, editor. New York: St. Martin's Press, 1964. Pp. 115-133.

Ryle, Gilbert. "Ordinary Language," *The Philosophical Review*, LXII (April, 1953), 167-186.

_____. "Philosophical Arguments," *Logical Positivism*, A. J. Ayer, editor. New York: The Free Press, 1966. Pp. 327-344.

Waismann, Frederick. "Language Strata," *Logic and Language*, Antony Flew, editor. Second series. Garden City, New York: Doubleday and Company, Inc., 1965. Pp. 226-247.

B. Books

Chisholm, Roderick M. *Perceiving: A Philosophical Study*. Contemporary Philosophy, Max Black, editor. Ithaca, New York: Cornell University Press, 1957.

_____. *Theory of Knowledge*. Foundations of Philosophy Series, Elizabeth and Monroe Beardsley, editors. Englewood Cliffs, New Jersey: Prentice-Hall, Inc., 1966.

Clifford, William Kingdon. *Lectures and Essays*. 2 vols. Leslie Stephen and Frederick Pollock, editors. London: Macmillan and Company, 1879.

Edwards, Paul. *The Logic of Moral Discourse*. New York: The Free Press, 1955.

Frankena, William K. *Ethics*. Foundations of Philosophy Series, Elizabeth and Monroe Beardsley, editors. Englewood Cliffs, New Jersey: Prentice-Hall, Inc., 1963.

Hampshire, Stuart. *Freedom of the Individual*. New York: Harper and Row, Publishers, 1965.

_____. *Thought and Action*. New York: The Viking Press, Compass Books, 1967.

Kierkegaard, Søren. *The Point of View for My Work as an Author: A Report to History*. Trans. Walter Lowrie. New York: Harper and Row, Publishers, Torchbooks, 1962.

Locke, John. *An Essay concerning Human Understanding*. A. S. Pringle-Pattison, editor. Oxford: Oxford University Press, 1934.

Ryle, Gilbert. *The Concept of Mind*. New York: Barnes and Noble, 1961.

Wellek, René, and Austin Warren. *Theory of Literature*. Third edition. New York: Harcourt, Brace and World, Inc., 1956.

Wimsatt, William K., Jr. *The Verbal Icon: Studies in the Meaning of Poetry*. New York: The Noonday Press, 1966.

Wittgenstein, Ludwig. *Lectures and Conversations on Aesthetics, Psychology, and Religious Belief*. Cyril Barrett, editor. Berkeley: University of California Press, 1967.

---. *Philosophical Investigations*. Trans. G. E. M. Anscombe. Second edition. New York: The Macmillan Company, 1958.